Foreign Policy of Bangladesh

Foreign Policy of Bangladesh

Kirti Singh Chauhan

Kaveri Books
New Delhi-110002

First Published in 2012
ISBN 978-81-7479-129-0

Published by
Kaveri Books
4832/24, Ansari Road
New Delhi - 110 002 (India)
Tel.: 011-2328 8140, 2324 5799
Fax: 011-2328 8140
E-mail: kaveribooks@vsnl.com,
kaveribooks@gmail.com
Website: www.kaveribooks.com

Laser Typesetting by : Deep Graphics, Delhi

Printed at : Salasar Imaging Systems, Delhi-110 052

PRINTED IN INDIA

Dedication

This book is dedicated to
my beloved children,
Miss Divyanshi Singh and
Mr. Bhavya Pratap Singh,
who are very caring and
always a real source of inspiration
and strength to me.

Acknowledgement

In the completion of this book, I received help and encouragement from a number of persons. I would like to express my sincere gratitude and thanks to all of them.

Dr. B.C. Upreti of South Asia Studies Centre, University of Rajasthan, Jaipur has been a great source of inspiration for me during the completion of this book. He took all pains, and devoted his precious time. I have learnt much from him and he also provided me valuable suggestions, moral support and blessings always.

I wish to express my indebtedness and gratitude to Dr. Krishan Gopal of South Asia Studies Centre, University of Rajasthan, Jaipur for his valuable suggestions, appreciations and academic support.

In the same vein I recall my great indebtedness and deep sense of regards and gratitude to the teachers and staff members of South Asia Studies Centre, University of Rajasthan, Jaipur. Specially 1 am very thankful to Dr. S.N. Kausik, Director, South Asia Studies Centre and Dr. Shashi Upadhaya for their valuable advice and appreciations.

In the University of Rajasthan, Jaipur I owe a great deal of respect for Dr. K.L. Sharma, Professor, Department of Law, Dr. Yashbir Singh, Assistant Professor, Department of Statistics, Dr. Jyant Singh, Assistant Professor, Department of Statistics, and Dr. Raka Singh, Assistant Professor, Department of Political Science for their support and encouragement at various stages of the present book.

I shall be failing in my duty if I do not recall my indebtedness to the librarians and staff members of Jawaharlal Nehru Memorial Fund, New Delhi, Jawaharlal Nehru University, New Delhi, Delhi University, Delhi, Central Library and Library of South Asia Studies Centre, University of Rajasthan, Jaipur along with High Commission of Bangladesh, Embassy of Myanmar, Nepal, Bhutan, Sri Lanka and High Commission of Pakistan in New Delhi, for providing valuable literatures, informations and data on foreign policy of Bangladesh.

I do not have appropriate words to express my gratitude and indebtedness to my parents Shri Digvijay Singh and Smt. Suman Singh, my father-in-law Shri Sohan Singh Chauhan and my mother-in-law Smt. Roopwati Singh Chauhan for their life long inspirations and for extending their unflinching moral support and encouragement during every stage of the book.

I wish to express the deep sense of indebtedness to my brothers-in-law Kr. M.S. Chauhan, Advocate, Kr. J.S. Chauhan, Advocate, Kr. B.S. Chauhan, Dr. D.S. Chauhan, Assistant Professor, Department of Geography, University of Rajasthan, Jaipur, and Dr. Yashwant Singh, Lecturer, Seedling Academy, Jaipur, my sister-in-law Dr. Sushma Chauhan, Assistant Professor, Government Women's Polytechnic College, Jaipur, my brother Mr. Surya Pratap Singh, my bhabi Ms. Gunjan Raje, my cousins Miss Anupama Singh, Miss Archana Singh, my nephews Mr. Abhimanyu Singh, Mr. Parmendra Singh, Mr. Ran Vijay Singh, my nieces Miss Kamakshi Singh, Miss Ojaswini Singh, Miss Sunena Singh, Miss Vasundhara Singh and other members of my family who have been an endless sources of moral support and inspirations for me during the preparation of the present book.

I want to convey my hearty thanks to my husband Dr. Surendra Singh Chauhan and my children Miss Divyanshi Singh and Mr. Bhavya Pratap Singh for their moral support, unstinted cooperation and encouragement. They gave a new direction to my academic life.

Finally, I am very thankful to Kaveri Books, New Delhi for timely completion of the book with utter neatness and quality.

Preface

Bangladesh which is officially known as the *Gano Prajatantri Bangladesh* (People's Republic of Bangladesh) is a new sovereign state in South Asia, other states of the region being India, Pakistan, Nepal, Bhutan, Sri Lanka, and the Maldives. Bangladesh is almost surrounded by India. It is bordered on three sides by the Indian states of West Bengal on the West and North, Meghalaya, Assam and Tripura on the North-east and East, and by Myanmar toward the South-east; on the South-the country extends to the Bay of Bengal, which provides direct access to the high seas. It is the 88 state in area in the world with total land of 147,570 square kilometers (56,977 sq. miles). In population, Bangladesh occupies 9 position in the world, total population being approximately 129 million. At present, the estimated population of Bangladesh is more than 141 million. It is one of the world's most densely populated countries where more than 920 people live per square kilometer.

The origin of Bangladesh can be traced back to the partition of India in 1947 when Pakistan was carved out of the subcontinent in response to the demand of the All India Muslim League, a party of the Indian Muslims, founded in Dhaka in 1906 for a homeland for the Indian Muslims. Bangladesh was then known first as East Bengal and afterwards when the first constitution of Pakistan was promulgated in 1956 as East Pakistan. East Pakistan was formed by combining together eastern part of Bengal and the Sylhet district of Assam, two provinces of the then undivided India.

Pakistan then had two wings-East and West, which were separated by 1600 kms. of "hostile" territory of India. East and West wings of Pakistan had few similarities but more dissimilarities. Soon there arose deep dissension between them over the issues of establishing democracy, according national language status of Bengali and of distribution of the national revenue. The Eastern wing wanted democratic system of government, recognition of its language Bengali as one of the national languages of Pakistan, and proportionate share of national revenue for its development. But its demands met with stiff resistance from the Western wing and in course of time Eastern wing was reduced into an internal colony of the West Pakistan. This situation gave birth to a national movement in the Eastern wing. The movement was led by Awami League (called earlier Awami Muslim League) which was founded in 1949 by a faction of the Muslim League. The faction left the Muslim League after it had failed to democratise the parent body. The national movement gradually developed into a war of independence. The war ended with total defeat of Western wing based Pakistan government in December 1971. East Pakistan, then emerged as a sovereign independent state, called Bangladesh.

Dr. Kirti Singh Chauhan

CONTENTS

List of Abbreviations

ADB	Asian Development Bank
AL	Awami League
ASA	Air Service Agreement
ASEAN	Association of South East Asian Nations
BDR	Bangladesh Rifles
BEPZA	Bangladesh Export Processing Zones Authority
BIISS	Bangladesh Institute of International and Strategic Studies
BIMSTEC	Bangladesh, India, Myanmar, Sri Lanka, Thailand Economic Cooperation
BNP	Bangladesh Nationalist Party
BOI	Board of Investment
BSF	Border Security Force
BTC	Bangladesh Trading Cooperation
BTPA	Bangladesh Trade and Payment Agreement
CHT	Chittagong Hill Tracts
CIS	Common wealth of Independent States
CPB	Communist Party of Bangladesh
D-8	Developing-8 (Islamic Organization)
$	Dollar (US Currency)
FACA	Fast Attack Craft Gun
FACP	Fast Attack Craft Patrol
FDI	Foreign Direct Investment
EPZs	Export Processing Zones

FTA	Free Trade Area
G-77	Group of 77
G-8	Group of 8
GCC	Gulf Cooperation Council
GPSA	Gas Purchase Sales Agreement
HANA	Humanitarian Assistance Need Assistance
ILO	International Labour Organisation
JBC	Joint Business Council
JCCES	Joint Committee for Commercial and Economic Cooperation
JEC	Joint Economic Commission
JMB	Jamuna Multipurpose Bridge
JRC	Joint River Commission
JRD	Joint Record of Discussions
LDCs	Less Developed Countries
LTTA	Long Term Trade Agreement
MFNs	Most Favoured Nations
MNF	Multinational Force
MOU	Memorandum of Understanding
MQM	Mohajir Quami Movement
NAM	Non-Aligned Movement
NAP-M	National Awami League-Muzaffar
NIEO	New International Economic Order
OIC	Organisation of Islamic Countries
ONGC	Oil and Natural Gas Commission
PCJSS	Parbottya Chattagram Jana Sanghati
PIA	Pakistan International Airlines
POWs	Prisoners of War
PNP	Pakistani National Party
PRC	Peoples Republic of China
RMG	Readymade Garments
RS	Rupees (Indian Currency)
SAARC	South Asian Association for Regional Cooperation
SAFTA	South Asia Free Trade Area

SAGQ	South Asian Growth Quadrangle
SAPTA	South Asia Preferential Trading Arrangements
SMES	Small and Marginal Enterprises
SOFA	Status of Forces Agreement
SPDC	Myanmar State Peace and Development Council
STA	Special Trading Arrangements
TK	Taka (Bangladesh Currency)
TNV	Tripura National Volunteers
USA/US	United States of America
UNGA	United Nations General Assembly
UN	United Nations
UNHCR	United Nations High Commissioner for Refugees
USAID	United States Agency for International Development
USPALOM	United States Pacific Command
USSR	Union of Soviet Socialist Republics
WHO	World Health Organisation
WTO	World Trade Organization

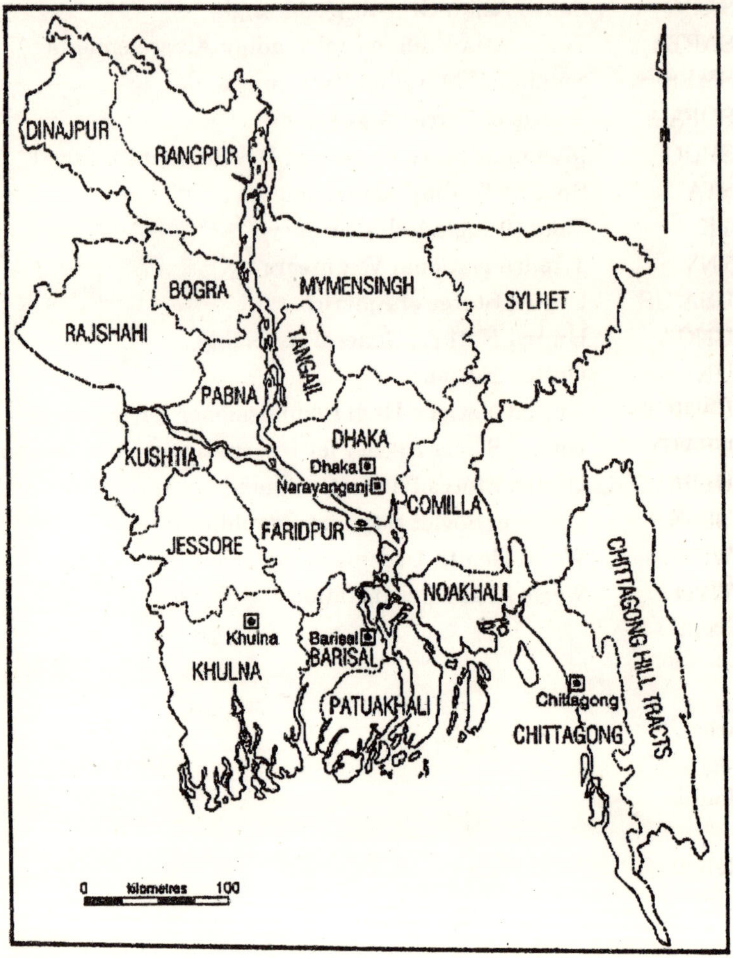

Map of Bangladesh

Bangladesh at a Glance

Official Name	:	The People's Republic of Bangladesh
Independent Day	:	16 December 1971
Capital	:	Dhaka: Area- 1416 Sq. Km.
Population	:	9.9 million
President	:	Mr. Md. Zillur Rahman
Prime Minister	:	Mrs. Sheikh Hasina
Geographical Location	:	Between 23° 34' and 26° 38' north latitude and between 88 41' and 92° 41' east longitude
Area	.	1,47,570 Sq. Km. including inland waters = 56,977 Sq. Miles
Boundary	:	North: India, West: India, East: India and Myanmar, South: Bay of Bengal
Religion (Census 2001)	:	Islam (88.3%), Hinduism (10.5%), Buddhism (0.6%) and Christianity (0.3%)
Unit of Currency	:	Taka
Gross Domestic Product	:	USD 230 Per Capita
GNI	.	USD 370 Per Capita
GDP Growth	:	3%
Income	:	USD 220-240 Per Capita
Import	:	USD 2709 Per Capita
Export	:	USD 2138 Per Capita
Trade	:	USD 43-54 Per Capita or 31.5% of GDP

Time	: GMT + 6.00 hours
Administrative Units	. Division : 6; Zila : 64; Thana : 507; Union : 4484; Municipalities : 254; Village : 87319
Major Cities	: Dhaka, Chittagong, Khulna, Rajshahi, Mymensing, Comilla, Barisal, Sylhet
Climate	: Average Winter temp (Max - 29° C, Min - 11° C) Average Summer temp (Max - 40° C, Min - 21° C)
Main Seasons	: Winter (November- February), Summer (May-June), Monsoon (July-October)
Population (Census 2001)	: Approximately 129 million; Growth rate 2.3% per annum; Density per square km. 920.
Language	: Bengali but English is also used.
Principal River	: Padma, Meghna, Jamuna, Brahmaputra, Teesta, Surma and Karnaphuli in all 700 rivers including tributaries and branches.
Principal Minerals	: Natural Gas, Lignite Coal, Limestones, Ceramic, Clay and Glass Sand.
Principal Industry	: Garments, Jute, Cotton, Textile, Tea, Paper, Newsprint, Cement, Fertilizer, Sugar, Engineering, Electric Cables, Leather, Fish.
Principal Exports	: Readymade Garments, Jute and Jute products, Tea, Leather and Frozen food.
Sea Ports	. Chittagong and Mongla.
Airports	: Dhaka, Chittagong, Jessore, Rajshahi, Iswardi, Sylhet, Cox's Bazar, Syedpur and Barisal.

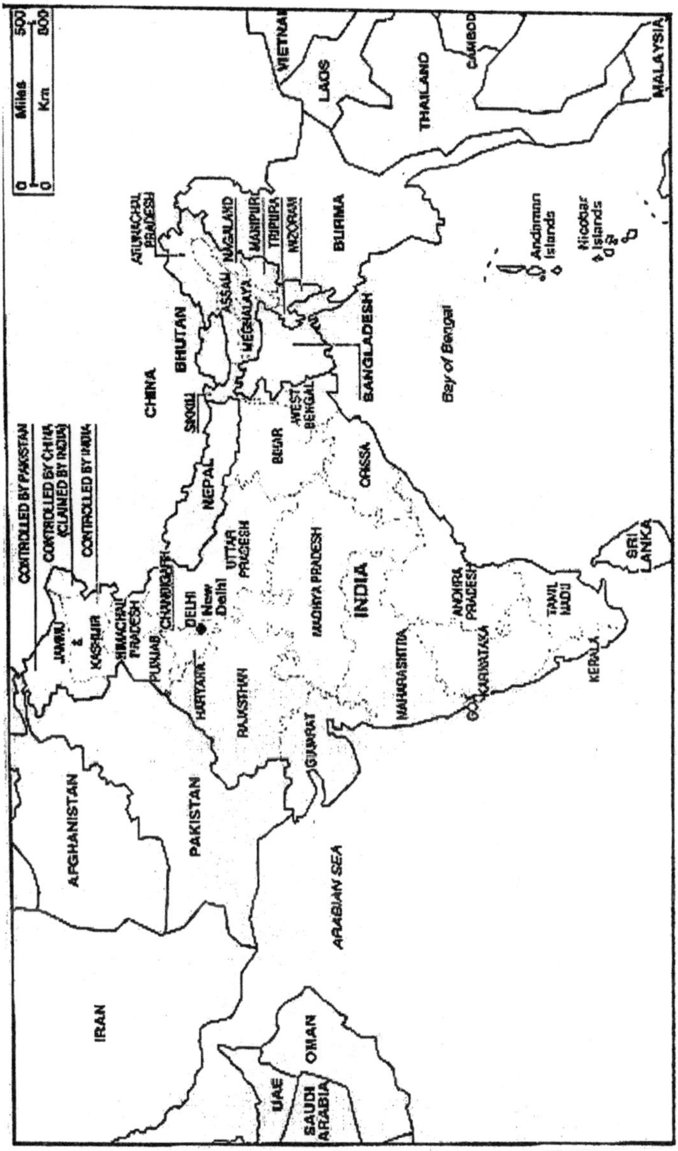

Map of South Asia

A FLOW CHART OF THE DETERMINANTS OF FOREIGN POLICY OF BANGLADESH

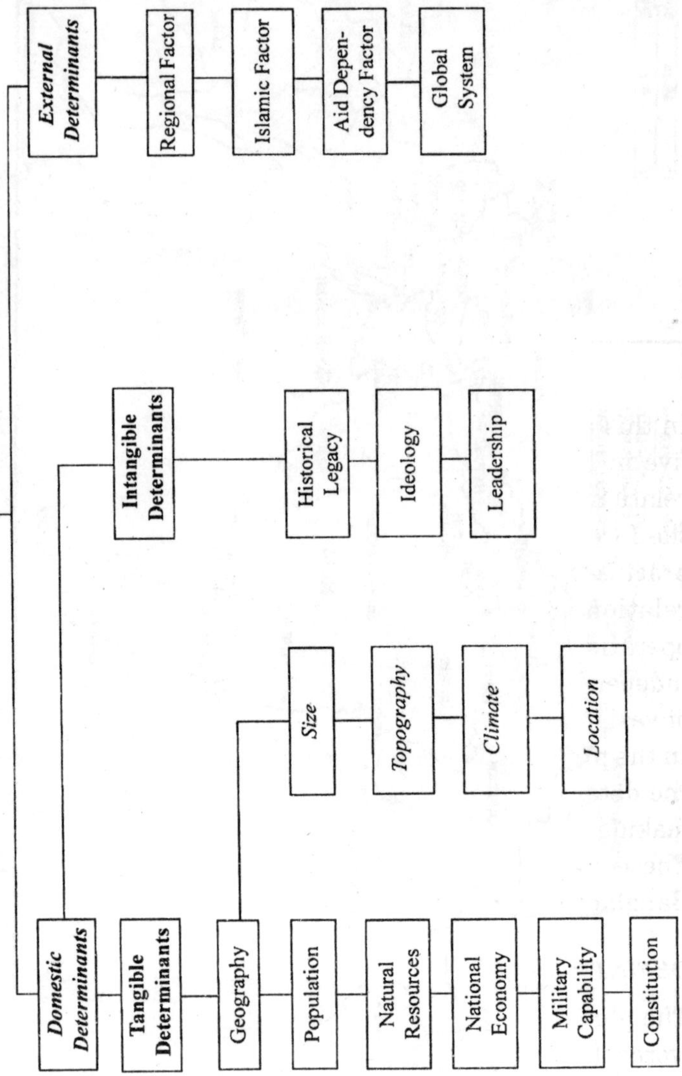

CHAPTER -1

Determinants of Foreign Policy of Bangladesh

In this age of global interdependence, where no nation can live in isolation, every state has to maintain some sort of relations with other states. This is usually done by pursuing the foreign policy. In keeping with this basic fact of state practice, Bangladesh also pursues a distinct course in its relations with the external environment. However, the operational isation of foreign policy of a country is not an independent variable. It is shaped and conditioned by a set of variables which includes both stable and dynamic forces. In the present chapter an attempt has been made to find out the determinants of Bangladesh foreign policy, its decision making structure and the nature of its continuity and change. These are important for understanding the bases on which Bangladesh formulates its foreign policy.

DEFINITION OF FOREIGN POLICY

The phrase 'foreign policy' is a combination of two separate words-'foreign' and 'policy'. But it does not mean that a state's foreign policy is 'foreign' to the hopes and aspirations of the people of that state. Usually by 'policy' we mean certain courses of action taken for the purpose of attaining specific goals and objectives. As Padelford, Lincoln and Olvey say, "policy is the over all result of the processes by which a state translates its broadly conceived goals and interests into specific courses of action in order to achieve its objectives and preserve its interests."[1] A state's overall national policy may be divided into domestic policy and foreign policy. Conceptually, foreign policy is that part of a state's national policy which relates to the external environment. In a nutshell, as it has nicely been expressed by the nineteenth century Prussian diplomat and statesman Prince Otto von Bismarck, the extension of domestic policy is foreign policy. For an operational definition of foreign policy, we may state that it consists of the courses of actions which a state usually undertakes in its effort to carry out its national objectives beyond the limits of its own jurisdiction.[2]

Foreign policy consists of both the long-term, i.e. relatively permanent interests which are to be maintained and enhanced, and declaration of specific policy objectives as they relate to a particular situation arising out of any event or occurrence in international affairs having vital link with the long-term objectives. For example, the foreign policy of Bangladesh in relations with the Arab countries has permanent basis. However, in the event of any development in the Arab world arising out of, say, any new Israeli aggression, the Foreign Minister of Bangladesh usually declares the position of his country as to what course the country is likely to take in that particular event, keeping in mind the long-term basis of her foreign policy. It thus follows that fulfillment of national interest is the main goal of foreign policy. In fact, national interest is the basic foundation on which the foreign policy of a country is built. This is true for Bangladesh as well as any other country of the world.

MAJOR DETERMINANTS

The determinants of foreign policy are simply factors, sources or variables which influence the nature, style, objective and strategy of the foreign policy of a country. It is expected that for a rational decision the foreign policy decision makers would take into consideration all or some of the relevant factors at the time of reaching a particular decision, or responding to a particular situation. A study of the determinants gives us an understanding of the reasons behind a particular decision or the options available to a decision maker in a particular situation.

The principal peaceful means to pursue goals and objectives of a foreign policy is diplomacy. Diplomacy is the inter-state communication of dialogue. The dialogue between independent states-the machinery by which their governments conduct it and the network of promises, contracts, institutions and codes of conduct which developed out of it-is the substance of diplomacy.[3] Foreign policy is the legislative aspect and diplomacy is the executive aspect of managing foreign relations. Communication has brought changes in roles and functions of policy makers and diplomats. Heads of governments, Foreign Ministers, and Bureaucrats now can meet personally with their counterpart. The policy making and negotiating roles have merged to a certain extent..While the administrative functions of the diplomat in the field has expanded but his negotiating role has probably decreased.[4]

The foreign policy of a state is directly determined by its power or capability. The diplomacy of a state is indirectly determined by its power. The extent to which a state can persuade others to act or refrain from acting in a certain way, depends on the power which each of them command, including the will to use it, and the extent to which other states support them that is, tend their power to one side or the other. The diplomatic objectives of a state and the tactics it adopts for their achievement are always a function of its overall capability of action, within the situation in which it is placed.

The power is relative, because one state can be strong to another but may be weak to a third. The nature of diplomacy-whether it will be aggressive, uncompromising with an ambition to create zone of influence or pacific, compromising and persuasive to achieve its national interests is determined by a state's capability. It dictates the style which will be suitable whether bilateral negotiations with the concerned state or a multilateral collective bargaining. A developed and strong state's diplomatic objectives are power projection and creation of influence area in addition to security, development and world peace, which are indeed the objectives of a weak state. Security threats faced by modern states have increasingly diversified and diplomacy is an essential element in the continuous process of defining, controlling, maintaining and enhancing security.[5]

The determinants of foreign policy are broadly of two types domestic and external. The domestic variables act as a capability or constraint for the foreign policy of a country depending on their nature. Any factor might be boon for one country and bane for another. Domestic factors can be divided into tangible and intangible. All tangible factors have some intangibility and all intangible factors have some tangibility. Tangible factors can be measured by analysts and intangible factors can be evaluated.

DOMESTIC TANGIBLE DETERMINANTS

Geography

The most permanent variable of a state and its capability is geography. Although the theory of the geographical determinism of foreign policy has undergone changes consequent to the technological development, but even then the influence of geographical factor on foreign policy of states remain considerable. It is not possible for any state to ignore its geographical realities i.e. facts of location, territorial space, boundary and terrain resources, etc. There are four geographical factors - *size, topography, location and climate* which affect the foreign policy of a country.

Size

The total land area of a state is in itself an element of power. Its significance varies considerably with changes in the other elements of national power. Other things being equal, the larger a state, the greater is its power of defence.[6] For a developing country with meagre resources sheer size may in some respect contribute to its weakness. To develop transportation and communication are burdensome and to bring the political unity of people in a widely dispersed area is difficult.

Bangladesh is a country of moderate size, neither small nor big. The total area of Bangladesh is 56977 sq. miles or 1,47, 570 sq. km. It is somewhat larger than England. But it is dwarfed by its neighbour India.

Topography

The configuration of topography is the location and direction of the flow of rivers, the mountains, the plains. Topography influences the nature of an economy and population density of a nation. Bangladesh is the world's largest deltaic area criss-crossed by an amazing network of rivers, rivulets and streams. The deltaic plain is formed by three great rivers - the Ganga, the Brahmaputra locally known as the Jamuna and the Meghana. The other important rivers are Tista, Karotoya, Atri, Mahananda, Karnafulli, Kabodak Rupsha, Anal Khan and Madhumati. One important reason of the high density of population is the fertility of the soil which attracted migration from the mainland to this part in the past.

Bangladesh has a flat land. Mymensingh and Sylhet constitutes the small hilly region in the north east which is an extension of the Meghalaya plateau of India. The coastline of Bangladesh along the Bay of Bengal extends from a western projection of Myanmar to the beaches of West Bengal. There is a dense forest in the south-west of the country known as Sunderban. In the south-east lies the Chittagong Hills, rising somewhere between 2,000 and 3,000 feet. This is also covered by forest. Absence of any plateau is the cause of the non-availability of minerals in Bangladesh.

Topographically, Bangladesh is linked and dependent upon India in many ways. The main rivers- the Ganga and the Jamuna pass through India before entering into Bangladesh. The third river Meghna has catchment area in Indian north-eastern plateau. The rivers have less than required water in the dry season, and bring flood in the monsoon. The river systems create ecological threat to Bangladesh. Optimum utilization of the water resources of Bangladesh require enhancement of river flow in dry season and control of the flow in monsoon. This is not possible without India's cooperation in the development of the water resources. India as upper riparian state is capable of unilaterally increase the intensity of the problem by diverting more water in dry season at Farakka, and by non-diverting the flow in monsoon which will increase the ferocity of flood in Bangladesh. The nature of topography of Bangladesh suggests to have good friendly relations with India.

Climate

Climatic condition is one of the important determinants of culture and economy, along with natural resources, political organization and religion of country. Climate influences the productivity of the soil and the vigour of the people. Continuous extremes of heat and cold and excessive aridity and rainfall are handicaps to human existence.

The climate of Bangladesh is sub-tropical monsoon. The climate is characterised by high temperature, heavy rainfall, excessive humidity, and marked seasonal variations. Rainfall sometimes is accompanied by cyclones, storms and tidal bores. Torrential and incessant monsoon rainfall in Bangladesh and the high flow of rivers bringing monsoon waters from India, often create heavy flood in this low lying land. Natural calamities are a great challenge to the economic development of Bangladesh.

Natural calamities are important in the history of Bangladesh. The devastating cyclone of November 1970 and the apathetic response by the Pakistan authorities, which was highlighted by the A L completed the alienation of the East Pakistan People, from West Pakistan. The sweeping victory of the Awami League in the December 1970 elections was greatly influenced by the cyclone. The flood of July 1974 caused great havoc in Bangladesh. Famine and crisis stalked the land like the big jungle cats. People in the countryside began to die like flies.[7]

Location

Location of a country is more important than size. Location figures in the diplomacy and war strategy adopted by a country. Every state has two types of location i.e. absolute location and relative location. Absolute location of a state is its permanent place on the earth surface which is expressed in terms of latitude and longitude. This decides the state, climatic zone, its maritime and land locked status etc. The relative location of a state is its proximity with other state i.e. its borders and frontiers. Some borders and frontiers due to their nature induce cross border human interaction and some borders due to their difficult terrain repel cross-border interaction i.e. migration, trade, inter-country marriage and conflict.[8]

Bangladesh is virtually surrounded by India on three sides. The total land boundary of Bangladesh is 4,246 km in which it has a small border of 193 km with Myanmar, the rest 4,053 km is with India. Most of the Indo-Bangladesh border is artificial passing through fields, villages and some towns. All sorts of good and bad interaction is prevalent and can not be controlled by either of the two states. Bangladeshi coastline in the south along with the Bay of Bengal is 580 km. Other countries located near Bangladesh without common borders are Nepal, Bhutan and China in the North. In the Bay of Bengal its maritime border with India has not been settled. India has a long sea coast from west to east extended deep into the Bay of Bengal, by the presence of Indian islands of Andaman and Nicobar. For practical purposes Bangladesh is indirectly surrounded by India even in the South. Bangladesh is a very weak state in comparison to India. Its location and comparative weakness with India make it rational to maintain good neighbourly relations with New Delhi.

Geography is more a restraint than a capability to Bangladesh. Its size, topography, climate and location have more negative features than positive. Bangladesh is sensitive to its geo-politics. It regards itself India-locked and geographically, strategically and ecologically vulnerable to India.[9]

Population

The second domestic tangible factor of national capability is population and human resources. At present, the estimated population of Bangladesh is more than 141 million. It is one of the world's most densely populated country where more than 920 people live per square kilometer and per capita income is 220-240 US $. Large population may be a source of strength and weakness depending on the ability of the state to support it at a tolerable standards of living, and the capacity of the state to provide productive engagements to the talents and energies of the human resources. In developed countries large population is a source of power, but in developing countries large population is a burden and hindrance in fast development.[10]

Population must be considered in terms of birth and death rates, age, sex ratio and land-man ratio. It should be examined in terms of population density, literacy, health facilities, skilled and unskilled, earning and dependent members. The population becomes a liability when any increase in overall population results in a reduction in the quality of goods and services, available for any individual. Higher population increases the number of younger people in the society i.e. dependents in the national population. Generally 3 per cent of national income saving is necessary to maintain 1 per cent increase of population at the same standard of living.[11]

The population explosion of Bangladesh is its paramount economic problem. The government has declared it as number one problem. Population density of Bangladesh is highest in the world except the city state of Singpore. It is three times more densely populated than India. There is extensive malnutrition, hunger and disease prevalent in the country. Large number of people are scantly clothed, illiterate, unskilled unemployed and underemployed. To provide the basic necessities to the fast growing population is a great challenge to the government of Bangladesh. Due to all pervasive poverty revenue generation is low, saving is small, capital formation is slow. Huge investment is required for the optimum utilisation of the exploited resources.

The population explosion is a great problem for Bangladesh. Over-size population is a bane, not a boon for Bangladesh. The unusually high population in terms of land-man and natural resources ratio has resulted in migration from Bangladesh, in search of better conditions of life to neighbouring countries towards the close of the nineteenth century. After the formation of East Pakistan heavy in and out migration began, but the reason was more religious and political than economic. The migration in this period changed the demography of Tripura, an Indian province. After the liberation of Bangladesh, the migration from Bangladesh into Assam and other parts of north east and north India mainly due to economic reason has heavily increased. It is one of the problems between India and Bangladesh in the perception of New Delhi.

Natural Resources

Natural resources includes minerals, flora and fauna, waterfall and soil fertility. Natural resources are gifts of nature and of immense utility. Resources are assets, and what constitute assets vary according to time and place. Raw minerals require labour, technology, capital to convert it into actual utility. If a state has minerals it has the potential to be an industrial power. The presence of exploitable non-human natural resources are neither essential nor a guarantee for economic development is proved by the development experiences of different countries. H.W. Arndt in his book - *Economic Development: The History of an Idea,* has shown that there is an inverse relationship between the availability of non-human natural resources in a country and its industrialisation. The country with abundant natural resources suffers from 'the temptation of lotus eating'.[12]

Bangladesh has limited mineral resources. The only important mineral which is present in abundance and being exploited is natural gas. Total estimated recoverable natural gas is 13.59 million cubic feet and the net available reserves after production of 2.96 trillion cubic feet till 2004, is about 10.63 trillion cubic feet.[13] Gas is the main raw material for power generation, fertilizer and other industries. It is also used for commercial and domestic purposes.

The second important mineral is coal and a total reserve of 1053.9 million tons of coal is available at the depth of

2800 to 3800 feet below the surface in western Bangladesh. The third important mineral available in Bangladesh is limestone, which is the basic raw material for cement production. One of the three deposits of limestone is presently mined. Cement factories have been set up for utilisation of the limestone. The minerals of the other deposits are under exploration. Other minerals, small quantity of which are being exploited are white clay and glass sand. Still unexploited but under the process of exploration are peat, construction material and mineral sand containing heavy metals. Extensive radio-active sand deposits have been found along with beaches of Bangladesh. There is possibility of off-shore oil availability. Full exploration is not possible without settling maritime boundary with India. Oil deposits were found in Haripur in north-eastern Bangladesh in 1986.

But the rivers and the high yielding deltaic soil are the most important natural resources of Bangladesh. The rivers are the living arteries of Bangladesh which have formed the delta, they provide irrigation water and cheap means of transportation and facilitate fisheries development. The fertility of soil has tremendous capacity. But it is grossly under utilised. Lack of irrigation facilities in dry season is also a factor for low productivity. River water management is essential for checking the damage done to the crops in rainy season by flood and provide water for irrigation in dry season. Presently the river systems are not properly controlled, so they create problems of abundant water in monsoon which cause flood and less water in dry season, which result into draught affecting the agricultural productivity in both ways.

In Bangladesh, despite huge availability of water there is not much scope for hydro-electric power as most of the land is flat. The only hydro-electric power station is on Karnafulli river at Kaptai in Chittagong hills, which generates 25 per cent of the country's electricity.

The forests of Bangladesh are important natural resource. Different industries like newsprint, match box, pencil timber are based on the forest. Wild honey and bee wax are collected from the Sundarban forests. In the rivers and creeks of Sunderban, shells, conches, skins of lizards, reptiles and crocodiles are available. The area is abound by fish. Fast growing foreign trees and commercial plants like rubber and coffee are being planted to generated more resources.[14]

National Economy

The strength of a country is determined by its national economy. The status of a country as developed and developing is basically on the basis of its national economy. A developed state is generally self-sufficient for its basic needs, financially strong and technologically advance. This becomes a leverage for the foreign policy of the state. An economically underdeveloped country is a weak power. It is dependent upon others for its needs. A developing economy has negative balance of payment to cope with, that it has to borrow from international money market which further weakens its economy, and consequently its bargaining power in diplomacy is weakened.

Problem of Economic Development

Bangladesh is the largest among the Least Developed Countries (LDCs). Taking into consideration the extreme nature of challenges before economic development of Bangladesh, some optimist economists have termed it as a 'test case of development'.[15] The economy of Bangladesh has four fundamental ailments which have been termed as 'ominous convergence' : 1. rapid population growth 2. ecological vulnerability 3. large number of absolute poor and 4. deeply rooted domestic and external macro-economic problems.[16]

Bangladesh national economy was surplus rich economy during the pre-colonial period. Three phases in the modern economic history of Bangladesh have led the economy to this position.

1. The agriculture economy of the region, presently Bangladesh, was restructured and converted from a self-sufficient prosperous economy into a hinterland region, for the supply of raw materials for the new industries of Calcutta, the imperial capital during the British period. The world famous textile industry of Bengal was slowly annihilated by discriminatory policies against the industries, and atrocities against the artisans for the promotion of textile industry in England. The interest of the colonial power demanded such policies and decisions which were favourable to it but which went against the interests of the colony.
2. Pakistan proved to be a false liberation for East Bengal or East Pakistan. The vested interests of the ruling elite of Pakistan, dictated them to turn East Pakistan into an internal colony of Pakistan. The internal colonialism of East Pakistan by West Pakistan is a fact established on the basis data given not only by Bangladesh economist, but also by the western economists. The irony is that, when West Pakistani rulers recognized the abnormal disparity and took initiatives to remove it the liberation war started. In the 50s there was stagnation but in the 60s, particularly in the late 60s the economy was growing with a satisfactory rate.[17]
3. The economy suffered a serious setback during the War of Liberation. Production declined in all sectors and the process of development was reversed. There was massive movement of population, huge destruction and damage to the infrastructures. The overall economic situation was worse than at any time in the recorded history of the country. Gigantic resource investment was done in the reconstruction and rehabilitation work, which extended from 1972-73 to 1975-76.[18]

During all these three phases of the modern economic history of Bangladesh, the national population increased, particularly in the second phase which resulted in progressive deterioration in the situation because there was not a corresponding growth in production.

The total GDP of Bangladesh in the year 2004 was taka 1610 billion or $ 46.7 billion. The GDP growth rate was stagnant below 5 per cent till 1994-95 since the creation of Bangladesh. It crossed the psychological barrier for the first time in 1995-96 and increased to 5.3 percent. It reached to 5.8 per cent in 2004. Still it is far below the desired rate of 7-8 percent which is required for a long period to make any real dent to the poverty scenario. Per capita income in Bangladesh grew from $ 100 to $ 210 during 1970 to 1990. The growth rate was 3.8 percent per annum which was 5.6 per annum in South Asia, and 7.9 per annum in South East Asia. In 1998 the per capita income was $ 230. At present (2005) the per capita income of Bangladesh is $ 240. The over all economic situation of Bangladesh has stabilised and has shown a trend of improvement after 1990s.

The status of Bangladesh as LDC is a great handicap on her foreign policy. The economic dependence of Bangladesh upon the developed countries, even for maintenance as a state, demands that its foreign policy must keep the benifactor countries always interested in it. Bangladesh can take only that much independent decision which is tolerated by the development partner. The structural problems of the national economy, food deficit and urgency of development of the Bangladesh economy, demand very active economic diplomacy to get foreign assistance, promote export and attract foreign investment. The weakness of the economy has made the economic diplomacy of Bangladesh more important, than the political□security diplomacy. Through aid diplomacy Bangladesh procures different kind of foreign assistance from different sources for its survival and economic development. The weak economy projects a bad image of Bangladesh in the international public opinion.

Military Capability

Foreign policy of a country is greatly influenced by its military capability. Military capability includes the size of the armed forces, arms and equipment of the forces and the quality of the manpower of forces. The size of the armed forces includes army, air force and navy. Arms and equipment must be considered in terms of quantity and quality, modernity and sophistication, fire power and delivery power. The quality analysis of the manpower in defence forces can be done on the basis of training, discipline, morale and character. Military capability of a country also depends upon the level of self-sufficiency in arms production as well as the arms imports from other countries.

Military capability is an important and essential factor for the protection and promotion of politico-security objectives of foreign policy. Diplomatic bargaining of state depends upon its military capability. A nation can negotiate effectively only from position of strength.[19] A weak state fears negotiation with a strong state, because it feels that it has to compromise its stand in favour of the strong adversary.

Despite the importance of military capability for any country's foreign policy and diplomacy, its role should not be over emphasised. If the negotiating states are antagonistic and hostile to each other, agreement is elusive even when there is relative equality in their military capability. On the other hand, if they have mutual interest and confidence, fruitful negotiation is possible in spite of power disparity.

The military forces of Bangladesh were organised after independence from the deserters of the armed forces of Pakistan, who were posted in East Pakistan and participated in the War of Liberation of Bangladesh and the Bengali repatriated soldiers from West Pakistan. There was a clear chasm between the 'freedom fighters' and 'repatriates' in the forces. The freedom fighters got politicised on ideological line in the process of liberation war. [20]

Bangladesh is heavily dependent upon other countries for its arms and ammunition. The chief suppliers of arms and equipment to the Bangladesh armed forces in the post-Mujib era, are China and Britain. Bangladesh armed forces are equipped with some light weapons and equipment. According to *World Military Expenditures and Arms Transfers* the annual arms import of Bangladesh during Mujib regime was $ 18 million and during Zia, and Ershad it was $ 30 million.[21] Some of the arsenals are unserviceable due to shortage of spares.

In Bangladesh civil and military relations are not clearly defined and have not been properly established. It seems that after the advent of democratic era the armed forces have accepted the civilian control. Lack of political stability and nature of hostility between the two major parties still keep open the option of the armed forces, to emerge as the 'saviour of the nation' in any political crisis. The armed forces made a number of successful and unsuccessful coups against governments. All the heads of government before Ershad were either killed or removed by the armed forces. Ershad wanted to institutionalize the role of the armed forces in government to remove the potential threat from them but he could not do it due to strong opposition.[22]

Bangladesh armed forces are an important institution influencing the foreign policy and diplomacy of the country. The military men have played active diplomatic roles during the regimes of Zia and Ershad. The armed forces were one of the important players in foreign policy decision making and its implementation due to the nature of these regimes. Zia used diplomatic posting as a strategy to minimise troubles from disgruntled elements in the forces.

Ershad also maintained the policy of diplomatic posting to appease potential coup leaders like Zia to mitigate coup threat. In addition to the diplomatic appointments of the military officers, they are also posted as military attaches in the diplomatic mission of Bangladesh for looking after the defence and security related interests of the country. The Military attaches are significant diplomatic personnel in all the important diplomatic missions of the country. Bangladesh armed forces are providing training assistance to friendly countries either by offering training facilities in Bangladesh or sending trainers to the country which requires such training.[23] Bangladeshi forces have been deputed in many countries as peace keeping forces. Bangladesh has become one of the important contributors of the peace keeping in the world. BDR guarding the international borders of Bangladesh represents Bangladesh in border talks, with Indian Border Security Force (BSF), if some tension occurs on the border.

Contrary to the traditional attitude of Awami League towards defence forces, Sheikh Hasina was accommodative to the armed forces in the seventh parliamentary elections. She recognised the military as a significant force in the politics of Bangladesh, which would be a potential threat to an elected regime if they would have grievances against the regime. All the three important parties gave tickets to ex-army men in the seventh parliamentary elections. All of them had MPs from the military background. Three important ministers in Sheikh Hasina's government were ex-army men.[24] Although she removed those military officers from diplomatic postings who were involved in the assassination of her father, there has not been any radical change in the influence of military in the foreign policy. Instead of serving officers retired military officers were engaged in policy formation and its implementation after the advent of the democratic rule in 1991.

In the present elected regime of Khaleda Zia (2001-onwards) there is no reduction in the role or influence of armed forces in foreign policy. BNP is identified by its critics as a cantonment party. Some ministers of her government are also from army. In earlier regime also (1991-1996) armed forces played and important role in guiding Bangladesh's foreign policy. Many parliament members from her party were ex- army men. Her Foreign Minister and other two ministers were from military background.

Constitution

It has become a tacit convention of constitution-making for the decolonised nations who achieved their independence after the second world war to express their faith in the United Nations Charter, international law and peaceful means for achievement of their diplomatic objectives. In order to become a member of the comity of nations it had become necessary for the newly independent countries, to express conviction to the international norms and conventions. Most of these states included in their constitutions the broader framework to be followed by the incumbent governments in their foreign policy. By identifying the ideals and strategies of foreign policy, the constitution of a post-second world war state become a variable for the foreign decision-making of that country.

The Constitution of Bangladesh defines the broader guidelines of Bangladesh's foreign policy and its objectives. The constitution is a determinant of foreign policy and diplomacy of Bangladesh. Part 2 of the constitution which deals with the 'Fundamental Principles of State Policy' in article 25 defines four principles which may be called the ideals of foreign policy of Bangladesh government. It is incumbent on the government of Bangladesh irrespective of the nature of the government, to keep into consideration these principles in their foreign policy. The four guidelines of the foreign policy of Bangladesh are

1. respect for national sovereignty and equality,
2. non-interference in the internal affairs of other countries,
3. peaceful settlement of international disputes,
4. *respect for international law and the principles enunciated in the United Nations Charter.*[25]

The constitution in article 25 identifies three general aims which ought to be followed by the government of Bangladesh. Through the inclusion of these principles Bangladesh expressed its solidarity with the foreign policy aspirations of the developing countries, and also its support to the struggling peoples who were still colonies at the time of Bangladesh liberation. The constitution expects that every government in Bangladesh should

A. *strive for the renunciation of the use* of *force in international relations and for general and complete disarmament,*
B. uphold the right of every people freely to determine and build up its own social, economic and political system by ways and means of its own free choice,
C. support oppressed peoples throughout the world waging a just struggle against imperialism, colonialism or racism.

Zia divided the article into two clauses. He added one more aim through clause (2) to be pursued by every government of Bangladesh by Proclamation Order No. 1 of 1977, which later on became part of the constitution through amendment. Placing of the whole original article in clause (1) and his new addition in a separate clause, expresses the relative importance he wanted to give to this new objective. Article 25 (2) reads : *'The state shall endeavor to consolidate, preserve and strengthen fraternal relations among Muslim countries based on Islamic solidarity'.* [26]

This addition of a new aim of the foreign policy of Bangladesh was part of his Islamisation programme. This amendment formally recognised the importance of the Islamic World for the foreign policy of Bangladesh.

Zia also included through amendment a new article-145 A about international treaties signed by Bangladesh. The article reads: 'All *treaties with foreign countries shall be submitted to the President, who shall cause them to be laid before Parliament; provided that no such treaty shall be so laid if the President considers it to be against the national interest so to do.*[27] The article gives full powers to the executive to conclude a treaty. The executive which includes the President and his cabinet led by the Prime Minister is not accountable to the parliament in this matter, irrespective of the nature of the government, viz. whether the actual authority lies in the Prime Minister or the President. By qualifying the parliamentary ratification on the consideration of the executive this article implies that the executive may sign even a secret treaty with another state.

DOMESTIC INTANGIBLE DETERMINANTS

Historical Legacy

History as the record of the accumulated experience of past generations is an important factor for the domestic policy as well as foreign policy of a country.

History of a country includes among other things, the history of ideas and institutions, which influenced it through the ages. The history of a nation also includes its peaceful and violent interaction with other peoples or states in course of trade, and invasions throughout its known history. Each generation inherits the memories and experiences of the preceding generation. 'The dead hand of the past' is not really dead, it continues to influence the living generations. The national outlook remains the same, unless the circumstances in which the nation exists alter radically and permanently. One of the cardinal principles of international relations is the principle of past-future linkages. For understanding the foreign policy behaviour of a state, its past must be understood. Modern history of a state is more important in this regard than ancient and medieval.[28]

Foreign Policy of a nation as a part of its overall national policy is a continuation of the world view that national leadership holds and which has been evolved over a period to time. In the case of Bangladesh it is necessary first of all to remember that this country is relatively a new entrant into the comity of nations, having emerged as an independent nation a little more than three decades ago, to be precise on 16 December 1971. Historically speaking, therefore, one has to go beyond its period of independent existence.

Bengal (of which East Bengal was a part) has long tradition to fight against domination. Although Bengal's participation in the first war of independence in 1857 was not noteworthy, there is ample evidence to show that the imposition of British rule was resisted by the native rulers as well as by the people. Nawab

Sirajudollah's heroic battle against the foreign invaders- the British East India Company, the revolt of the Indigo plantation workers and the consciousness that it generated among the intelligentsia created a situation which later on developed into a powerful movement against British imperialism. Anti-imperialism remained an important plank of East Bengal's struggle for autonomy when opposition to imperialist-sponsored military alliances and pacts was a consistent theme of that struggle. In fact as the struggle against Pakistani domination got momentum in East Bengal, the anti-imperialist edge became sharper since the general belief among the leadership of the struggle was that Pakistan's military dictatorship was being sustained by the imperialists-the USA and other western powers.

Historically, therefore anti-imperialism could be an important determinant of the foreign policy of Bangladesh. In other words Bangladesh was expected to bear in mind that by pursuing an anti-imperialists foreign policy, she would be acting in conformity with a historical legacy.

Role of Ideology

Ideology is a comprehensive framework of doctrines inculcated into the society by its political leadership. Ideology provides the intellectual framework through which policy makers observe real ity.[29] Ideology prescribes for policy makers an image of the future state of the world, established the long-range goals of a state's external behaviour to be promoted through diplomacy, propaganda or force. It also serves as a means of rationalisation, justification, legitimisation and guidance for the choice of more specific domestic or foreign policy strategies.

The constitution of independent Bangladesh adopted nationalism, socialism, democracy and secularism as elements of state ideology. The four doctrines were propagated by the Awami League as *Mujibbad* (Mujibism). Nationalism was defined as the unity and solidarity of the Bengalee nation based on Bengali language and Bengali culture which achieved independence and sovereign Bangladesh through war of independence. The non-Bengali ethnic communities of the country, the Islamists, and the pro-Chines Communists, had reservations of identify themselves with the version of nationalism.[30] The constitution did not explicitly define socialism. The purpose of socialism was to achieve just and egalitarian society free from exploitation. In its implemented form it was mixed economy modeled on Indian socialism. Mujib nationalised the abandoned industries owned by west Pakistanis and Biharis before independence.

Democracy established by Sheikh Mujib was parliamentary democracy which guaranteed fundamental human rights, freedom and dignity of human person. He curtailed human rights through amendment in 1974 to cope with the opposition to his regime. When he thought that governing the country was becoming difficult due to continuously increasing opposition, he amended the constitution in January 1975 to change the parliamentary form of government into presidential form. He established his absolute autocratic rule through single party presidential system.

The fourth doctrine of the national ideology was secularism which for practical purposes meant elimination of communalism, neutrality of state towards religion, prohibition of any political use of religion and absence of any discrimination or persecution on religious ground. The critics viewed it also as Indian type i.e. negative and non-discriminatory. According to some the adoption of secularism in the constitution was a historical necessity.[31] Due to many compulsions Mujib himself began the use of religion for political purposes which weakened secularism.[32]

Zia redefined the state ideology through proclamation order as Chief Martial Law Administrator and later on by constitutional amendment. Zia propounded Bangladesh nationalism at the place of Bangalee nationalism which is constituted by race, religion, territory and economy in addition to language, culture and independence war. Ershad also followed Bangladeshi nationalism. Zia also removed the pledge to establish socialist economic system. Socialism remained in the constitution, but in its amended version it simply mean economic and social justice. Zia adopted capitalist path of development on the advice of the donors which was further strengthened by the succeeding regimes.

Zia retained the presidential from of government but ended single party system and limited the executive and legislative powers of the president. Ershad continued the same system of governance. Khaleda Zia though favoured continuation of the same system but due to pressure from her party men the constitution was amended in 1991, to change the system of governance from presidential to parliamentary. This is the only principle of the original national ideology over which both the major parties i.e., the B.N.P. and the Awami League (Sheikh Hasina) have reached consensus and which re-established through amendment.

Bangalee vis-a-vis Bangladeshi Nationalism

Zia completely removed secularism from the constitution and substituted it *by 'absolute trust and faith in the Almighty Allah'* in the Preamble and article 8. A new article 1A was added which reads: *absolute trust and faith in the Almighty Allah shall be the basis of all actions.* Article 12, which defined secularism was totally omitted. *'Bismillah-ar Rahman-ar Rahim* (in the name of Allah, the Beneficient, the Merciful)' was added above the Preamble. Ershad used Islam more explicitly and extensively in his politics. Through the 8 amendment of the Constitution in June 1988 he made Islam the state religion of Bangladesh. Article 2A which he inserted through the amendment reads: *The state religion of the Republic is Islam, but other religions may be practised in peace and harmony in the Republic.* The name of the country and the rights of the non-muslims remained unchanged in the constitution.

The Awami League government under Sheikh Hasina again adopted Bangalee nationalism and the spirit of secularism in its politics and policies, but could not amended the constitution because of not having two-third majority in the parliament, which is required for any constitutional amendment. Socialism was discarded even by Sheikh Hasina's Awami League. Both the major parties (AL and BNP) have common viewpoint on the form of government and the form of national economy. Nationalism and secularism, place of religion in national polity and politics are still controversial. Bangladesh is facing a problem of 'identity crisis'.[33]

In Bangladesh, on the question of identity the whole middle class is divided into two camps: *Bangalee nationalists and Bangladeshi nationalists.* The conflict on the issue of national identity has its implications in domestic policy and foreign policy. The Bangalee nationalists are generally biased for India and against Pakistan in their foreign policy approaches and the Bangladeshi nationalist have generally reverse biased in their attitudes in foreign policy issues.

In the post-Mujib era from August 1975 to June 1996, Bangladeshi nationalism was the dominant viewpoint. In the realm of foreign policy it implied opening up and development of good relations with China, Pakistan, Saudi Arabia and other Islamic countries. Bangalee nationalism again became ruling ideology in 1996 under Sheikh Hasina. Her coming into power heralded a new era of relationship with India based on reciprocal faith and confidence. From 2001 onwards, Khaleda Zia again came to power and maintained good relations with China, Pakistan, Saudi Arabia and other Islmaic countries which have matured and proved beneficial to Bangladesh irrespective of regimes. Now again Bangladeshi nationalism viewpoint is dominant under Khaleda Zia regime.

Role of Leadership

Leadership is an intangible determinant of power. Democratically elected popular, strong and legitimate leaders are a capability for foreign policy. Autocratic rulers who have usurped power through military coups with controversial legitimacy are not taken seriously by other countries, with which their governments negotiate on any issue. The leaders through their will (conscious and subconscious) convert the resources into power. Dynamic leadership can mitigate the weak power status of a country through its active and prudent diplomacy. Without the utilisation of the leadership the resources of a country cannot become power.

Image of a particular situation in the mind of leadership is very important determinant for the foreign policy of a country. Decision makers act according to their perception of reality, not in response to reality itself. The elite image constitutes a number of inter-related perceptions : (1) *of the external environments - global, regional and bilateral; and (2) of the internal environmental - military capability, economic capability, political structure, interest groups, and competing elites.*[34] From these perceptions emanates the elite's definition of their state's foreign policy. These images taken together constitute a world view, which creates a general psychological framework for decision making. The difference between image and reality is partly due to physical impediments to the flow of information and partly as a result of the distortion of reality caused by attitudes, values, beliefs or faulty expectations.

Every society, regardless of its form of government, has pyramidical elite structure comprising primary, secondary and tertiary elites and below them the masses. Every state has governmental elite, bureaucratic elite (including military as a vertical subsection), commercial-industrial elite, religious, intellectual, labour, agricultural, racial or ethnic and in some cases particularistic elite-each consisting primary, secondary and tertiary layers. These elites pressurise the top government elites to define the national interest in terms compatible with their own interests. The most influential among the groups of elites are most benefited through the diplomacy of the country.[35]

The reign of Zia had features of an intermediate regime and the politics of this period was of praetorian nature.[36] During his regime civil and military bureaucracy was restored to its earlier position of Pakistan period, which had been disturbed during the parliamentary regime of Mujib (1972-74). After the coup of 7 November, 1975 they re-emerged as the ruling elites. The Martial Law regime in Bangladesh was a partnership between the military elite and the civil bureaucracy. During Zia's period, particularly in its second phase the partnership between them was more or less equal but under Ershad the military elite subordinated the civil bureaucracy. The top echelon of civil and military bureaucracy in Bangladesh, who were very influential during 1975-1990 were recruited and trained during Pakistan days. These officers had fully imbibed the values and orientation of the West Pakistani civil and military bureaucracy. One of the important reasons for the change in the threat perception of Bangladesh during the post Mujib regimes are the similarities of attitude, belief and perception of the ruling elites of Bangladesh with that of Pakistan. The pattern of foreign policy in the post-Mujib Bangladesh was similar to Pakistan in many respect i.e. friendly attitude towards the Islamic countries, the US and China.[37]

Intellectual and religious elites are the other elite groups which are influential in foreign policy making. The teachers and students of Dhaka University are the primary intellectual elite, and the teachers and students of other institutions of higher learning are secondary and tertiary intellectual elite. A student leader of Dhaka University was appointed in the Bangladesh High Commission in Australia by Ershad, as a reward for his role in creating dissention in the students political groups in the university.

In 1991, with the restoration of parliamentary democracy in Bangladesh, the majority party in parliament has recovered its right to power. The civil and military elites are participating in governance indirectly through nomination, and election of the retired personnel to the parliament from different parties. Civil and military bureaucracy still plays important role in policy formation in the era of democratic regimes. The non-cooperation of the military with Ershad during anti Ershad movement of 1990 resulted in his fall, and the non-coperation of the civil services with Khaleda Zia forced her to accept the demand of neutral caretaker government, for free and fair election in 1996.

One of the important reasons for friendly relation of Bangladesh with India during Mujib regime was its sub-conscious faith and confidence in Indian leadership and its people. They developed personal relations during their stay in India at the time of Liberation War, and before with the India leadership and the ruling elite in general, and with West Bengal leaders and ruling elite in particular. The change of leadership in Foreign Ministry in 1973 by Mujib and removal of Tajuddin Ahmed from Finance Portfolio in 1974, were changes done by Mujib to bring changes in the foreign policy and economic policy of the country. An important factor influencing the positive foreign policy behaviour of Hasina's regime towards India, was the good experiences of the leadership during their stay in India during the Liberation War as youth leaders and the stay of Hasina in Delhi during the bad time of her family and her party, as a guest of the government of India from August 1975 to May 1981.

EXTERNAL DETERMINANTS

Regional Factor

The most important external factor for Bangladeshi foreign policy is its big neighbour India. Every country's first priority in foreign policy is its neighbourhood. In the perception of Bangladeshi security analysts few countries have to face the *tyranny of geography,* as it is faced by Bangladesh. Dictates of geo-politics have rendered Bangladesh literally India-locked.[38] India is the pre□eminent power in the South Asian region. This fact makes India an important determinant to be taken into account by the foreign policy decision makers of all the regional states. Bhutan and Nepal since 1950s and Sri Lanka since 1987 have formally accepted Indian role in their foreign policy decision-making through bilateral treaty agreements with New Delhi. Indo-Bangladesh treaty through which both the countries had decided to keep each other's foreign and security policy in harmony, and which was practically defunct in the post-Mujib era expired without renewal in 1997. India signed bilateral Shimla Agreement with Pakistan in 1972 which is recognised by both states as the basis of their bilateral relations. Indian help to the Maldivian government in the removal of the threat to its existence in 1988 has proved the utility and dependability of New Delhi in any military threat to the security of Maldives.

There are three policy options before Bangladesh in relation to India: *a policy of intransigence, a policy of indifference and a policy of accommodation.*[39] A policy of intransigence is not feasible considering the comparative capabilities of both the countries and the vulnerability of Bangladesh to India. A policy of indifference towards India is not a sane policy due to geographical, historical and social linkages *of* Bangladesh with India. Indo-Bangladesh border is artificial viz. the result *of* the unaccmodative politics *of* the major two religious communities *of* the sub-continent during a particular period *of* time. The bonds *of* topography, hydrography, culture and the economy linkages evolved during colonial period are so strong that neither *of* the two states can afford to be indifferent to each other. Only the policy *of* accommodation is a proper policy. Indis's cooperation is necessary for development and prosperity *of* Bangladesh and Dhaka's support is essential for the development *of* North-East India.

India watches carefully the foreign policy pursued by Bangladesh. It is difficult for any government in Bangladesh to take a foreign policy decision, which is considered hostile and antagonistic to its national security by India. No government in Dhaka can go beyond a limit in its pronouncement and posture against India. Bangladesh is forced by its location to maintain at least normal if not closer relations with India. Its location has seriously circumscribed its manoeuverability. India factor is and will remain an important concern in the minds of Bangladesh foreign policy decision makers. It influences its politico□security diplomacy both at bilateral and multilateral level.[40]

Islamic Factor

Islam is an influencing factor on the foreign policy of all muslim states either as a capability or as a constraint. The degree of its role on the foreign policy may vary from country to country depending on the state ideology. The unity and universality of the Islamic world and muslim people has weakened. During colonial period the western powers introduced modernisation and secularisation, which resulted in the emergence of territorial national sovereignty, abolition of Caliphate and supersedence of European systems of law over *Shariah law.* But the feeling of single Ummah has survived and rather strengthened among the muslims everywhere in the post-colonial period. The doctrine of Islamic brotherhood, the scriptures, the rites and rituals and past history provides a bond for the muslims of all states. The urge for Islamic solidarity is expressed in the form of the organisation like OIC. The OIC has gradually emerged as a forum for the muslim states to collectively deliberate on the problems of the Muslim Ummah and the Islamic states.[41]

Islam is an independent determinant for the foreign policy and diplomacy of Bangladesh. The process of opening up of bilateral relations with the Islamic countries was initiated by Sheikh Mujib which grew and matured during the post-Mujib regimes, and is maintained on the same pattern under Khaleda Zia. There are push and pull factors influencing Bangladesh's relations with Islamic countries. The first push factor is the religiosity of the masses who desire closer relations with the Islamic countries, and identification of Bangladesh government with Islamic issues. The second push factor is the presence and development of religious institutions, organisations and personalities. They work as a pressure groups for Islamic orientation of the foreign policy. The pro-Bangladeshi nationalism, fundamentalism forces and the Islamic parties are in favour of closer relations with the Islamic countries. The fifth constitutional amendment done by Zia in 1979, made it a duty for any government in Bangladesh to strive for strengthening bilateral and multilateral relations with the Islamic states. Another push factor is the absence of any Islamic country as a close neighbour unlike other Islamic countries. The consciousness of this isolation has made its unique contribution to Bangladesh's desire for Islamic solidarity.[42]

The pull factor include political and economic utility of the Islamic states individually and collectively for Bangladesh. Politically the Islamic countries are important for Bangladesh's diplomacy. They supported Bangladesh on the water dispute with India in the UN in 1976 and its candidature to the Security Council as a non-permanent member in 1978. Economically the oil rich Arab Islamic countries are very helpful in different ways. They provide economic aid to Bangladesh most of which is in the form of grant. The Islamic countries have become the largest market for Bangladeshi labour force-both skilled and unskilled. The remittance money sent by these Bangladeshis is a vital source of foreign exchange. Trade between Bangladesh and these countries has good prospects which is increasing in volume and value. The terms of trade is favourable to Bangladesh, because a major share of the import bill is paid through loans and grants.[43]

The push and pull factors influence Bangladeshi foreign policy towards Islamic countries. Bangladesh adopts Islamic posture on every opportune occasion. The Islamic countries particularly Saudi Arabia, indirectly influenced the Islamisation process in Bangladesh as an external factor. Bangladesh actively participates in the diplomacy of the OIC and has won a credibility for its active diplomacy. Bangladesh highlights and takes definite stand on problems of Islamic countries in the UN and other international organisations. It co-sponsored the resolutions against the Soviet intervention in Afghanistan, along with Pakistan in the General Assembly. On dispute between Islamic countries, Dhaka maintains neutrality and impartiality and diplomatically strive to solve the problem. Bangladesh supports the peace process between Palestine and Israel. Dhaka participated in the special ministerial meetings of the OIC in Bosnia and contributed troops for the United Nations Protection Force to save Bosnian Muslims.

Bangladesh has hosted many official and semi-oifficial conferences and congregations of the world Muslim dignitaries since 1982. As the second largest Muslim state in the world and as the leader of the LDCs among the OIC countries Bangladesh has a position in the Islamic world. The present regime of Khaleda Zia has a great believe that the role of Islam, as a determinant in Bangladesh's foreign decision-making is very prominent and essential.

Aid Dependency Factor

One of the universal features of the third world countries is their aid dependency for economic growth and development. Foreign aid performs two functions in the receiving country. Firstly, aid provides the necessary capital for investment which is scarce in developing economy due to low saving rate. Higher investment is essential for economic growth. Secondly, it provides foreign exchange for necessary import. The import is higher than export in these countries. Higher import is required for industrialization. Aid maintains balance of payment position in the receiving country. In developing countries like Bangladesh aid performs a third function. It provides revenue to government through taxes on aid-financed imports and sale of the food aid. Bangladesh and other LDCs needs aid not only for development but even for recurring regular government expenditure and for survival.

Bangladesh receives large quantities of foreign aid. The total amount of aid progressively increased from 551 million dollars in 1972-73 to 1.03 billion dollars in 1978-79. It reached 1.5 billion dollars in 1986-87. The highest amount of aid which Bangladesh got was in 1989-90 after which a downward trend is observed in the succeeding years. The total amount of Bangladesh aid was 1.4 billion dollars in 2003-2004.

In Bangladesh, the extent of aid dependence can be perceived from the fact that employment for rural poor, domestic revenues, development expenditure, fixed investment, imports, the balance of payments deficit and level of output in some sectors of the economy are directly or indirectly dependent on levels of aid flow. The total average annual aid of 1.5 billion dollars to Bangladesh is not large, when compared to other larger aid recipient states with smaller populations. Aid dependency of Bangladesh is greater than other aid recipient countries because the share of aid is very high than the share of domestic resources in the development budget. Bangladesh is integrated into the world economic system as any classically dependent Latin American or African country.[44]

The Bangladeshi policy makers look for the decisions taken in Washington, London, Tokyo, Bonn and Paris before formulating their annual development budgets, import policy, food policy and desicison even about the number of children to be born. Annual World Bank country report about Bangladesh and Bangladesh Aid Consortium meeting to decide annual aid for Bangladesh, and the representation of the Finance Minister before the consortium are major political news for the media in the country. Any negative reporting or commitment of lesser amount of aid by the consortium makes time difficult for the government and a positive reporting by the Bank and a pledge of higher aid by the consortium, give an opportunity to the government to celebrate its achievement. There is no aspect of life they do not interfere.[45] The sovereignty of Bangladesh is a polite fiction which is prevailing by the courtesy of the donors, as long as it does not challenge their strategic assumptions and ideological perceptions.

Aid requirement has influenced the direction of Bangladeshi foreign policy. The western countries are the major donors of Bangladesh both multilaterally and bilaterally. Bangladeshi diplomacy is concentrated outside

South Asia in West and the Islamic world, because they are the important donor states. The value of aid by a particular donor given to a particular recipient depends largely on the image of the recipient and its utility for the foreign policy of the donor. For creating goodwill among the donors Bangladesh has identified its foreign policy with the West and the Islamic world.[46] In its pronouncements on international issues and diplomatic moves Bangladesh always keeps into consideration not to annoy the aid donors.

Bangladesh cancelled exports of jute bags to Cuba when America insisted for it in 1974 in exchange of its food aid.[47] Dhaka did not condemn the Camp David Agreement, the American attack on Granada and Libya keeping in view the American sensitivity. It followed the American foreign policy line on Afghanistan and Kampuchea. In recent years, Bangladesh has announced some of its important foreign policy decisions from abroad. General Ershad announced his decision to establish diplomatic ties with democratic Kampuchea from China, during his November-December 1982 visit. These instances show that aid dependency factor is an important external constraint on the foreign policy of Bangladesh.

Impact of Globalisation

The international political scene confronting the new nation of Bangladesh in 1971 was characterized by antagonistic and even confrontationist relationship between major powers of the world. Bangladesh had to charter the course of her foreign policy in a manner so as to protect her freedom under the pulls and pressures of antagonistically divided international world. Anti-imperialism, being a crucial ingredient of her national liberation struggle and the fact that powers generally characterized as imperialist-the Western World led by the USA had opposed her emergence as independent sovereign political entity, were important determinants influencing her foreign policy orientations. Her commitment to non□alignment, support to anit-colonial struggles in different parts of the world and signing of friendships and cooperation treaties with the Soviet Union and India were logical consequences of her comprehension about the kind of role that different major powers had played in her liberation struggle. China's hostility towards Bangladesh's independence had determined the nature of Bangladesh's relationship with China, which remained cool for a considerably long time, and China did not recognise Bangladesh till Pakistan did it after the Lahore Conference of the Organisation of Islamic Countries. Therefore, the role of major powers is very essential external determinant of Bangladesh Foreign Policy.

SUMMING UP

The determinants or variables which determine the nature, style, objectives, instruments and strategies of Bangladesh foreign policy are of general nature. They can be applied to analyse the foreign policy of any Third World country. The tangible domestic factors like geography, population, economy and natural resources of Bangladesh have more negative aspects than positive. They act as constraints rather than capabilities of Bangladesh foreign policy. The defence establishment as a capability grew during the post-Mujib period but it is not strong enough to play an important role in the foreign policy decision making. The Constitution of Bangladesh acts as a determinant of its foreign policy because it defines the guiding principles and objectives of Bangladeshi foreign policy.

Among the intangible variables historical legacy as perceived and interpreted by the ruling elites of Bangladesh particularly modern and contemporary history, sub□consciously influence their foreign policy towards India and Pakistan. The national ideology is a divisive issue among the middle classes of Bangladesh. It indirectly determines Bangladesh's attitude towards the neighbouring countries particularly India and Pakistan. Change in national ideology in the post-Mujib era influenced the change of the regime's perceptions of India and Pakistan. Leadership in the post-Mujib period was restored in the hands of military and civil bureaucracy as it was during Pakistan days. The section of the leadership which became more powerful was the repatriated personnel whose values, attitude and images were not drastically changed because they did not participate in the Liberation War. The biases and the images of a situation perceived by the leadership have an imprint upon the foreign policy of Bangladesh. The restoration of democracy in 1991 did not affect the national ideology and the political character of leadership. The national ideology and the nature of leadership both changed in 1996 which have its implications on Bangladesh's neighbourhood policy.

The external variables of foreign policy are very important particularly for the least developed countries including Bangladesh. The pre-eminent state in the South Asian regional sub-system is India which surrounds Bangladesh from three sides. The situation is perceived by ruling elites of Bangladesh for the purpose of foreign policy decision making as 'India factor'. The approach of the regimes of Zia, Ershad and Khaleda Zia towards India was to minimize or if possible remove the influences of India upon the foreign policy of Bangladesh. The Indo-Bangladesh Treaty of Peace and Friendship became redundant for all practical purposes. Common national ideology and similar world view was the basis of the bilateral treaty which changed after the violent removal of Mujib regime. Dhaka's perceptions of the international and regional issues were divergent from New Delhi in many cases during the post-Mujib era. The Bangladeshi approach towards India again became positive and its perception's on regional and international issues became similar or at least non- hostile to the Indian perceptions with the advent of the Awami League into power.

REFERENCES

1. Norman J. Padelford, Gerorge A. Lincoln and Lee D. Olvey, *The Dynamics of International Politics* (New York, 1976) p. 201
2. *Ibid.*, p.211.
3. Adam Waston, *Diplomacy. The Dialogue Between States* (Philadephia, 1986), p.14.
4. K. J. Holsti, The Study of Diplomacy in James N. Rosenau and others (eds.), *World Politics: An Introduction* (New York, 1976), p. 295.
5. R. P. Barston, *Modern Diplomacy,* (London, 1988), p. 198.
6. Charles P. Schleicher, *International Relations: Cooperation and Conflict* (New Delhi, 1963), p. 236.
7. A. Mascarrenhas, *Bangladesh: Legacy of Blood* (London, 1986), p. 13.
8. W. East Gordon and J. R.V Prescott, *Our Fragmented World: An Introduction to Political Geography* (London, ,1 975), pp. 74-75.
9. Iftekharuzzaman, Changing Global Scenario: Challenges for Bangladesh, in M. G. Kabir and Shaukat Hassan (eds.), *Issues and Challenges Facing Bangladesh Foreign Policy* (Dhaka. 1989), p. 257.
10. Norman D., Palmer and Howard C. Perkins, *International Relations: The World Community in Transition* (Delhi, 1985), pp. 63-66.
11. Mizanur Rahman Khan, The Global Population Problem: A North-South Dimension, *BIISS Journal* (Dhaka), Vol. 7, No. 3, July 1986, pp. 380-1.
12. H.W. Arndt, *Economic Development: The History of an Idea* (Chicago, 1987).
13. *Bangladesh Economic Review, 1997,* Ministry of Finance, Government of the people's Republic of Bangladesh (Dhaka, 2004), p. 19.

14. Nafis Ahmad, *A New Economic Geography* of *Bangladesh* (New Delhi, n.d.), pp. 117- 20.
15. Just Faaland and J.R. Parkinson, *Bangladesh: The Test case of Development* (New Delhi, 1977).
16. *Bangladesh Observer,* 30 September 1991.
17. *Bangladesh Observer,* 26 April 1985.
18. *Bangladesh Year Book 1983* (Dhaka, 1984), p. 86.
19. R. Ruthnaswamy, *Principles and Practice of Foreign Policy* (Bombay, 1961), p. 14.
20. Habibul Haque Khondaker, Bangladesh: Anatomy of an Unsuccessful Military Coup, *Armed Forces and Society* (Chicago, Maryland), Vol. 13, No. 1, 1986, p. 136.
21. Talukder Maniruzzaman, *Politics and Security of Bangladesh* (Dhaka, 1994), p. 123.
22. Ali Riaz, *State, Class & Military Rule: Political Economy of Martial Law in Bangladesh* (Dhaka, 1994).
23. Ataur Rahman, Foreign Policy Making in Bangladesh: Institutions and Processes, *BIISS Journal, Vol.* 6, No. 3, July 1985, p. 335.
24. Rupak Bhattacharya, The Bangladesh Army and the Awarmi League, *Newsletter,* Maulana Abul Kalam Azad Institute of Asian Studies (Calcutta) Vol. 3, No. 2-3, February 1997, pp. 24-27.
25. *The Constitution of the People's Republic of Bangladesh, As modified up to 30 June 1988,* Ministry of Law and Justice, the Government of the People's Republic of Bangladesh (Dhaka, 1988), p.15, 17.
26. *Ibid.,* p.17
27. *Ibid,* p.131
28. Fredrick H. Hartman, *The Relations of Nations* (New York, 1978), p. 57.
29. K. J. Holsti, *International Politics: Framework for Analysis* (New Jersey, 1967), p. 163.
30. Abul Fazl Haq, The Problem of National Identity in Bangladesh, *The Journal of Social Studies* (Dhaka), No. 24, April 1984, p.50.

31. Zillur R. Khan, Islam and Bengali Nationalism, *Asian Survey,* Vol. 25, No. 8, August 1985, pp. 846-8.
32. M. G. Kabir, Religion, Language and Nationalism in Bangladesh, *Journal of Contemporary Asia* (Nottingham), Vol. 17, No. 4, 1987, p. 484.
33. Azizul Haque, Politics in Bangladesh: Conflict and Confusion, *Foreign Affairs Reports* (New Delhi), Vol. 35, No.], January 1986, p. 7.
34. Michael Brecher, *The Foreign Policy System of Israel : Setting Images, Process* (London, 1972), pp. 1-4.
35. James N. Rosenau, *National Leadership and Foreign Policy: A Case Study in the Mobilisation of Public Support* (Princeton, 1963).
36. Peter J. Bertocci, Bangladesh in the Early 1980s: Practorian Politics in an Intermediate Regime, *Asian Survey, Vol.* 22, No. 10, October 1982.
37. Farah Kabir, Bureaucracy in Bangladesh: The Political Involvement and Influence, *BIISSJournal,* Vol. 12, No.2, April 1991, pp. 258-9.
38. Iftekharuzzaman, The India Doctrine: Relevance for Bangladesh in Kabir and Hassan, op. cit., n. 9, p. 18.
39. Muhammad Tajuddin, *Foreign Policy of Bangladesh* (New Delhi, 2001), p. 75.
40. M. Rashiduzzaman, Changing Political Patterns in Bangladesh: Internal Constraints and External Fears, *Asian Survey,* Vol. 17, No. 9, September 1977, pp. 793-808.
41. Muhammad Tajuddin, *Bangladesh and the Islamic World,* Azad Institute Paper- 9 (Calcutta, 1998), pp. 7-10.
42. Tabarak Hussain, Domestic Inputs in Foreign Policy in S.R. Chakravarty and Virendra Narain (eds.), *Bangladesh: Global Politics,* Vol.3 (New Delhi, 1988), p.26.
43. Md. Golam Mostafa, Bangladesh Foreign Policy: The Middle East Factor, *BIISSJournal, Vol.* 7, No. 1, January 1986, p. 51.
44. Rahman Sobhan, Bangladesh and the World Economic System: The Crisis of External Dependence in Chakravarty and Narain, op. cit. n. 42, p. 43.

45. James J. Novak, *Bangladesh: Reflections on the Water* (Dhaka, 1993), pp. 4-5.
46. Iftekhar A. Choudhury, *Bangladesh's External Relations: The Strategy of Small Power in a Subsystem,* Ph.D thesis submitted to Australian National University (Canberra, 1980) p. 136.
47. Rehman Sobhan and Debapriya Bhattacharya, Aid Conditionality in Bangladesh : The Case of PL 480, *Journal of Contemporary Asia, Vol.* 17, No. 4, 1987, p.489.

CHAPTER-2

Foreign Policy of Bangladesh: A Backdrop

The emergence of Bangladesh as an independent state in 1971 was a significant event with its manifold implications for the South Asian region. India played a major role in the emergence of Bangladesh. The formative years were important in identifying the nature, trends, goals and direction of the foreign policy of Bangladesh.

The evolution and implementation of Bangladesh's foreign policy, as a small state, have not been easy, and at times indeed difficult. Since the end of the Cold War in 1990, all nation states, big or small, have been restructuring their foreign policy orientations. And Bangladesh is no exception. An analysis of Bangladesh's foreign policy will indicate certain objectives and principles, which have governed it since the emergence of the country. There have been changes of government in Bangladesh through military coups, sometimes causing bewilderment, nonetheless its foreign policy has shown certain consistent features. The technique and *modus operandi* for attaining those objectives varied from time to time in accordance with changing circumstances both at home and abroad. The attitudes of the superpowers' patterns of alignment in the subcontinent, inter-state relations in South Asia, historical experience under the neocolonial rule of Pakistan and trauma of Bangladesh's birth, international as well as regional political and economic structures all have profoundly affected the policy makers in Dhaka and prompted them to enunciate the following foreign policy principles: (i) friendship for all, malice to none; (ii) preservation of national sovereignty, territorial integrity and political independence in line with UN Charter 2(4); (iii) non-interference in the internal affairs of other countries as per the UN Charter 2(7); (iv) a policy of peace; and (v) relations with the muslim world. These are the guiding principles of the foreign policy of Bangladesh.

Let us now examine the aims and objectives of Bangladesh's foreign policy which are enshrined in articles 25(1) & (2), 63 and 145A of the Constitution. The fundamental aims have been stipulated- (i) self-preservation, (ii) economic advancement, and (iii) national self-respect. To preserve territorial integrity and political independence, article 25 explicitly spell out that the state shall base its international relations on the principles of respect for national sovereignty and equality, non-interference in the internal affairs of other countries, peaceful settlement of international disputes, and respect for international laws and principles of the United Nation's Charter. These principles indeed make Bangladesh's intentions clear in the context of its weak military status and geopolitical position vis-a-vis India. Thus Bangladesh has believed in peaceful coexistence. This intention was further demonstrated by the authority for the declaration of war being made the prerogative of the parliament under article 63.[1]

The aim of this chapter is to analyse the foreign policy as well as its implementation under three major regimes since Bangladesh's independence, i.e. 1972 to 1990. This will form as a background of our study.

THE MUJIB PERIOD

Bangladesh's revolutionary birth as an independent and sovereign state in 1971 brought world-wide sympathy for it. But at the same time there was scepticism in certain quarters, especially among the countries aligned with the "Washington-Beijing-Islamabad axis". Opinions were expressed in those quarters that Bangladesh had fallen in the arena of "Indo-Soviet sphere of influence". There were apprehensions that the newly born South Asian nation would indirectly or directly come in the orbit of Soviet leader Brezhnev's "Collective Security Plan for Asia." [2]

Bangladesh had to shape up its foreign policy at a difficult time, when the bipolar international order had not yet given way to a fully emerged multipolar world. And the emergence of Bangladesh was being considered as a victory for the Indo-Soviet bloc in south Asia. As such, compulsions like the then existing international order as well as the role of the major powers during the liberation war of Bangladesh had more or less restricted Mujib's options in formulating the foreign policy. It was no wonder that Dhaka would tilt towards the Indo-Soviet bloc in spite of its officially proclaimed policy of non-alignment and its desire to turn into a'Switzerland of the East'.[3]

As Mascow, with its enhanced prestige in South Asia, embarked on a determined policy of cultivating cordial and close links with Dhaka with increased political, economic and trading ties, the Bangladesh's response was obviously positive. Contact between trade unions, youth and public organizations were established. The Soviet Communist Party had established good party-to-party relations with both the Awami League and the NAP (M)-CPB faction and in fact influenced Mujib's foreign policy. A broader trade agreement between the two countries was signed. Furthermore, a state visit to Moscow by Mujib underscored the development of close links between the two countries. Moscow also became the major arms supplier and helped organised Bangladesh's nascent armed forces.

On the political level, Moscow and Dhaka demonstrated not only a convergence of views on international issues but also on the principles underlying the conduct of their foreign policies. Bangladesh was in complete agreement with the Soviet Union on the issues like, the resolution of the Kampuchean problem without outside interference; the Soviet Union's and socialist countries' efforts to convene an all-European conference on security and co-operation in Europe; and the proposed seven-point plan of the Provisional Revolutionary Government of the Republic of South Vietnam, which was considered to be a a realistic and constructive basis for peaceful settlement of the Vietnam Problem. Thus, during the Mujib regime the relationship between the two countries remained very close in spite of some minor irritants such as Moscow's prolonged involvement in salvaging Chittagong port (removing sunken vessels and clearing mines), and Dhaka's unwillingness to join Brezhnev's Asian Collective Security Plan.[4]

Bangladesh's relations with India during the Mujib regime were unique in character. Sheikh Mujib made clear his intention of a special relationship and assured New Delhi that friendship with India would be a central feature of his country's foreign policy, due to the dictates of geography and other factors. So relations with India and India's attitude towards this new south Asian nation were of paramount importance.

The bond of fraternity with India was not confined to exchange of friendly statements. Dhaka soon institutionalized this relationship of eternal friendship by signing the Indo-Bangladesh Treaty of Friendship and Co-operation in March 1972. It was, no wonder that there would be similarities in their foreign policy objectives. It was with a perceived mutuality of interests that both countries went ahead with specific economic, security and political policies and signed a number of agreements in order to forge a close bond.

Despite these friendly links, Indo-Bangladesh relations started showing signs of stress and strain as early as 1972 over the outstanding issues inherited from Pakistan days, namely, boundary demarcation, Farakka problem and trade deficit. And the issues remained unresolved until the fall of the Mujib government. Dhaka's close links with the Indo-Soviet bloc were certainly not pleasing to either the US or China. The displeasure over perceived Soviet penetration in Bangladesh was evidenced by the delay in US recognition of Bangladesh and in the closure of the Chinese consulate at Dhaka. But the policy makers in Dhaka were painfully aware of the necessity to develop ties with both these counties as well as the muslim states. The main reason was its gigantic unsolved economic problems. It needed massive economic assistance which neither India nor the Soviet Union was in position to provide. The problem became all the more evident after Mujib's disappointing state visit to Moscow in March 1972 as the Soviet pledge of economic assistance was meagre.[5]

Since economic development of the country was essential, and Dhaka needed massive external assistance which only the United States was in position to pledge, the Mujib government started its bid to win Washington's goodwill. But the relationship between Dhaka and Washington was far from satisfactory, despite the US's recognition of Bangladesh on 4 February 1972, and its declaration of financial assistance. At this stage, US involvement in Bangladesh was partially motivated by the desire to inhibit Moscow's influence in the region. The US was also worried that any possible internal upheavals stemming from domestic difficulties could threaten regional stability, thereby drawing the USSR into the affairs of Bangladesh.[6]

Though economic imperatives had compelled Mujib to repudiate the then Finance Minister Tajuddin's earlier statement and express his willingness to accept American aid, the task of improving ties was difficult due to Dhaka's close relations with Moscow and New Delhi. As such, US-Bangladesh relationship was correct but not cordial.

Similarly, Mujib's attempts to diversify Dhaka's foreign policy options by having links with the muslim world and China ran counter to his overwhelming dependence on India and Moscow. Initial Sino-Bangladesh relationship also suffered a setback due to China's alleged siding with Pakistan during the liberation war of Bangladesh in 1971. In spite of this, Dhaka made a number of overtures to Beijing in the hope of developing a friendly relationship. China did not, however, respond, on the contrary, in August 1972 it vetoed against Bangladesh's application for UN membership. But by 1974 the political situation in the subcontinent had somewhat eased as a tripartite pact was reached between India, Pakistan and Bangladesh under which a settlement of the unresolved issues of the subcontinent was sought.

China's welcome to this pact was evidenced by the withdrawal of opposition to Dhaka's UN membership. Thus ended a period of acute tension in the nascent relationship. Although China did not recognize Bangladesh until 1975 but there were various unofficial contacts between the two countries during 1974□1975.

Turning to Dhaka's relations with the Arab world, it was discernible that the entire Arab world was unhappy with the dismemberment of the largest muslim county, Pakistan and was annoyed at the Israeli recognition of Bangladesh. However, the relationship between Bangladesh and the muslim world started to grow when Mujib attended the non-aligned conference held in Algiers in September 1973 and Dhaka wholeheartedly supported the Arab countries during the Arab-Israeli war of 1973. The relationship further improved after Mujib's attendance at the Lahore Islamic Summit in February 1974 where the Arab diplomats played a crucial role in bringing about a rapprochement between Dhaka and Islambad. It was widely believed that the Arab leaders persuaded Mujib to drop the proposed trial of 195 Pakistani officers for war crimes before Islamabad agreed to recognize Bangladesh as an independent nation.[7]

As mentioned earlier, Sheikh Mujibur Rahman's foreign policy options were constrained by Bangladesh's tumultuous birth, complexities of the South Asian international system and alignments of the major powers. He tried to diversify Dhaka's foreign relations without making a major breakthrough.

THE ZIA PERIOD

After the military take over on 15 August 1975 and violent overthrow of Sheikh Mujib's regime, a significant departure took place in Bangladesh's foreign relations and international alignments. The process gained momentum after the assumption of state power by General Ziaur Rahman in November 1975. The change was characterized by Bangladesh's shift from Indo-Soviet axis and its attempts to get closer to the western alliance led by the United States. Cultivation of special relations with the Islamic world was also observed.

With the major changes in the county's foreign policy there was a corresponding change in the constitution. The Zia regime inserted certain fundamental change in the preamble. As such, two significant principles of state ideology, namely, 'secularism' and 'socialsim' were deleted and in their place 'absolute trust and faith in Almighty Allah' and 'economic and social justice' respectively were included. An amendment with Islamic flavour was added in the Constitution by Proclamation Order No. 1 of 1977 which declared that the state shall endeavour to consolidate, preserve and strengthen fraternal relations among muslim countries based on Islamic solidarity.[8] Subsequently, two significant clauses were inserted in the Constitution to signify a shift in the fundamental principles. Clause (2) of article 25 sought to consolidate, preserve and strengthen fraternal relations among muslim countries and was ostensibly added to attract petro-dollars from Middle Eastern countries. But actually it was the outcome of Dhaka's domestic compulsions as well as Zia government's attempt to diversify his country's foreign policy and created a support base for his regime. Insertion of article 145 A made a major shift in the foreign policy making process by empowering the President to enter into secret agreements with foreign government thus making him the final arbiter in the matter. This clause, however, has been amended and now any such treaty has to be placed before a closed meeting of the parliament.[9]

The relationship of euphoria between Bangladesh and India ended with the August 1975 *coup d'etat* and there followed a sharp worsening of bilateral relations. Mixed feelings against the big neighbour became more pronounced in the country. There was an attack on the Indian High Commission on 26 November 1975 and the newspapers reported frequent border clashes and skirmishes between the security forces of the two countries. Anti-Indian sentiment among the new leadership, recognition of the new regime by the People's Republic of China, and major policy changes initiated by Zia greatly hardened the attitude of India towards Bangladesh. During this time Indo-Bangladesh relations were dominated to a great extent by politico-security issues. At home General Zia exploited Indian support for pro-Mujib and the water dispute in the own favour to consolidate and stabilize his regime. There was a widening of differences leading to bitter relationship between the two nations. Due to Indian pressure tactics and uncompromising behaviour, bilateral relations worsened with the following unsettled problems, aid to pro-Mujib guerrillas; the demarcation of maritime belt; the Muhurir Char border dispute; ownership over South Talpatti Island, and, above all, the dispute over the sharing of Ganges waters.

India's continued large-scale and unilateral withdrawal of Ganges water became a special concern for Bangladesh. Being unable to receive concession form India on water sharing, the Zia regime tried to internationalise the Farakka issue. As such efforts were made to seek support of the muslim countries at the Islamic Foreign Ministers Conference at Istanbul and the issue was also raised at the non□aligned summit in August 1976 at Colombo. Moreover, the Zia government issued a white paper on the dispute in September 1976 highlighting the grave crisis that had arisen for Bangladesh on account of India's diversion of the Ganges water.[10] It mentioned the repercussions on the country's agriculture, navigation, fisheries, population, environment, etc. Later, on 31 September 1976 the Zia regime raised the issue at the United Nations General Assembly and submitted to its Special Political Committee the text of a draft resolution by which the Assembly could call upon the two sides for a quick solution. But following opposition from India and her allies the Committee postponed discussion on the issue and, after consultation, Bangladesh withdrew its draft resolution, enabling the Committee to approve a consensus statement calling for a bilateral solution to the dispute. Improvement in relations, however, was discernible after the Janata government's accession to power in 1977 as exemplified by Indian Prime Minister Morarji Desai's initiatives in solving the water issue and his subsequent visit to Dhaka. An interim arrangement on Ganges water was reached in April 1977, but in 1980, with the assumption of power in India by Congress (I), there was a relapse.

After the August coup d' etat Bangladesh obtained necessary recognition and support from the United States and its allies in the region. She began to improve relations with China, Pakistan and the Islamic world. General Zia became increasingly distrustful to the countries belonging to Indo-Soviet axis. Throughout Zia's five-and-half-year rule Soviet-Bangladesh relations remained cool. However, there were indications from the two sides to at least maintain a reasonably normal bilateral relationship along with trade ties and the like.

Bangladesh's growing relationship with the People's Republic of China became consistent with the Chinese strategy of extending co-operation to smaller nations of South Asia, and President Zia's strategy of neutralizing India's threat and pressure tactics. Thus, Chinese support became available to Bangladesh on the Farakka issue and on different international issues, including Kampuchea and Afghanistan, both Bangladesh and China held similar views. Chinese friendship was given special emphasis in Ziaur Rahman's external measures and this was manifested by his official visits to Beijing and signing of economic, technical co□operation, cultural and trade agreements. China offered interest-free loan, food aid and other assistance and emerged also as one of the Bangladesh's major sources of military aid.

Bangladesh's shift away from the Indo-Soviet bloc paved the way for closer ties with the principal western aid donors led by the United States. General Zia's policies of denationalization and privatization were also acclaimed by these donors. As such there was a massive inflow of western aid which enabled the regime to embark on development projects and strengthened Zia's initiatives to consolidate his governance. The average annual commitment of aid during the Zia regime was US $ 1,218 million as compared to Mujib's US $ 828 million.[11] The economic steps and foreign policy measures undertaken by Zia enabled him to come closer to Washington which was supportive of his above actions. Zia's external policies, therefore, witnessed a convergence of views of both Bangladesh and United States on a number of international and regional issues.

Zia's foreign policies highlighted the Islamic line and emphasized special relations with the Muslim countries. AS such Dhaka's support to the Arab cause was reiterated with greater vigour at OIC summits and mediation was offered to end Iran-Iraq conflict. Zia also developed very cordial and warm personal relations with the liberal Arab statesmen. His policies convinced the oil-rich Middle Eastern countries like Saudi Arabia, Kuwait and UAE which thus provided economic aid to Dhaka and recruited its manpower in greater numbers. Bangladesh's dependence on Arab economic aid had the impact of bringing pressure on the country's government to conform to Islamic values.[12]

As part of its continued endeavours to enlarge Bangladesh's foreign policy operations and to bring for the nation international prestige, the Zia government managed to get the country elected to the Security Council of the United Nations in November 1978.

Bangladesh's external policy measures during the Zia regime were also geared towards cultivating good-neighbourly relations with the smaller nations of the region and solving existing problems. Intensive diplomatic negotiations took place to solve the Bangladesh-Burma dispute over the unprecedented flow of Burmese muslim refugees (Rohinghas) from Arakan to Bangladesh territory.

The two countries also signed a boundary demarcation agreement.

Another important initiative of Zia at the regional level was his attempt to induce the seven countries of South Asia to move towards co-operative relationship within a regional framework. During 1977 and 1980 Zia paid visits to South Asian capitals and through his envoys and letters tried to convince the South Asian Governments to develop more concrete proposals for regional co-operation. Thus, his ideas became a reality through the formal launching of SAARC after his demise in May 1981.

Zia's foreign policy measures and international alignments marked a significant shift from the policies pursued by his predecessor. His external policy orientation made a deep imprint and provided guidance to his successors.

THE ERSHAD PERIOD

Bangladesh once again came under martial law after a short span of Justice Sattar-led BNP rule, when General Ershad seized state power in a blood less coup in 1982. Dhaka's main concerns during that time were its dealings with India as Indo-Bangladesh relationship was far from satisfactory. None of the outstanding issues had been solved by the tow previous regimes, and new areas of conflict had been added to the long list of existing one such as proposed fencing of the Bangladesh-Assam border by India and the Chakma issue.

Ershad's first visit abroad was to India in 1982 to discuss a variety of bilateral irritants, most important being the Farakka problem which continued to bed evil relations ever since the feeder canal started operating on a temporary basis under the interim agreement of 1974 between then Prime Minister of Bangladesh, Sheik Mujibur Rahman, and Indian Prime Minister Indira Gandhi. Ershad's hope of getting the issue resolved was dashed. The reason was quite simple.

Ershad, whose domestic support base was extremely shaky and needed external help to consolidate his rule, was naturally negotiating from a weak position and as a consequence got a raw deal.

In the joint communique issued at the end of the visit, it was stated that the actual working of the 1977 Farakka agreement had not provided a satisfactory and durable solution.[13] It suggested for fresh efforts for a long-term solution after its termination. Hence two MOU were signed during the Ershad regime - in 1982 and 1985 - neither of which was better than the agreement of 1977. Till 1990, no long-term solution was found. On the contrary, Ershad, in order to allegedly appease India, did not incorporate the guarantee clause with respect to water sharing, which had safeguarded the interests of Bangladesh during the 1978-1982 period. This clause of the 1977 agreement had guaranteed a certain quantity of water Bangladesh needed during exceptionally low flows of the Ganges at Farakka. In lieu of this, however, the two sides agreed on a burden-sharing formula in case of exceptionally low flows. Ershad also stated that he would not internationalise the Farakka issue, though at the time Dhaka had cordial relations with both USA and the People's Republic of China. New Delhi's sensitivity with regard to non□involvement of third pary was also given due consideration. In spite of such gestures no long-term water-sharing formula had evolved even when the second MOU expired in 1988. Since then till the fall of the Ershad government, India continued to draw Ganges water at Farakka unilaterally.

Besides Farakka, Indo-Bangladesh relations remained bogged in suspicion over maritime border dispute, issue of sovereignty over Talpatti island and insurgency in Chittagong Hill Tracts. These irritants, which posed direct threats to Bangladesh's territorial security were not resolved in spite of Dhaka's earnest desire to have good neighbourly relations with India.

Other irritants like Dhaka's changed attitude towards Sri Lanka's proposal for turning the Indian Ocean into a peace zone, was detested by New Delhi, as the ocean was, and still is, a strategic component in India's security perception. Dhaka's pragmatic approach to India's growing naval power and its proposal for withdrawal of the navies of the major powers without settling the maritime boundary between the two affecting Bangladesh's direct interest in the share of the ocean and its resources, could not be appreciated by India.

There came a genuine opportunity to improve bilateral relations when Rajiv Gandhi took over powers in 1984. Both the leaders had a chance to shed their pre□independence and inherited inhibitions, and there were hopes when the new Indian leader demonstrated a number of gestures to improve relations. But, unfortunately, without the resolution of the outstanding issues, the relationship remained as it was during Zia's rule.

Ershad tried to take full advantage of Dhaka's relations with China which had a qualitative and deepening aura. The relationship which flowered during the Zia regime was mutually beneficial. China was the only country which provided some psychological security to Dhaka against its fear of India's designs in the area. With China's help, Bangladesh's won the election for the presidency of the 41 General Assembly session of the United Nations in 1986. Similarly, Dhaka sought Chinese support in getting positions in other international organizations such as the World Food Council and the Industrial Development Board of UNIDO (United Nations Industrial Development Organisation). China sought Bangladesh's support for its admission to the Asian Development Bank and in endorsing China's compromise formula describing Taiwan as Chinese Taipei in the Asian Development Bank.

All this Mutual co-operation and support in international forums and on global issues made Sino-Bangladesh ties closer and closer. This was reflected through exchange of high-level visits between the two countries and statements like "the two nations are friends and have no conflicts,[14] and glowing tributes to each other. The deepening relationship was once again demonstrated during Ershad's third visit to Beijing when the sincerity of their bilateral relations was stressed repeatedly. As a matter of fact Ershad even sought Beijing's support during a domestic upheaval against him in 1987.[15]

Since the deterioration of relations with the Soviet Union, which was the only arms supplier to Bangladesh during the Mujib regime, Dhaka had been groping to establish a security link with China. The emerging security relationship between the two countries was evidenced by the fact that by late 1979 Bangladesh was one of the eight Asian countries in which China maintained a military attache and Bangladesh, along with Pakistan and North Korea, was principal recipient of Chinese arms. By 1987, the Bangladesh Army possessed 20 Chinese T-59 tanks; the Air Force had 18 Chaining J-6 FGAs (fighter/ground attack) and CJ-6 training aircraft; and the Navy was equipped with 14 Chinese-built FACPs (fast attack craft patrols), six Hainans, eight Shanghais and four Chinese-made FACGs (Fact attack craft guns).[16]

As part of cooperation in the field of defence, the exchange of high-level visits of military personnel contributed to the promotion of understanding between the Bangladesh armed forces and People's Liberation Army. China, during the Ershad regime, had also given valuable assistance by providing arms and equipment, technical assistance and training facilities. Beijing also sent 70 advisers to advise and cooperate in building an arms factory at Joydevpur and a tank workshop at Rajendrapur.

With regard to US-Bangladesh relations, the initial reaction of Washington was one of disappointment with the *coup d' etat* of General Ershad. Later, however, the US took a softer attitude towards the regime as signified by the statement given by the White House spokesman, '*During recent months, we have repeatedly stressed to Bangladesh leaders the importance which we attach to constitutional and democratic government and to the economic development in Bangladesh*'.[17] The implications were to see Bangladesh follow a constitutional route while pursuing the foreign policy of the Zia regime. Dhaka promptly issued a statement promising a return to democracy within two years and allowing political activities, which had been banned under martial law, within six month. Ershad also appealed to the donor countries to understand the situation and to continue the flow of aid.[18]

During his meeting with President Reagan in Washington in 1983, General Ershad discussed a wide range of bilateral, regional and international issues. Dhaka's approach to international issues such as Afghanistan and Kampuchea, as an active member of the Non-Aligned Movement (NAM) and the Organisation of the Islamic Conference (OIC), was considered pragmatic, constructive and moderate by Washington[19] but such moves by the regime undoubtedly steered the country away from its declared principles, whose budding process was initiated during the Mujib regime, continued during the Zia period and had fully blossomed during General Ershad's regime.

The closer relationship evolving between the two countries was indicated by the agreement signed on 26 October 1982, which corrected the Title-3 of the 1982 PL480 Programme. Under the new arrangement, Washington agreed to supply $60 million worth of extra food to Bangladesh as well as short-and long-term loans totaling $200 million for the augmentation of food grains production and food distribution in the following three years. This gesture of goodwill was demonstrated by the USA even before the civilianisation process of General Ershad's martial law had begun. It seemed that General Ershad's consistent efforts to impress upon the policy makers of the US that, due to his disinvestments policy and other policies, the United States would be able to play a bigger role in the economic development of Bangladesh, eventually paid off. He was able to secure the much need US support for his regime and successfully used American goodwill gestures for domestic consumption.[20]

Relations between the US and Bangladesh thus improved considerably between 1982 and 1983. The trend continued during the rest of Ershad's regime. Bangladesh not only received economic assistance from USA but also received tacit support for the continuation of his rule, much to the dissatisfaction of the majority of Bangladeshi people. General Ershad ostensibly followed and furthered Zia's policy towards the USA but, as pointed out earlier, he aligned Bangladesh totally with the USA and the West. The policy served his personal objective to such an extent that during the Iraq-Iran war, he saw to it that Dhaka tilts in favour of Iraq ignoring one of the fundamental principles of foreign policy and violating article 25(2) of the Constitution which calls for maintaining fraternal relations with all muslim countries. A similar constitutional violation was made when Ershad sent Bangladesh troops under UN auspices during the Gulf war without the approval of the parliament.

The US had been giving huge quantities of military aid to the South Asian subcontinent, particularly to Pakistan of which Bangladesh was a part until 1971. Military aid, unlike humanitarian aid like food, is given only when there is a strategic interest. Since Bangladesh had hardly any strategic importance, it is, therefore, no wonder that it had not received any military aid from the USA. Bangladesh, like any other independent country, wanted to build up its defense capability but the policy makers in Washington did not attach much importance to its request for defense equipment. The US, however, maintained minimum defense relations in the form of US Military Assistance Programme, US Military Assistance Sales Programme, International Military Education and Training Scheme, etc. [21]

The relationship between Bangladesh and the erstwhile Soviet Union on the other hand plummeted soon after Ershad's coming to power. Dhaka had some unhappy experience with Moscow in 1980 over the importation of electronic monitoring equipment. Another incident involving two Soviet diplomats who were trying to burn 588 rolls of Soviet film at a place 20 miles north of Dhaka set rumours afloat in Dhaka that Moscow was trying to stage an Afghan style revolution in Bangladesh.[22] Soon after this incident in 1982, General Ershad said in an interview that he believed that the Soviet Union was very dangerous.[23] In another remark he expressed his distrust and fear about Moscow.[24] Besides, the government request to cut down the Soviet embassy staff and close its cultural centre indicated the new regime's sensitiveness about alleged Soviet intentions in Bangladesh.

The unhappy relationship between Moscow and Dhaka was reflected in the media of both countries. Through November-December 1983, the Dhaka press printed negative reports about the Soviet Union, and Moscow painted a dismal economic picture of Bangladesh and its economic and financial dependence on the west, particularly the US.[25] It criticized Dhaka's denationalization policy, which Moscow thought was responsible for the slow growth of its economy. Moscow also showed some reservations when SAARC was formally launched in December 1985. While welcoming SAARC as a significant step towards solving urgent problems of the South Asian countries, Moscow warned about the activities of imperialist forces and neo-colonialists who were creating distrust and suspicion between the countries of the region. Moscow implicitly blamed Beijing which, by 1978-79, showed a desire to improve relations with India in the context of Moscow's military intervention in Afghanistan. This was a period of intense struggle for influence in countries like Vietnam and Kampuchea by both the Soviet Union and China. Bangladesh aligned with the US and China to meet its dual needs of securitv and economic assistance.

An opportunity for positive trends in the relationship with the Soviet Union emerged with Mikhail Gorbachev's Vladivostok speech on 28 July 1986,[26] which outlined a number of important foreign policy measures calling for an Asian Pacific System involving all countries in the region. The peace and stability in the Asia Pacific region sought by the Soviet Union required friendly and cooperative bilateral relations with each country of the region. Moscow now wanted to deal with Dhaka on proper terms. The visit by Gorbachev's special envoy in 1986 signalled that it wanted to establish a more pragmatic and correct relationship with Dhaka. However, since 1985 till the demise of the Soviet Union, the bilateral relations remained static.[27]

AID DEPENDENCY VIS-A-VIS FOREIGN POLICY OF BANGLADESH

One of the fundamental characteristics of Bangladesh foreign policy is to ensure foreign aid and it was always given top priority in the foreign policy mechanism. Economic assistance of any kind was regarded as vital to the development of the country. Ever since independence, there has always been a tremendous need for foreign aid. As aid from the socialist bloc was insignificant and even the aid from the rich Arab countries was not upto expectations, western aid became attractive for the policy planners of Dhaka. The dependence on western aid had in reality put the donor countries in a position where this can dictate the economic policy of the country and influence its foreign policy behavior.

In the initial years of independence, external economic assistance was mainly geared to support the relief and rehabilitation efforts for the recovery of the war-ravaged economy. But to procure foreign aid, particularly western aid, was not easy in the initial stage of nation building. Bangladesh adopted a socialist economy, and acceptance of western aid was opposed by some powerful member of the ruling party. But later on, meagre aid from the former Soviet Union and the socialist bloc forced Mujib to seek the membership of the Paris Aid Consortium, a club of major donor countries sponsored by the World Bank. Since then Bangladesh's dependence on western aid grew enormously, and despite changes of government in the last 34 years, the nature and condition of western aid has not changed. Dependence is still there and will certainly continue.

During the 1972-1991 period a total $ 31,136.184 million of external assistance was committed. Of the total amount, 16.7% was in the form of food aid, 28.1% commodity aid and 58.2% project aid. But the total amount was never disbursed. Only $ 25,746.6 million was disbursed, of which 48.8% was in the form of grants, and 51.2% loans. Out of the total aid received, 19.7% was received as food aid, 32.5% as commodity aid and 47.8% as project aid.[28]

Among the donors, the IDA (International Development Association, the soft loan window of the World Bank) toped the list in terms of aid disbursement, followed by Japan, USA, ADB, etc. The socialist countries, particularly the erstwhile Soviet Union and China's aid disbursement was much lower than that of the western countries. While IDA and Japan provided $ 4412 million and $ 3586.5 million respectively, the erstwhile Soviet Union disbursed an amount of only $ 393.9 million. China provided $ 120.782 million.[29]

During the 1972-1991 period, the OECD countries committed an amount of $ 14851.346 million, but disbursed $ 13116.284 million. The OPEC countries disbursed only $ 1130.81 million.[30]

Analysing the pattern of aid, one can find that the donor countries were interested in project aid rather than food aid, though Bangladesh remained a food deficit area. Due to natural calamities, the demand for food aid was always immense. But the donor countries failed to demonstrate proper response in this sector. The available data shows that during 1972-1991, Bangladesh was offered $ 5184.693 million worth of food aid, but disbursed only $ 5067.0 million.[31] The amount of project aid was much more than that of food aid, which shares the bulk of foreign assistance to Bangladesh. From independence to 1991 project aid has accounted for $ 12310.5 million or 47.8% of the total foreign aid disbursement. It is interesting to note that IDA and ADB did not provide any food aid. Soviet Union and India disbursed only that amount of food aid which they had committed during the 1972-74 period when both countries maintained good relations with Bangladesh. Since then no food aid was offered to Bangladesh from the Soviet Union. India also did not offer any food aid after 1975-76. Political considerations were the main factor in reducing the aid commitment.

Moscow's role in the liberation war was widely appreciated in Bangladesh. But the meagre aid form Soviet Union no doubt damaged its image. During the period 1974-75, when Bangladesh was suffering from acute food crisis, the Soviet Union reacted with a business-like attitude. It diverted 200,000 tons of wheat procured abroad to Bangladesh to help bridge the food gap on the understanding that it would be returned. Eventually the Soviet Union was approached to defer repayment or convert it into grants. The Soviet Union agreed to neither, and Bangladesh, in spite of acute food crisis, had to commit itself to return the amount in five instalments.[32] Many Bangladeshis saw it as an unfriendly attitude.

According to the statistic available, during the 1972-91 period, Bangladesh exported goods worth Tk. 38.54 billion, while at the same time imported goods of about Tk. 100.98 billion.[33] This indicated that Bangladesh is very much dependent on imported goods, including food, oil, garment accessories, etc.

During 1980-91, Bangladesh exported to Japan goods amounting to Tk. 17.5 billion, but imported goods worth Tk.10000 billion.[34] With India, an alarming figure is emerging. During the 1972-91 period, Bangladesh imported goods worth Tk.33 billion from India, but exported only Tk.6.25 billion. During 1981-91, Bangladesh export to China amounted to Tk. 6154 billion, while at the same time it imported Tk. 28.8 billion. During the 1973-91 period, Bangladesh exported goods amounting to Tk. 84.26 billion to the United States and imported an almost equal amount.[35]

CONCLUSION

In nutshell, it can be said that Bangladesh's foreign policy had two important phases, which are guiding foreign policy orientations, even now a days, one being the era of Sheikh Majibur Rahman (1972-August 1975) and other the Ziaur Rahman-Ershad eras (August 1975 to December 1990). In the Mujib era, as pointed out in the chapter, it followed a foreign policy which, though apparently nonaligned, in practice, was heavily tilted towards New Delhi and via New Delhi towards the Soviet Union. During the first phase of Bangladesh's foreign policy under Mujib, it was ostensibly nonaligned, but in reality Mujib relied on India in external policy. Similarly, with regard to the two superpowers, the United States and the former Soviet Union, although Mujib did not formally become an ally of either, his preference was for Moscow in view of the fact that the Soviet Union supported the movement for Bangladesh while United States under President Nixon allegedly favored Pakistan. It was a difficult task to maintain good neighbourly and friendly relations with both superpowers as well as neighbours in an era which was ridden with conflicts and acrimonious bilateral relationships between the powers. It was no wonder that Mujib had no diplomatic relationship with China presumably because China's relations with both Moscow and New Delhi were strained. Similarly, Mujib was not fully successful in winning the friendship of the majority of muslim countries.

A shift in foreign policy orientations was, however, discernible during the end of Mujib's rule. The domestic compulsions, such as aid for much needed economic development, and desire for fraternal relationship with the muslim world, were already influencing his foreign policy formulation. As mentioned earlier, by contacts with the Arab world through his attendance of the Islamic countries summit conference in Lahore in 1974, he was already gets closer to the Islamic countries; and the need for aid also compelled him to seek friendly ties with the west, including with the US, which, however, remained aloof due to Mujib's tilt towards the socialist bloc and his publicly proclaimed socialist ideology. He was also aware of the need for diplomatic relation with a country like China and limited contacts were made between the two countries but again his commitment to the Indo-Soviet bloc constrained his desire to diversify Bangladesh's foreign policy options. As such Bangladesh's relations with the United States, muslim world and Beijing remained warmless.

The significant changes in Bangladesh's foreign policy were, however, evidenced with the coming of Ziaur Rahman to power. Zia wanted to remove Bangladesh from the orbit of Indian influence. He sought to have greater autonomy for

Bangladesh in external relations by widening diplomatic relationship with different countries, particularly with China and the muslim world. Zia also realised that in order to solve Bangladesh's basic economic problems the country needed large-scale external economic aid which could come only from the United States and Western European countries. Zia, therefore, vigorously applied himself to cultivate closer relationship with the United State and the western world as well as Japan. He also sought to cultivate closer links with muslim countries, particularly Arab Countries.

During Ershad period, foreign policy orientation continued and further developed Zia's foreign policy, as discussed in the chapter. He brought Bangladesh closer to both Washington and Beijing and consolidated and developed further friendly bonds with the muslim countries.

REFERENCES

1. *The Constitution of the People's Republic of Bangladesh,* as amended up to February 1979.
2. Dilara Choudhury, *Bangladesh and the South Asian International System,* (London, 992).
3. *Ibid.,* p.26.
4. *Ibid.,* p.39.
5. *Ibid.,* p.121.
6. Ibid., p.151.
7. Talukder Maniruzzaman, Banlgadesh in 1974: Economic Crisis and Political Polarisation, *Asian Survey,* February 1975.
8. *The Constitution of the People's Republic of Bangladesh,* op.cit., n. 1, p.49.
9. *Ibid,* as amended up to July 1991.
10. S.S Bindra, *Indo-Bangaaesh Relataions,* (New Delhi, 1982), p. 88.
11. Adbul Bayes, *Foreign policy and External Economic Relations of Bangladesh : Direction, Nature and Implications,* paper presented at the First Annual Conference of the BLISS, 21 January 1988, p. 6.

12. Akmal Hossain, Bangladesh and the Muslim World, in Emajuddin Ahamed (eds.), *Foreign Policy of Bangladesh : A Small States's Imperative* (Dhaka, 1984), p. 91.
13. *Bangladesh Observer,* 7 October 1992.
14. *Being Review, 16* July *1985.*
15. *Bangladesh Observer, 30* November *1987.*
16. *The Bangladesh Times, 15* January *1991.*
17. *The New York Times, 24* March *1982.*
18. *Ibid, 28* March *1982.*
19. *The Daily Ittefaq, 28* March *1983.*
20. *Daily Independent, 17* April *1985.*
21. *Bangladesh Observer, 15* May *1985.*
22. *Bangladesh Observer, 16* January *1982.*
23. *The New York Times, 11* April *1982.*
24. *The Daily Ittefaq, 24* December *1983.*
25. *Dainik Bangla, 30* December *1983.*
26. *Bangladesh Observer, 29* July *1986.*
27. *Bangladesh Observer, 11* January *1989.*
28. *Flow of External Resources into Bangladesh,* Economic Relations Division, Ministry of Finance, People's Republic of Bangladesh, Dhaka, *1993, p. xvii.*
29. Ibid., p. 41.
30. Ibid., p. 45.
31. *The Bangladesh Times, 25* December *1993.*
32. Iftekhar A. Chowdhury, *Bangladesh's External Relations: The Strategy of Small Power in a Sub-system* (Canberra, *1980), pp. 162-163.*
33. *The Annual Export Receipts and Annual Import Payments,* Different issues, Published by Bangladesh Bank.
34. Ibid
35. Ibid.

CHAPTER -3

Bangladesh Relations with USA

The independence of Bangladesh in 1971 was a unique historical event as it symbolized a social revolution in terms of rising expectations among a large segments of the people for better life. These expectations, heightened by relative deprivations, enabled the predominantly middle class and subsequently an overwhelming number of people to undergo a bitter and bloody war of independence. Bangladesh's independence was the result of its people's aspirations for democracy, self identity, equality, freedom and progressive society. In the present chapter an attempt has been made to discuss trends and direction of Bangladesh-USA relations.

Bangladesh has however, shown considerably resilience and is trying to overcome its various problems, with the aim of acquiring a respectable position in the comity of nations. For its development needs, it considers US as a reliable partner and has cultivated friendship with it over the years in a fruitful manner. Thus Bangladesh-US relations have evolved over the years in domestic, regional as well as global contexts.

Bangladesh which was once called a basket case, is today a leading moderate muslim democratic country of the world, and has immense geo□strategic and geo-economic importance for the US. Being a member of important world bodies including, SAARC, OIC, D-8, BIMSTEC, NAM, G-77 and because of its contribution to the UN, the US feels that Bangladesh is capable of contributing effectively in the peace and stability of the world. It is also not a conjecture that Bangladesh has same agenda as the US, which includes democracy, human rights, peace keeping, and nuclear issues, such as NPT, CTBT, etc. These similarities have brought the two countries closer, and both have benefited through their mutual relationship.

The US wants to take advantage of Bangladesh's membership in various fora to express its concern over the issues, which are crucial to the US economic and strategic interests. Emergence of Bangladesh as potential source for oil and gas has also not gone unnoticed in the US.

During the Cold War period, the US interests were mainly geo□strategic and humanitarian, and Bangladesh depended on the US mainly for economic aid and certain other interests like obtaining recognition for itself, and the membership of UN, etc. In the post Cold War period the interests have been redefined. For the US geo-strategic interests assumed less significance than geo-economic interests in the context of globalization, liberalization and democratization.

PROGRESS IN RELATIONSHIP

In the post-Cold War era, under the influence of liberalised and globalised trade and investment regime, this relationship grew further during the democratic governments of Khaleda Zia and Hasina Wajed. Trade and investment relationship has grown much beyond expectations and subsequently the US aid has declined. However, project aid is still very important for long term socio-economic development of Bangladesh. During 1991-92 trade between Bangladesh and the US amounted to the tune of $ 91.49 million. This further increased to $ 2268.50 million by the years 2004□2005.[1] Most significant feature of this trade relations is trade balance in favour of Bangladesh which helps in financing its consumption as well as investment needs.

Investment has also gained momentum in four years between 2000□2001 to 2004-2005. The total US investment in Bangladesh, which was roughly estimated at US 30 million dollars till October 2001 has sharply risen to US 780 million dollars in 2004.[2] This has happened in the light of prospect of potential reserves and exploitation of oil and natural gas and lucrative returns in telecommunications and energy sector.

Though the US also provided technological knowhow to Bangladesh, this was limited to the input and physical infrastructure in the fields of agriculture, rural electrification, health and nutrition, and military training besides providing some hardwares for its use by the Bangladesh military.

Technology cooperation has been widened in post 1995 phase in the fields of energy, telecommunication, oil and natural gas sector, even though this has largely been done by private firms of the US. Further cooperation is now expected in computer hardware and IT, biotechnology and genetic engineering, renewable energy, environment management, oceanic resource exploration and management, and meteorology and plant medicine.

Cultural interaction between Bangladesh and the US has not been as close as economic relations though steps have been taken by both the countries to strengthen it. The US provides scholarships to Bangladesh students and teachers for study in the US, and to develop mutual understanding in the field of culture, and exchange of ideas in the field of science and technology and socio-economic aspects. In 1998, a MOU was signed between the US Peace Corps and

Bangladesh government to provide English language training to primary school teachers of Bangladesh.[3]

One area where Bangladesh has received continues support of the US is aid and assistance during natural calamities such as cyclones and floods. The US continues to give support during cyclones and floods in the form of food, money and technology to meet disasters. In fact now the US concentrates on socio-economic and technological infrastructure in Bangladesh to meet natural disasters.

Presently, the US is concentrating on protection of human rights and curbing of fundamentalism in Bangladesh. Thus, at present the two countries are marching on the path of fruitful mutual cooperation, with increased vigour.

Bangladesh-US relations have elevated from a state of mere existence to a state of close cooperation. The two countries presently cooperate in several areas. As for political relations, overcoming phase of hostility, both have developed understanding and cooperation on several national, regional and international issues. However, there are some contentious issues like extradition deal, curbing of Islamic fundamentalism, development and its linkages with environment, eradication of child labour, etc, which need to be resolved.

Now the US intends to help strengthen democracy in Bangladesh in the context of liberal-individualistic perspective. The institutionalization of democracy will help strengthen the nation building process and preservation of socio-cultural ethos of Bangladesh.

In the military and strategic areas, there is vast scope of expanding the existing cooperation in areas like military training, joint exercises, joint rescue and rehabilitation efforts, and procurement of equipments.

Bangladesh-US relations are excellent at present. But to get the real picture of the relations between Bangladesh and US, it will be fair to examine these relations during the different regimes in Bangladesh. Therefore, Bangladesh-US relations were as follows during different regimes.

BANGLADESH AS AN INDEPENDENT STATE

The great diplomatic challenge before Bangladesh as an independent sovereign state and also before the government of Sheikh Mujib, was to get recognition from different states and the United Nations system. Recognition was essential for establishing the legitimacy and legality of the nascent state. Secondly, it was not possible to get aid for the reconstruction of the war-devastated economy and for the rehabilitation of the returning refugees from different international sources without their recognition. Another important diplomatic task before the government was the repatriation of about 100,000 Indian troops from Bangladesh, which was necessary to prove complete independence and sovereignty of the state. The government of Sheikh Mujib pursued active diplomacy to attain these objectives. He succeeded in achieving most of them and took initiatives for the rest which were completed by the successive regimes.

At the time of independence on 16 December 1971 Bangladesh was recognized only by India and Bhutan.

BANGLADESH-US RELATIONS DURING MUJIB'S REGIME

It was Nixon administration's policy during the 1971 Bangladesh crisis which greatly jeopardized the Bangladesh-US relationship. A majority of Bengalees had expected for a solid US support during their struggle; however, they were frustrated by the US official policy, specially when the crisis culminated in the Indo-Pak war. From then until the early years of independence there was a wide gap in the Bangladesh-US relationship. However, it was dring Mujib's period, that slowly and gradually the relations between these two countries started improving. These emerging relations can be seen in the light of the socio-economic condition prevailing in Bangladesh. After its creation, Bangladesh was landed in acute economic crisis; there was paucity of food and money. This not only led to widespread discontentment among the people but also ensured the emergence of political corruption and evil practices. This economic crisis not only made the country heavily dependent upon the rich nations for its survival but prompted it to formulate a foreign policy that could be helpful in obtaining maximum foreign help and economic assistance. Thus, the economic compulsion placed Bangladesh in a position to accept anything from any quarter irrespective of its political and ideological principles. Mujib had declared, 1 *need help from all the nations of the world.*[4]

The economic condition of Bangladesh however, provided Washington an opportunity to enter into Bangladesh. Though Bangladesh maintained close relations with both India and the Soviet Union, the economic aid it received from these two countries was not sufficient to meet its need. In fact, the US was the only country, which was in a position to meet its financial requirements. It may be recalled that the economic channel between Dhaka and Washington had always remained alive.[5] Despite their diplomatic hostility and even during the war, the US had provided large economic relief to the country through the UN, in spite of the fact that diplomatically it tried to prevent the breakup of Pakistan. Even during the period when Bangladesh had no diplomatic relation with the US, Dhaka received $ 119 million American aid. The economic factor, therefore, provided a positive rationale for the US to legitimize its relations. There were several projects in Bangladesh, financed and promoted by the US, that were lying incomplete. For the development of Bangladesh economy, completion of these projects was necessary. With this view the Mujib government tried to reestablish the lost link with the US.

QUESTION OF RECOGNITION

The official recognition of Bangladesh by the US was somewhat delayed because of Washington's determination not to impair its relations with China and Pakistan. In early February 1972 Nixon said, *with regard to the political side, we have under study our whole relations with the subcontinent and as a part of that relationship, of course, the 70 million people of Bangladesh are involved. We have not made a decision with regard to recognition, and you should not expect a decision prior to the time 1 return from China.*[6]

The United States was indirectly against the creation of Bangladesh, since it was not in favour of the disintegration of Pakistan. American arms supplied to Pakistan were used by the Pakistani armed forces against the Bengalee liberation fighters. Washington also supported Pakistan at the UN, and sent its seventh fleet into the Indian Ocean to express its solidarity with Pakistan. Anti-American feeling was overt in the Bengalee middle class after the liberation of Bangladesh. Despite this the government of Bangladesh was conscious of the importance of Washington for its security and development.

Sheikh Mujib did not castigate the American administration for its negative role in the Liberation War. In his first speech after his arrival in Dhaka he expressed thanks to the people of the United States for their support in the liberation of Bangladesh. President Nixon also expressed similar sentiments, we have never been hostile to Bengalee aspirations. We have no intention of ignoring these 70 million people.[7]

The administration had not totally withdrawn its diplomatic personnel accredited to its Dhaka Consulate during the war period. The United States was willing to give aid to the new state even without formal recognition. An agreement was signed on March 30, 1972 between Bangladesh and the US, through which a cash grant of 90 million dollars was given to the Bangladesh government. The US government had reservations about the sovereignty of Bangladesh till the presence of Indian army on its soil. Washington gave formal recognition to Bangladesh on April 4, 1972 after the withdrawal of the Indian forces from Bangladesh.

In the autumn of 1974 Sheikh Mujib visited the United States to address the UN General Assembly. He met Bangladesh- friendly members of the Congress, the State Department officials, Secretary of State Henry Kissinger and President Ford. 1n November 1974 Kissinger went to Dhaka during his visit to the South Asian countries. He had a two hour meeting with Sheikh Mujib.[8]

Sheikh Mujib succeeded in establishing formal relations with the United States during his regime but the bad memories of independence war and his lndo-Soviet oriented foreign policy kept the relations cool.

BANGLADESH-US RELATIONS DURING ZIAUR RAHMAN'S REGIME

Bangladesh during Zia regime followed equidistance policy towards the two super powers. In reality the foreign policy had a clear bias towards the United States. The United States was the single larger donor to Bangladesh. Bangladesh was always conscious to maintain good relations with the largest donor. Sometimes it worked in the international fora according to the advice of the US. As a member of the Security Council, it co-sponsored a resolution condemning Iran for holding American diplomatic hostages and the Bangladeshi representative abstained from condemning the Camp David agreement signed between Egypt and Israel, with the active

American support. Good relationship was also maintained with other western countries.

Previously, the development of closer working ties with the US were hindered by Bangladesh's proximity with India and the Soviet Union and its emphasis upon socialism. But now the new regime adopted anti-Soviet and anti-Indian stand favouring capitalism rather than socialism. Socialism was redefined to conform to the Islamic ideas of social justice and economic equality. In view of the large scale aid requirements of the country, the new government sought to cultivate political ties with richer countries, particularly the US in order to secure more economic benefits and thereby to ensure political and economic stability of the country.[9] Middle East countries also became Bangladesh's major aid donors on Islamic grounds.

Another significant change at international level that went in favour of Bangladesh's pursuit of foreign policy goals was the establishment of the Carter government in Washington. Carter government was also keen to improve US relations with Bangladesh. This resulted in positive development in US-Bangladesh relations.

The amendment of the 1972 Constitution, the pursuit of friendly relations with China and the muslim countries, and the consequent fading away of the predominating Indian and Soviet influence, were all indication of the new priorities of the Zia's regime that did not appear to go against US calculations.[10] In fact, the US began to take Bangladesh more seriously since the removal of Awami League government and the establishment of a pro-west regime in its place. Thus, within a year of Mujib's death, the US indicated its willingness to consider Bangladesh's request for export license for the cash sales of military equipment.

The US also showed great interest in Bangladesh affairs. A political and economic appraisal of the country was placed before the US Congress on the eve of the Presidential elections in Bangladesh and surveys of US□Bangladesh relations were frequently in the general assessment of US-South Asian relations, signifying the importance of the country in the US's regional calculations.[11] The appointment of Mr. Tabarak Hossain, who was considered to be the chief architect of the country's foreign policy, as Bangladeshi ambassador in the US signified the country's interest in developing closer relationship with the US.[12]

Bangladesh also indicated its tilt towards Washington by signing Non-Proliferation Treaty (NPT). Since India and Pakistan, the two powerful nations of subcontinent were non-signatories, the US attached special significance to Bangladesh accession to the treaty. Convergence of views on the NPT became a strong bond in the US-Bangladesh friendship.[13]

The development of bilateral economic relationship between the US and Bangladesh during Zia's period was the most significant achievement between these two countries. In 1978, Bangladesh became the first country in Asia to receive new PL 480 Title III Food for Development programme. The inclusion of Bangladesh in the Title III programme signified the US interests in playing a more influential role in the Bangladesh's development efforts. Moreover, with the liberalization of private investment ceiling and the government's encouragements to foreign and private enterprises, several US firms engaged themselves in offshore oil exploration in Bangladesh.

Bangladesh signed a Peace Corps Agreement with the US on 13 July 1978, solidifying the relationship which allowed American voluntary activities in Bangladesh. In the past, Mujib had asked the US to withdraw its peace corps members. However, the Zia government faced sharp flak over its decision to allow American volunteers to work in

Bangladesh and therefore agreement could not come into force.[14]

The US government was highly supportive of the Zia regime which was evident from several political events.[15] The parliamentary elections of 1979 in Bangladesh were accepted by the US as a part of the democratization process though the opposition parties were intensely critical of its fairness. Zia's attempt at civilizing the country's political system was interpreted as a deliberate gesture made to appease the US. Washington deemphasized the alleged human right violations in Bangladesh. In 1977, Zia executed many people involved in the coup to destabilize his government. But for understandable reasons, the State Department started acclaiming Zia government for improved human right's situation. In its 1978 report it observed that since 1975 there had been a modest but broad-based improvement in public order.[16]

Zia's visit to the US in August 1980 further strengthened relations between the two countries.[17] His hour-long talks with President Carter over bilateral relations as well as regional and international issues were conducted in a friendly atmosphere. The two leaders expressed identical views on Afghanistan and Kampuchea and called for immediate withdrawal of all foreign troops from these places. Bangladesh took active part in the drafting of the resolutions, while voting on both the issues at the UN. [18] Moreover, the US President expressed his personal admiration for the Zia's economic and political leadership and assured him of all possible cooperation in the successful implementation of the Second Five Year Plan of Bangladesh.[19]

BANGLADESH-US RELATIONS DURING ERSHAD'S REGIME

On 30 May 1981, Ziaur Rahman's regime came to an end. In a coup, Ziaur Rahman was killed at Chittagong by a group of army rebels called "Biplabi Parisad" led by Major General Manzur Ahmad. Soon after the coup, the Vice President Abdus Sattar took over as the acting President and elections were held in November 1981, which confirmed the Presidency of the 71 year old Abdus Sattar. On 24 March 1982, the government was overthrown in a bloodless coup by General H.M. Ershad on grounds of corruption in public life and fight of power.[20]

General Ershad, who was known to be loyal to Ziaur Rahman, followed Zia's domestic and foreign policies. Ershad tried to consolidate US-Bangladesh relationship on the grounds made by Zia during his regime. He sought the US support by referring to the Soviets as dangerous.[21] Soviet diplomats were expelled from the country and the Soviet Cultural Centre was closed down. This diplomatic move earned a plus point for Ershad regime especially from those who did not like the alignment of the Bangladesh with the USSR. Therefore during Ershad period, Dhaka-Moscow relations came under serious strains. A complete shift from the Indo-Soviet axis was clearly discernible.

Ershad, at the domestic level, followed the policies of Zia. He took bold steps towards creating conductive atmosphere for a market economy to work. On the domestic front, his regime followed the World Bank and USAID prescriptions for privatization of the supply of agricultural inputs and the withdrawal of subsidy from agriculture. Various other steps were taken to promote and expand private sector's role in the economy. All these policies, foreign and domestic, provided leverage to the Ershad regime in its negotiations with the US.

Bangladesh's desire for peace, disarmament, and a new international economic order was reiterated by General Ershad in June 1982. In his address to the second special session of the United Nations on Disarmament, he urged the developing nations to cut down their spending on armaments and divert the money to promote the economic well being.[22] General Ershad had, to his great pleasure, the opportunity to meet President Reagan at the United Nations.

ERSHAD'S VISIT TO THE U.S.

Ershad was formally invited to the United States by President Ronald Reagan, the first invitation for a Bangladeshi head of government. Ershad's two predecessors, Mujib and Ziaur Rahman, had only brief meetings of less than an hour with American Presidents, Ford and Carter, respectively. Ershad's working official visit was, therefore, a positive development between the US and Bangladesh relations.[23]

The evolving closer relationship between the two countries was confirmed by the agreement signed on 26 October 1982, which corrected the Title-III of the PL 480 Programme. Under the new arrangement, Washington agreed to supply $ 60 million worth of extra food to Bangladesh as well as long term loans totaling $ 200 million for the augmentation of food grain production and distribution in the following three years.[24]

During his meeting with President Reagan in Washington, General Ershad discussed a wide range of bilateral, regional and intentional issues. Bangladesh's stand on Afghanistan and Kampuchea and active membership of Non-aligned Movement (NAM) and the Organization of the Islamic Conference, were highly commended by President Reagan.[25] Washington was highly pleased when Bangladesh, as a Third World country, abstained from voting at the UN General assembly resolution condemning the American invasion of Granada.[26] Even in 1986, when the US mounted an air attack on Libya, the Government of Bangladesh remained tight-lipped, giving enough indications of its willingness to remain friendly with the US.

WIDENING SPECTRUM OF RELATIONSHIP

The improved trends in the US-Bangladesh relations were also in the exchange of visits by the high dignitaries of both countries after 1983. Senator Larry Preslar, visited Bangladesh in 1985 and C. Whitehead, Deputy Secretary of State visited Bangladesh in October 1985. These were followed by Ambassador Vernon Walters, US President Representative to the United Nations, in June 1986, who had discussions with both President Ershad and the Bangladesh Foreign Minister. At the invitation of the government of Bangladesh, former US President Jimmy Carter and his wife Rosalyn visited Bangladesh between 1-2 November 1986. They met President Ershad during their stay and initiated the Bangladesh Programme of a voluntary organization, Global 2000, of which Carter was Chairman.[27]

Senator Larry Preslar, the first US Senator to visit Bangladesh raised the issue of American policy towards the smaller states of South Asia, vis-a-vis India and Pakistan. The Senator perceived that other smaller countries were not getting enough attention in US South Asian foreign policy objectives and hence were suffering psychological disadvantage vis-a-vis India. In this context he recommended giving more emphasis to the US-Bangladesh relations and suggested that the US would benefit from greater political and economic stability in South Asia. He recommended that an exchange of high level visits would foster enduring and mutually beneficial ties between the two countries.[28]

Growth in military ties between the US and Bangladesh was also witnessed during Ershad's regime. Contacts between senior military officials of the two countries began with the visits to Bangladesh by Lieutenant General Charles Wilson Bagral, Commander of the United States Army Western Command, and Admiral Ronald J. Hays, Commander in Chief of the US Pacific Command, in January and November 1986 respectively. During their visits they met the President and high ranking military officials and discussed matters of mutual concern. A goodwill visit was paid by the US ship *Capondanno* to Chittagong port in December 1986.[29]

During his tour in 1982 General Ershad consistently tried to impress upon the policy-makers of the US that, due to his disinvestment and other policies, the United States would be able to play a bigger role in the economic development of Bangladesh. In a meeting with journalists in Houston, Texas, General Ershad emphasized the favourable conditions created by the recent adoption of new policies to attract foreign investment. Prior to his visit, Ershad had taken a number of economic measures to develop a comprehensive structural adjustment programme. During Ershad's period, foreign private investment was about two per cent of the total investment in which a significant investment came from the US. In the wake of such measures adopted by Ershad, Reagan labeled Ershad as a "man of private enterprise".[30]

Ershad again visited the US on an official tour in November 1988 with twin objectives of addressing the UN General Assembly session and meeting the President of the US. During Ershad's meeting with President Reagan the latter assured Ershad of adequate aid and assistance for rehabilitation and reconstruction. President Ershad's visit to the US had brought the two countries closer as never before, and that his talks with the American leadership resulted in far greater understanding of Bangladesh's problems and aspirations of the people.[31]

However, Bangladesh domestic policies and the United State's strong reservations against continuation of military regime, did not affect the converging perceptions of both the countries on international issues. Rather, both the countries shared common perceptions on global and regional issues.

In the aftermath of the Iraqi invasion of Kuwait in August 1990, Bangladesh supported UN Security Council's sanctions against Iraq. Bangladesh and the US were also partners in a common enterprise in trying to reverse the effects of Iraq's aggression in the Gulf. Bangladesh dispatched 2,300 troops to Saudi Arabia for defensive purposes and participated in the US led Multinational Force (MNF) that fought against Iraq in January-February 1991.

BANGLADESH-US RELATIONS DURING KHALEDA ZIA'S REGIME

Begum Khaleda Zia, widow of General Ziaur Rahman, came to power after the 1991 elections. The basic framework of Khaleda Zia's policy with regard to the external relations of Bangladesh were greatly based on the policies of Ziaur Rahman and H.M. Ershad.

Realizing the state of affairs prevailing in Bangladesh, Begun Zia adopted a policy of economic restructuring, she directed her attention from obtaining aid and assistance to boosting the country's export and investment. She strongly suggested that Dhaka should be projected to world community in general, and to Washington in particular, in a proper perspective and that foreign relations must be utilized for prospect of trade and investment in the country.[32]

EMPHASIS ON POLITICAL-ECONOMIC RELATIONS

Soon after the restoration of the democratic government, Bangladesh was struck by a devastating cyclone in April 1991, causing widespread destruction. According to an estimate the total amount of damage was assessed to the tune of $2.5 billion.[33] In response, international relief efforts were mounted quickly from many countries. In the wake of this crisis, the largest assistance came from the US Marines who were returning to home bases from operation desert storm.[34] These forces were diverted to Bangladesh with the objective of assisting the cyclone hit people. These American relief efforts earned great appreciation from the Bangladesh government and its people, especially in areas where only the specialized equipments used by the Marines could be effective. The assistance of the US naval task force was credited with having saved as many as 200,000 lives. On the other hand, for the cyclone, the USAID provided $4,662,000 as disaster grants to non-government organizations.[35] In March 1992, Bangladesh and the US signed PL 480 agreement. The agreement contained a 4 year programme for up to $268 million US food aid to Bangladesh. The assistance was to be used not only to meet Bangladesh's food security needs, but was also meant to generate local currency to finance the annual development investment programme, much of which was used for agricultural development.[36]

The US became the most important trading partner of Bangladesh. One noteworthy feature of trade relationship was the export of garment and knitwear which in 1993 constituted 85 per cent of all Bangladesh exports to US. The garment industry became a key source of foreign exchange for Bangladesh.[37]

During Khaleda Zia's period Bangladesh garments industries became a subject of intense debate in the US. Use of child labour in textiles industries was opposed by a US pressure group, Child Labour Coalition. The coalition threatened to launch a boycott campaign against Bangladeshi garments for using child workers under the age of 14 years. The US Senator Tom Harkin tabled a bill in this regard in US Congress. Senator Tom Harkin also maintained that the MOU would benefit Bangladeshi garment industries by allowing the country the maximum access to the US market[38]. However, an agreement for eliminating child labour from the Bangladeshi garment industries was signed on 4 July 1995. In return, Bangladesh government expected an increase in export of Bangladeshi garments to the American market by increasing the quota.

During Khaleda Zia period, Dhaka liberalized and deregulated Bangladesh economy.[39] Bangladesh sought the US businessmen and entrepreneurs to utilize the new opportunities that created an atmosphere for unfettered trade and investment in Bangladesh. Dhaka stressed that Bangladesh would provide the US the opportunities to establish mutually beneficial commercial and trade relations.[40] In response to this attractive market and investment opportunities the US framed several positive policies designed to improve trade and investment in Bangladesh. Roger C. Altman, Deputy Secretary of the US Department of Treasury, hailed the "bold and dynamic" economic policy measures undertaken by Bangladesh government and the tangible results that folowed.[41]

In addition, growing trade and investment relations between the US and Bangladesh were epitomized by the organization of the US trade shows in Dhaka known as the premier trade events in Bangladesh. The first Trade Show was held in Dhaka in 1992, the second in 1993, the third in 1994, and the fourth in 1995 demonstrating sustained US business interest in the market potentials of Bangladesh.

Khaleda Zia opted for the parliamentary democracy in place of presidential form of government. The logical argument for such a transformation was to ensure people's participation in the government of the country and effective role of the opposition, as against the authoritarian regimes. Bangladesh stand on the democratic form of government was reflected again in 1994 during Haiti Crisis Bangladesh maintained and supported US perception of democracy.[42]

In August 1995 US Navy and Bangladesh Navy carried Operation Sea Bat, a joint exercise as a symbol of their collaboration in the Bay of Bengal. This exercise focused on cooperation between US and Bangladesh naval forces in the fields of surveillance, search, and rescue operation during natural calamities. It was also aimed at forging a cooperation between the US Navy and Bangladesh Air force in search and rescue operation.[43]

The US had been responsive to Bangladesh's economic needs and security concerns and it indeed came forward with aid and support whenever the latter needed. Bangladesh, in return, reciprocated by being sensitive to US calculations in respect of policies adopted by the US on several global issues like Kuwait and Haiti, during Khaleda Zia period.[44] It could be safely concluded that Bangladesh and the US made serious effort to enlarge the area of cooperation, especially in the field of trade and development. The American government recognized Khaleda Zia's attempt towards expanding press freedom, independence of judiciary and local elections that were free and fair. The process of democratization in Bangladesh, under Khaleda Zia's rule was successful in alleviating the US's earlier reservations against Bangladesh due to its previous bad record in forming and sustaining democratic institutions.

BANGLADESH-US RELATIONS DURING SHEIKH HASINA'S REGIME

The general elections were held on 12 June 1996, with the participation of all major political parties of the country. The Awami League won the largest number of seats and its leader Begum Sheikh Hasina Wajed was sworn in as the new Prime Minister of Bangladesh on 23 June 1996. Begum Hasina Wajed also followed the policy of her predecessors. She also recognized and reinforced traditional friendship with the US. She tried to project Bangladesh as one of the leading muslim countries being moderate in its orientation, this to her was an important virtue at a time when many leading muslim countries have pursued radical and fundamental policies.

The other credit was for being a democracy. Not many muslim countries have made a success of democracy. At a time when the Islamic world was in deep political turmoil, strengthening of democracy in Bangladesh was of considerable strategic value to the United States.[45] Parliamentary elections held in Bangladesh in June 1996 made a tremendous impact on the Clinton Government which held the elections as free and fair and particularly appreciated the large turnout of the voters. The US President consequently sent a letter to Begum Wajed congratulating on her commendable achievement.[46]

STRENGTHENING OF RELATIONSHIP

Prime Minister Sheikh Hasina paid a visit to the United States in October 1996. Although ostensibly the visit was to address the fifty-first session of the UN General Assembly, she availed the opportunity of her stay in New York to meet potential investors and the chief executives of major oil companies in order to explain to them her government's policies and priorities.[47] Congressman Bill Richardson met Sheikh Hasina along with a group of senior executives of US companies. Sheikh Hasina briefed them on the liberal foreign investment policies of her government, the incentive package offered to investors and urged them to invest in Bangladesh.[48] Richardson and his delegation assured the Bangladeshi Prime Minister that they would seriously consider investing in Bangladesh. She also discussed double avoidance treaty, with the US Assistant Secretary of State Ms. Robin Raphael on 25 October 1996.[49]

However, an important landmark in the US-Bangladesh relationship undoubtedly was Sheikh Hasina's visit to Washington in February 1997 to chair the Micro-credit Summit. During her stay she met President Bill Clinton twice and held discussion on issues of national, regional and international importance. The US officials described these meetings as highly successful.[50] During her meeting Sheikh

Hasina apprised the President of the opportunities Bangladesh had decided to offer to foreign investors. She also requested President Clinton to waive Bangladesh's outstanding debt of US $318 million to US on account of PL-480 assistance. In October 2000, Sheikh Hasina once again visited US and discussed bilateral ties with US government.

President Clinton on his part commended Bangladesh for its success in reducing poverty level, increasing food self sufficiency and also applauded the Bangladesh government's vision in recognizing the important role that economic liberalization and foreign investment play in continued success in these areas. He also paid tributes to Bangladesh for leading the way in exploring new ideas that hold promise for the poor, and particularly cited, "successful micro credit lending programme developed by Grameen Bank during the democratic regime of Hasina Wajed as well as successful implementation of the oral dehydration therapy that has saved so many lives all over the world".[51]

The US Assistant Secretary of State for South Asian Affairs Karl Inderfurth visited Bangladesh in September 1997 and had detailed discussion with Bangladesh officials. He conveyed the US appreciation on the foreign policy achievements as well as the economic policies and performance of the Government of the Bangladesh. He commended Bangladesh government for eliminating child labour from the garment industries and the role played by the Grameen Bank in removing poverty.[52] Speaking before the House International Relations Subcommittee on Asia and Pacific, Karl Inderfurth described Bangladesh as a friendly country and appreciated the advancement Bangladesh had made in democatization of polity, elimination of child labour and empowerment of women. He also spoke at length about the US interests in energy and oil sector.

At the ground level, significant measures were taken by the government to attract the US investment in Bangladesh. This includes signing of the Bangladesh-US Bilateral Investment Treaty.[53] In addition, the Bangladesh-US Business Council set up with active financial assistance of the Bangladesh government and USAID, tried to project and promote trade and investment opportunities in Bangladesh through investment meetings. There had been several meetings between the two countries in connection with trade and investment.[54] Due to these efforts and policies, the total US investment in Bangladesh, which was roughly estimated at US $20 million till June 1996, had sharply risen to US $750 million in 1999. Most of these investments have been made in the energy sectors.[55] In December 1998, US and Bangladesh signed a joint statement on cooperation in energy sector. During Shaikh Hasina regime, several officials of the US visited Bangladesh and action plan to develop power sector was signed.[56]

As regards aid and assistance, the US concentrated on long-term development in Bangladesh. The objective of US assistance included reduction in population growth, protecting human health, encouraging broad based economic growth, and strengthening democracy. During the devastating floods of 1998 the US was the largest supplier of food grains to Bangladesh. It provided 700,00 metric tons of wheat and a variety of other relief measures.[57] This marks the strengthening of relationship between US and Bangladesh.

BANGLADESH-US RELATIONS DURING KHALEDA ZIA'S REGIME

The general elections were held in Bangladesh on 1 October 2001. The Bangladesh Nationalist Party (BNP) led four party coalition government and Begum Khaleda Zia sworn in as a new Prime Minister of Bangladesh for second time. The foreign policy of Khaleda Zia almost remained the same as was in her earlier regime.

During the present regime of Begum Khaleda Zia Bangladesh-US relations have attained a new height. The most significant transformation of Bangladesh-US relations has been its evolution from the one that was based on aid dependence, to the present one that is based on trade and investment. Begum Zia has adopted a policy to believe on trade and investment in place of aid as well as economic reform measures and opening of the market. Begum Khaleda Zia restructured the content of foreign policy and economic policy to drive diplomatic initiatives for trade and investment with US.

Begum Zia's main foreign policy objectives are as follows

1. Sustaining the current flow of foreign aid and removal of conditionalities as far as possible,
2. Strengthening trade relations with particular emphasis on promotion of export, and
3. Attracting foreign investment and joint ventures, especially from US.

It can be said that her initiatives has brought a shift in the foreign policy of Bangladesh from being a mere recipient of foreign aid and assistance, to a country which is earnestly striving for promotion of trade and investment, and which is following a policy of liberalization and globalization that also suits the US and proved to be a milestone in the relations of Bangladesh and US.

At present, Bangladesh-US relations are cordial. Both the countries are cooperating each other in many areas like promotion of democracy, human rights, war on terror and protection of peace and security in the world. The depth of relations between Bangladesh and US can be seen by the high level of deliberations of their leaders in last four years. One improved trend in the Bangladesh-US relations is also reflected by the exchange of visits by high dignitaries of both the countries after October 2001.

US President George W. Bush Congratulated Prime Minster Begum Khaleda Zia on 29 October 2001 on telephone for her party's victory in the parliamentary elections and also discussed bilateral issues with her. Bush assured Khaleda Zia that the relations between the US and Bangladesh would grow further. Furthermore, he added that his country has nothing against Islam and immensely honors Islamic values.[58] Khaleda Zia assured US president to provide full support against terrorism anywhere in the world and for the peace-keeping efforts.

Then Foreign Minister of Bangladesh A.Q.M. Badruddoza Chowdhary visited United States on 5 November 2001 and hold official talks with the US Secretary of State Colin Powell. Bangladesh argued for the US support for quota free, duty free access of readymade garments to the US market and the US assured Bangladesh for a positive decision on this issue.

The US Assistant Secretary of State Christian Rocca visited Bangladesh on 11 March 2002 and discussed national, regional and international issues with the Bangladesh government including military cooperation in the form of exchange of programme and training of officers in the United States and its military headquarters of Asia-Pacific in Hawaii. She also met Prime Minister Khaleda Zia and assured US help to Bangladesh in all sectors. In March 2002 America gifted four C-130 B transport aircraft to Bangladesh.[59]

Prime Minister of Bangladesh Begum Khaleda Zia visited the United States on 6 May 2002 to attend a special session of the United Nations General Assembly (UNGA) on child rights. This was her first visit to the US since she returned to power. During her stay she discussed many issues with the US government for strengthening the ties between Bangladesh and the US. This visit proved to be a landmark in the relations of the two countries.

On 20 May 2002 Foreign Minister of Bangladesh Morshed Khan went to America and met US Secretary of State Colin Powell in Washington. Morshed Khan discussed with Powell the issue of duty free access of Bangladeshi goods, including readymade garments to the US and US assured Bangladesh to consider it.

The US Secretary of State Colin Powell arrived in Dhaka on 19 June 2003 on a brief but important visit. Both the countries discussed bilateral and economic relations and decided to take steps to further strengthen bilateral relations. US assured Bangladesh of unwavering help in eliminating poverty and achieving economic progress. US thanked Bangladesh for unflinching support to the war against terror. In January 2004, Bangladesh signed a pact with the US embassy with a view to eliminating terrorism and financial sources of terrorists. As per the agreement both the government had decided to work together to expose the activities and fund raising initiatives of the international terrorist and Islamic militant organizations.

The United States Secretary of Defence Donald Rumsfeld visited Dhaka on 5 June 2004 and discussed bilateral and defense ties with Prime Minister Khaleda Zia and Foreign Minister Morshed Khan. America appreciated Bangladesh contribution to numerous peacekeeping efforts around the world. The US also appreciated Bangladeshi stand on the Iraq issue.

The US Assistant Secretary of State for South Asian Affairs, Christina Rocca, arrived in Dhaka on 9 May 2005. Both the countries discussed a number of issues, including the Dhaka-Washington bilateral relations. This visit of Christina Rocca was significant in further consolidating US-

Bangladesh cooperation in certain fields. The US assurance for support to Bangladesh bid for duty free access of her goods including readymade garment to the US market was an important issue.

Bangladesh, a muslim majority democracy, hopes for greater US cooperation in not only fighting terrorism but also economically changing her lot. In the present scenario, Bangladesh and US have been engaged in a long-term relationship and, significantly, that bilateral ties between the two have developed and grown stronger over the last four years. America praised the government of Bangladesh for her commitment to fighting terrorism and its success in improving the law and order situation in the country. The US also appreciated the primitive steps that Bangladesh has taken to prevent the rise of extremism and militancy.

Foreign Minister of Bangladesh M. Morshed Khan visited USA on 19 May 2005 and met the new US Secretary of State Condoleezza Rice. Both the Foreign Ministers expressed their intention to forge closer economic and political cooperation between the two countries. The US decided to extend more trade opportunity and greater economic assistance for Bangladesh. US termed Bangladesh "a good friend, a democratic force and voice of moderation" and decided that both the countries will continue the work together as partners for further strengthening of democratic institutions, maintain law and order and protect the rights of minorities.[60] Both the countries reiterated their commitment to continue to work with all in the fight against international terrorism and observed that the two countries are cooperating closely on this issue. America also praised Bangladesh economic and social advancement and termed its achievement in empowering women as fantastic. On 23 June 2005 the government of US decided to provide financial help to Bangladesh in buying Boeing aircraft B 777.[61]

The US Under Secretary of State for Political Affairs Nicholas R Burns arrived in Dhaka on 26 June 2005 for discussion on political climate and bilateral issues of mutual interest with government officials, political party leaders and members of civil society. Burns discussed bilateral, economic, political and religious minority issues with Khaleda Zia and Morshed Khan.

Describing US-Bangladesh relations as very good, strong and sound, Burns said, US has great admiration for democratic practices and institutions in Bangladesh. US is proud of the positive development in the Bangladesh-US relations under the able leadership of Prime Minister Begum Khaleda Zia.[62] US is greatful to Bangladesh for its stand against international terrorism and hailed Bangladesh's role in UN peacekeeping missions. Therefore, it seems that bilateral relations of Bangladesh and USA have greatly improved in the present regime of Begum Khaleda Zia and the regular visits of important officials of both the countries is a clear reflection of strengthening of ties between Bangladesh and USA.

MILESTONES IN BANGLADESH-US RELATIONSHIP

Bangladesh foreign policy recognizes the role of the US in the establishment o1 world peace and stability and therefore it continues to support areas of common and shared interests. Bangladesh also shares with the US similar perception with regard to the regional and international peace and security. Bangladesh is one of the leading countries in South Asia who has signed the CTBT.

CTBT AND NPT

Bangladesh has fully supported the Comprehensive Test Ban Treaty (CTBT) and Non-Proliferation Treaty (NPT). Bangladesh was the second South Asian country to sign CTBT, and this was particularly appreciated by the US in view of Pakistan and India's refusal to signing it.[63] Bangladesh firmly believes that CTBT is not an end in itself, but a significant step towards the ultimate goal of general and complete disarmament.[64]

Bangladesh has become the member of the Conference on Disarmament in Geneva in June 1996.[65] In the 1995 NPT Review Conference, Bangladesh joined the consensus decision for an indefinite extension of the NPT. Bangladesh has played a more constructive role in all the three Prep Coms for the 2000 NPT Review Conference in New York and Geneva. In the Third Prep Com in New York, Bangladesh reaffirmed that NPT is the legal cornerstone of the nuclear non-proliferation regime and most widely ratified arms control treaty in history.

SOFA AND HANA PROPOSALS

The US proposed Bangladesh to sign Status of Forces Agreement (SOFA). The SOFA was first proposed by the US diplomat, Bill Richardson during his visit to Bangladesh. The US had suggested that some kind of a legal cover should be created which would enable the troops to conduct joint exercises in Bangladesh and take part in rescue and relief operations during natural calamities.

But this proposal was opposed by media, intelligentsia and the Leftist politicians. They argued that the proposed agreement would work against Bangladesh's sovereignty and dignity. The Research Director of MISS, Abdur Rob Khan held that US wanted this provision for the security of its investment in the country.[66] India clearly opposed the SOFA and even expressed its concern over its own security and sovereignty. At one point it seemed that Bangladesh would relent and would sign the agreement. But after deliberating over the issue for months, the government expressed the view that Bangladesh has nothing to gain by signing SOFA in the form it was presented. Finally in July 1998, the Bangladesh government rejected the US proposal to sign the controversial SOFA.[67] However, despite all this, both countries reaffirmed their commitment to work in the areas of mutual interests.

The Humanitarian Assistance Need Assessment (HANA) was also signed by the two countries. Under the HANA programme the US defense department was expected to complete a survey of the country's need in times of calamities and disasters.[68] Further improvement in relationship between the two countries was reflected by the visit of Chief of the US Armed Forces General Dennis Joe Reimol in April 1998 who was heading a 97 member goodwill delegation to Bangladesh. He met the Prime Minister, President and senior defense officials of Bangladesh. On 5 July 1998, a MOU was signed between Bangladesh and US peace corps to implement peace corps programme in Bangladesh. Moreover, Bangladesh had no military agreement with any country in the world, but preliminary negotiations were made with the US to facilitate the holding of joint military exercises and for the participation of American Army personnel in time of natural disaster.

HUMAN RIGHT ISSUES

The theme of human rights feature prominently in the US-Bangladesh relations. Promoting human rights is an integral part of the US foreign policy. For promoting human rights in the country, Bangladesh, on the occasion of the 50 Anniversary year of the UNHR, acceded/ratified/signed the International Covenant on Economic, Social and Cultural rights, prevention and punishment of the crime of genocide, political rights of women against torture and other cruel inhuman or degrading treatment.[69] The Bangladesh government in fulfilment of its obligations under these Human Rights instruments has made efforts for their effective and timely implementation and practices by creating a national machinery, formulating new policies and programmes of action, and legislating new laws. During the 55 Commission of Human Rights Session held in Geneva in 1999 Bangladesh cosponsored and voted in favour of the resolution tabled by the US on Promotion of the Right to Democracy. This decision was taken in keeping with the Bangladesh deep commitment to the rights of people of Bangladesh to the democratic process and its institutionalization.[70]

THE CONCEPT OF DEMOCRACY

Bangladesh maintained and supported the US perception on democracy. In September 1994, Bangladesh agreed to participate in the UN sponsored Multi National Force (MNF) formed under the UN Security Council resolution concerning military intervention in Haiti, designed to force Haiti's military Director General, Raul Cedras, to step down and to restore democratically elected President, Jean Betrand Aristide, to his office. The decision came after a direct request from President Bill Clinton to Bangladesh Prime Minister Khaleda Zia. In an attempt to justify its position, Bangladesh announced that it would help in maintaining public safety and basic civil order after restoration of legally elected government in Haiti. The Bangladeshi Foreign Minister announced that the decision of Bangladesh was based on its abiding commitment to fully support the UN and to uphold the cause of democracy and peace around the world.[71] The US welcomed Bangladesh stand and the Secretary of State Warren Christopher commended Bangladesh for its commitment to democracy demonstrated by its stand "to give democracy a chance" in far away Haiti.[72] It implies that Bangladesh support to the US on issues like democracy and peace, projected Bangladesh as an important partner in protecting American political and strategic interests even in the remote Carribean region. In Bangladesh, this was seen as an opportunity to work closely with the country like America, while these decisions of the government were not free from strong resentments and opposition in many quarters.

AFGHANISTAN AND TERRORISM

During the Cold War days, the United States had a special interest in Afghanistan. The US was the main supporter of the Mujahideen in terms of weapon supplies and direct and covert military involvement against the Soviet invasion of Afghanistan. After the Soviet pull-out, and the subsequent collapse of the administrative machinery in Afghanistan, the US became wary of it fearing that it might become an Islamic theocracy and threaten US strategic interests. The US concerns became even more pronounced with Taliban gaining control of Afghanistan and its close links with Osama bin Laden. Osama bin Laden has been indicted and convicted by the US courts for his involvement in the bombing of the US Embassies in Tunisia and Kenya. The UN Security Council Resolution called upon the Taliban to hand over bin Laden or face sanctions.

In the context of Afghanistan and Taliban, Bangladesh has a stand similar to the US. Bangladesh had urged the Taliban to comply with the UNSC resolutions. Bangladesh also does not support any acts of terrorism from the Afghan territory.

PEACE-KEEPING MISSIONS: THE BANGLADESHI COOPERATION

The United States is a strong supporter of UN peace-keeping operations and one of the contributors to the peace-keeping budget although it is seeking support to its proposal to scale down its contribution from 31% to 25%. Bangladesh is also committed to the cause of international peace and security.

This is manifested in its active participation in various UN peace keeping operations. As of December 1999, Bangladesh ranked the second largest contributor of peace-keeping troops. In the 54 UNGA and in the 1999 session of the Special Committee on Peace-keeping, Bangladesh maintained that adequate financial resources and support were crucial for effectiveness of peace keeping operations.

NUCLEAR EXPLOSIONS BY INDIA AND PAKISTAN

The US came out with its severest criticism after both India and Pakistan carried out nuclear tests. It termed the tests as unjustified and capable of creating destabilizing impact in South Asia.

Similarly, Bangladesh government also expressed her apprehensions at the development. Bangladesh was of the view that this issue was no longer an issue between the two countries (India and Pak) only, since in the event of an Indo-Pak nuclear exchange the entire region would suffer from terrible consequences. Moreover, Bangladesh may face a physical threat in a nuclear environment that may occur out of any miscalculation or mistargeting. Bangladesh also expressed her hope that all the states in South Asia would refrain from further increasing the nuclear arms race.[73]

GEO-STRATEGIC LOCATION OF BANGLADESH - THE CHINA FACTOR

The geo-strategic interests that guide the US foreign policy today make it imperative for it to have presence in areas where it can counter China effectively.

The emergence of China as a major power, especially after the disintegration of the USSR, has become a cause of concern for the US. In the Middle East it has reliable friends in Gulf countries. In East Asia, its close relationship with South Korea provides it with an advantageous position. Yet, its presence in the Bay of Bengal could grant it more leverage. Therefore, besides India, it is trying to cultivate friendship with Bangladesh with renewed vigour. Besides Tibet, Taiwan can also prove to be a flash-point, since there have been strong reactions by China on utterances by the US on these two issues. On the issues of democracy and Human Rights violation also the US and China do not see each other eye to eye. As such, in the calculations of the US, Bangladesh has the potential of becoming a dependable US ally in the event of any mishap with China.

However, we also need to keep in mind that Bangladesh has friendly relations with China as well. Therefore, in order to have an upper hand the US needs to frame its policies in regard to Bangladesh, in a way that it can take advantage of geo-strategic location of Bangladesh. Bangladesh is also on the route of oil rich Gulf countries and South East Asian tigers. Besides Bangladesh can also take advantage of the US might in view of two strong neighbours - China and India - who are not so friendly with it.

INCREASE IN QUOTA AND ELIMINATION OF CHILD-LABOUR

The government of Bangladesh requested the US government through the Department of State for an urgent increase in the base quota by 30 per cent for export of textile and apparels. Bangladesh has also requested the merger of the single category item (RMG) into combined category items and also duty free access of RMG. According to Bangladesh the proposed increase will help accelerate economic development, alleviate poverty and provide opportunity for empowerment and emancipation of rural women and marginalized sections of the society.

Bangladesh Garment Manufacturers and Exporters Association (BGMEA), with the support of the US

Government, has eliminated child labour from garment industries. As a result, more and more US companies are now showing interest in buying garments from them. The BGMEA has set an example by eliminating child labour and making arrangement for their education and providing income support for the affected families on the basis of a MOU signed with ILO and UNICEF. On this ground BGMEA requested the increase in the garment quota by 30 per cent.

DEBT RELIEF

Bangladesh has a huge external debt liability. It stood at $14.03 billion in 2004-2005 accounting for 4.1 per cent of GDP.[74] For a developing country like Bangladesh with per capita GDP of US $240, it is a huge burden. The US has been providing substantial development assistance to Bangladesh in terms of loans and grants. Past loans, provided with extended grace periods, are now becoming mature for repayment. The debt problem could be perceived in the light of the huge debt/export, since a major portion of the export earnings of the country goes towards debt servicing. This has a drag and pull effect on the growth of foreign exchange earnings of Bangladesh, resulting in reduced domestic resource mobilization, which in turn implies that very less amount of finances are available for development purposes. In a high debt service scenario, the process of globalization will place Bangladesh at a particularly disadvantageous position. It will reduce capital inflow and capacity enhancement. Consequently, during the present regime of Begum Khaleda Zia the relations between Bangladesh and US are good and Bangladesh expects to the US to play a dominant role in reducing the debt burden both by converting a part of its loan to Bangladesh into grants and by influencing other donors to provide similar debt relief. Bangladesh as coordinator for the least developing countries (LDCs) for international meetings has always been demanding that the

LDCs should be assisted in their efforts to grow rapidly and attract foreign investment. For this the LDCs need preferential access to the global markets, measures to promote their capacity building steps to enhance their managerial and technical skills and assistance for building their institutional and physical infrastructure.

BILL CLINTON'S VISIT TO BANGLADESH

One of the brightest moments of Bangladesh-US relation was President Bill Clinton's visit to Bangladesh. His visit to Bangladesh proved that Bangladesh gets significant place in the US calculations in South Asia.

During his visit, the President acknowledged the role Bangladesh has played in past, and in promoting human rights, peace and democracy in the recent times. He also recognized significance of Bangladesh in the wake of growing Indo□Pak tension and their possession of nuclear arms as an established factor. He announced partial debt cancellation under PL480 debt for tropical forest protection.

President Clinton's visit was also an occasion to cement the bonds of friendship and cooperation between the US and Bangladesh. This visit brought Bangladesh in sharper focus in international affairs. President Clinton not only assured America's continued support to the economic development and democracy in Bangladesh but also recognized its role in peace-making in region, and in the world at large. Clinton remarked, I *think this is a nation with very bright future.*

SUMMING UP

It can be said in conclusion that Bangladesh-US relations are at their best today with both the countries cooperating in wide variety of areas. The degree of closeness can be measured by the high level of deliberations between their leaders. Bangladesh attaches particular importance to its relations with the United States not only because of its preponderant role in international affairs, but also for the commonality of interests of the two countries in many areas including promotion of democracy, human rights and protection of peace and security in the world. The US today is most important development partner, which has also assisted Bangladesh during the time of natural disasters, like floods and cyclone. Bangladesh has come to realize that in a unipolar world Bangladesh could derive benefit by promoting friendly relations with the US.

During the past few years, especially after the end of the Cold War, Bangladesh-US relations have attained a new height. The most significant transformation of Bangladesh-US relations has been its evolution from the one that was based on aid dependence, to the present one that is based on trade and investment. This is the result of fall of Soviet Block and promotion of liberalization and globalization in the world by the US and multilateral agencies. Begum Khaleda Zia has adopted a policy of dependence on trade and investment, rather than on aid as well as economic reform measures and opening of the market. On the other hand, Bangladesh today figures prominently in the US map of countries which matter to it for a number of reasons. In the first place, the US looks at Bangladesh as a leading developing country where democracy is taking firm roots.[77] During the 1990s, Bangladesh promoted democracy and the US helped the Bangladesh government in institutionalizing democracy. As the US Under Secretary of State, Thomas Pickering, in March 2000 commented, Bangladesh in less than 30 years of independence has turned itself into a model both of a moderate muslim democracy and as a grassroot based economic development.[78] Secondly, Bangladesh has been able to attract attention of leading US companies to invest in gas and power sectors in view of the country's huge reserves of natural gas. US companies have invested about $2 billion in Bangladesh and the investment is expected to reach about $ 3 billion in the near future.

Further, Bangladesh is being viewed by the US policy makers as a stabilizing factor in South Asia. The US after nuclear explosion by India and Pakistan and Indo-Pak tension, sees Bangladesh as a ray of hope. The US has also supported SAARC and integration of market in South Asian Region. US also appreciated Bangladesh initiatives to resolve the problem of Chittagong Hill Tracts insurgency and the Ganges water sharing dispute with India through peaceful means.

Hence, the Bangladesh-US relationship, which was hostile at the time of independence, has been hugely expanded and both countries are making effort to build a forward-looking relationship from which both countries can benefit. However, it can be said that the US approach towards Bangladesh is not beyond her politico-strategic considerations in the South Asian region. US has its long term interests. Therefore, Bangladesh as a developing country having its own problems of poverty and development needs to follow a cautious approach.

REFERENCES

1. *Bangladesh Observer, 15* October *2005.*
2. *The Independent, 27* January *2005.*
3. *New York Times, 17* April *1999.*
4. *The Economist, 16* January *1972.*
5. S.M. Ali, *After the Dark Night Problems of Sheikh Mujibur Rahman* (Delhi, *1973), pp. 163-165.*
6. *Bangladesh Observer, 6* March *1972.*
7. Mizanur Rahman Shelley, Bangladesh : The Quest for International Recognition, *Asian Affairs* (Dhaka), *Vol.5, No.4,* October-December *1983, p.405.*
8. Maidul Hasan, *Muldhara* (Dhaka, *1985), p.13.*

9. Rahman Sobhan, *The Crisis of External Dependence. The Political Economy of Foreign Aid to Bangladesh* (Bangladesh, *1982), pp. 122-23.*
10. Jayashree Biswas, *US-Bangladesh Relations* (Calcutta, *1984), p.56.*
11. *Ibid, p.58*
12. *Bangladesh Observer, 19* September *1978.*
13. *The Bangladesh Times, 21* September *1978.*
14. Ehsanul Haque, Bangladesh and the United States : Dimensions of an Evolving Relationship in Abul Kalam (ed.), *Bangladesh-Internal Dynamics and External Linkages* (Dhaka, *1996), p.238.*
15. Ibid, p.238.
16. Ibid , pp.133-134.
17. *New York Times,* 29 August 1980.
18. *UN Chronicle, Vol. XVII,* January 1980, p.6.
19. Virendra Narain, *Foreign Policy of Bangladesh (1971-81). The Context of national movement* (Jaipur, 1987), p. 13 1.
20. *New York Times,* 25 March 1982.
21. *New York Times,* 19 April 1982.
22. *Bangladesh Observer,* 25 June 1982.
23. Dilara Chowdhury, *Bangladesh and the South Asian International System* (Dhaka, 1992), p.116.
24. Ibid., p.117.
25. *Daily Ittefaq,* 26 October 1983.
26. Ibid, 28 October 1983.
27. Dilara Chowdhury, op.cit., n.23, p.117.
28. Ibid., pp. 117-18
29. Ehsanul Haque, op. cit., n.14, p.169.
30. Dilara Chowdhury, op. cit., n.23, p.117.
31. *Bangladesh Observer,* 20 November 1988.
32. S.R. Chakravarty, *Foreign Policy of Bangladesh* (New Delhi, 1994), p.56.
33. *Bangladesh Observer,* 5 June 1991.
34. Ehsanual Haque, op. cit., n.14, p.245.
35. Ibid, p.251.

36. Ibid., p.246.
37. Cornelia M. Weierbses, US-Bangladesh Trade Relations-Looking to the Future, *The Daily Star,* 12 January 1995.
38. *The Independent,* 12 July 1995.
39. Ehsanul Haque, op.cit., n.14, p.247. *40. Ibid*
40. *The Daily Star, 18* May, 1994.
41. Ehsanul Haque, op. cit., n.14, p.249.
42. *Ibid.,* p.244.
43. *Ibid.,* p.250.
44. *Bangladesh Documents,* Ministry of Foreign Affairs, Government of Bangladesh, February 2000.
45. *Ibid.*
45. *Bangladesh Foreign Policy Survey,* BUSS Publications, Vol.2, No.4, October-December 1996, pp.6-9.
46. *Ibid.,* p.9.
46. *Ibid.,* p.21.
47. *Ibid, Vol.3,* No. l, January-March 1997, pp.45 and *13.*
48. *Ibid.,* p.13.
49. Ibid., Vol.3, No.3, July-September 1997, p.19.
50. Government of Bangladesh, Ministry of Foreign Affairs, *Bangladesh Documents,* February 2000, pp.25-26.
51. *Ibid.*
51. Wahiduddin Mahmud, US-Bangladesh Economic Links, *The Daily Star,* 20 March 2000.
52. *BFPS* op. cit., n.47, p.16.
53. *Ibid., pp.* 14-15.
54. *Bangladesh Observer,* 5 November 2001.
55. *Bangladesh Observer, 31* March 2002.
56. *The Independent,* 25 May 2005.
57. *Bangladesh Observer,* 29 June 2005.
58. *The Bangladesh Times,* 29 June 2005.
59. *BFPS,* op. cit., n.47, Vol.6, No. l, January-March 2000, *p.13.*
60. *Ibid.,* p.23.
61. *Bangladesh Documents,* op. cit., n.45.
62. *Bangladesh Observer,* 28 March 1998.

63. *BFPS,* op. cit., n.47, Vol.4, No.3 July-September 1998, p.2. 64. *Ibid.*
64. *Ibid,* Vol.4, No.], January-March 1998, p.15.
65. *Bangladesh Documents,* Ministry of Foreign Affairs, Government of Bangladesh, February 2000.
66. *Bangladesh Observer,* 28 October 1994.
67. *Bangladesh Observer,* 30 October 1994.
68. BIISS Papers, *Nuclearisation of South Asia : Bangladesh Perspective,* Monograph Series, BIISS Publication , 1999, p.25.
69. *Bangladesh Observer,* 28 October 2005.
70. *The Bangladesh Times,* 19 November 2000.
71. *Daily Star, 21* March *2000.*
72. *Bangladesh Documents 2000,* MFA, GoB, *p.26.*
73. Medeline Albright's statement, *Daily Star,* March *2000.*

CHAPTER-4

Bangladesh Relations with China

From time immemorial Bangladesh has had close relations with China. In the pre-historic period Mongoloid and Bang people migrated from Indo-China and settled in Bangala. Buddhism spread to China from Bangala and during Palla rule Chinese Buddhist monks and devotees used to visit Bengal for learning Buddhism in Mainamati and Lalmai monastery and Bihara (institution). China and Bengal had trade relations. Hossain Shahid Suhrawardy, Prime Minister of Pakistan, for the first rime established diplomatic relations with China. He, along with Sheikh Mujibur Rahman, Secretary, East Pakistan Awami League, visited China on 22 October 1956. On 29 December 1956 Zhou Enlai, Prime Minister of China, visited Dhaka and he was given a rousing reception. Sheikh Mujibur Rahman led a parliamentary delegation to China in August 1957. During the military rule of General Ayub Khan Pakistan diverted its relations with China against India. India went to war with China in 1962. In 1971 China opposed the Liberation War of Bangladesh. During the liberation war the USA developed diplomatic relations with China through Pakistan. This chapter discusses Bangladesh's relations with another major Asian power China, which has its significance for a country like Bangladesh in many respects.

CHINA AND THE EMERGENCE OF BANGLADESH

Because of the compulsion of the cold war politics interplaying in the Liberation War of Bangladesh, China supported the integrity of Pakistan and so indirectly opposed the liberation of Bangladesh. The Chinese government had no ill will against the Bengalee people.[1] In the Chinese perception, the independence of Bangladesh was at the cost of the territorial integrity of its ally Pakistan and secondly, it was supported by the alliance of its number one enemy - the Soviet Union and the hostile neighbour- India. China vocally opposed the struggle and supported Pakistan unheeding the appeals of the pro-Chinese organizations participating in the Liberation War.

In independent Bangladesh, Sheikh Mujib and his government were well aware of the importance of the recognition by China, at least to get its support for Bangladesh's membership of the United Nations.[2] The Foreign Minister of Bangladesh, Abdus Samad Azad wrote a letter in January 1972 to the Chinese Premier Zhou Enlai, in which he expressed his country's desire to have good neighbourly relations with China as with any other country and indicated the hope that China would reciprocate the sincere feelings of the people and the government of Bangladesh. China ignored the letter with indifference.[3]

At the time when the issue of Bangladesh's membership came in the Security Council Beijing used its veto power for the first time and blocked the entry. Despite this open hostility Bangladesh's reaction was polite, though anti-China feelings were growing in the country. Sheikh Mujib in a public meeting said, *we do not want to maintain hostility with our neighbour China. We have nothing against the biggest country in the world.*[4] China progressively softened its tone against Bangladesh in the Security Council. When Pakistan recognised Bangladesh in February 1974 and a Tripartite

Agreement about POWs between India, Pakistan and Bangladesh was signed in April !974, China removed its veto and Bangladesh was admitted in the UN in September 1974. In October 1974 the Bangladeshi Foreign Minister met his Chinese counterpart in New York.

In 1974, the Red Cross Society of China sent aid for the flood victims of Bangladesh. Dhaka continued its effort for recognition and establishment of diplomatic relations with India. Emissaries were sent to meet the Chinese leaders in 1975. China allowed Bangladeshi delegation in the Canton Trade Fair in May 1975, in which four trade agreements were signed between Bangladesh and China. Beijing also agreed to recognise Bangladesh soon.[5]

The close relations of Bangladesh with India and the Soviet Union were a limitation on Sheikh Mujib's side and an abhorrent reality for China. China had opened its relations with Bangladesh and was slowing moving in the direction of recognition. The sudden and violent assassination of Sheikh Mujib and the positive signals conveyed by the new regime provided an opportunity to China to recognise Bangladesh without any reservation.[6]

BANGLADESH-CHINA RELATIONS ON THE MOVE

Bangladesh was recognised by China after the 1975 coup when it was established that the new regime was not pro-Soviet and pro-India. In October 1975 the Foreign Ministers of China and Bangladesh signed a joint communique in New York about establishing diplomatic relations with immediate effect at ambassadorial level.[7]

After assuming power, Ziaur Rahman gave special importance to improve relations with China. After sending several delegations to China he visited China in January 1977, which further consolidated the bilateral relations. China sent a number of delegations to Bangladesh in 1978 which was followed by Vice-Premier Li Hsien Nieu's visit the same year. A five year trade agreement was signed in March 1980 and a scientific and technical cooperation agreement in May 1980 between the two countries. China began to supply fighter planes and training-team to Bangladesh after Zia's visit. The importance of China in Ershad's diplomacy can be assessed from the number of visits he took to China in November 1982, July 1985, July 1987 and after 1988-flood. Joint Economic Commission was established in 1983 to expand areas of-economic cooperation between the two countries. Chinese aid and trade with Bangladesh progressively increased. The Chinese President visited Bangladesh in March 1986 and the Premier Li Peng visited Dhaka in November 1989.

Bangladesh and China developed good relations not only in political and economic fields but also in military field. Bangladesh Chief of Naval Staff visited China in April 1983 and Chief of Air Force in January 1984. These visits were reciprocated by the visits to Bangladesh of the Chinese Commander of the Navy and the Commander of the Air Force. China emerged as chief source of defence supplies to Bangladesh.[8]

In the 1990's the global scenario acquired increasing importance in determining international and internal relations of all powers. During Ershad's visit to Beijing on 29 June, 1990 increasingly the interest and anxiety of both the countries with regard to the peace and stability of South and South-East Asia were recalled in their talks.[9] The Chinese Premier Li stressed that the South and South East-Asian countries were China's close neighbours and laid hope for peace and stability in these regions. Both the countries were willing to continue to make efforts in this respect. During his visit they signed three agreements and two letters of exchange that covered new areas of cooperation, building of a bridge by China on the river Mahananda in northern Dinajpur District and institutionalising of periodic consultations between officials of the Foreign Ministries of the two countries. In technical cooperation, they agreed to exchange experience, scientific cooperation, data and personnel.[10]

It may be recalled that China had given assistance to build the young Navy of Bangladesh and other wings of the armed forces. Chinese Premier Li said the training facilities provided by China to Bangladesh officers and sailors enabled the country to raise her trained manpower to operate the sophisticated and modern machines and ships of the Navy. He further mentioned the continued assistance and training facilities provided by the Chinese Army and Air Force to modernise and build up the Bangladesh Army and Air Force.[11]

BANGLADESH-CHINA RELATIONS AFTER 1990

In 1991 Chinese-aided Bangla-China Friendship Bridge was completed and the defence workshop for the maintenance of defence equipments was commissioned in 1992. Bangladesh dependence upon China for its defence had progressively increased during Begum Zia's regime (1991-1996).[12]

With the coming of Begum Khaleda Zia to power there was no basic change in Bangladesh's attitude to China. Khaleda Zia visited China in 1991. The Chinese Communist Party (CCP) delegation visited Bangladesh in 1992 and 1994. Sheikh Hasina went to China in 1993 on the invitation of the CPC. On 2 June 1991 Khaleda returned to Bangladesh from a three-day official visit to China. She held talks with her Chinese counterpart Li Peng on bilateral, regional and international issues. She also exchanged views with the Chinese President, Yan Simpru and the Communist Party General Secretary Jiag Zamas. China agreed to provide

Bangladesh a soft loan of about Rs 20 crore. He said the two sides were agreed that poorer nations in South Asia were not getting their due share in the world economy and that their voice must be heard by the developed world.[13] This was Begum Zia's second official visit abroad after taking over as Prime Minister three months earlier. She had paid a visit to New Delhi to attend Rajiv Gandhi's funeral, and then was in Saudi Arabia for a pilgrimage and talks with the Saudi leaders. Her visit to China was her first real business trip. In continuation of the policy of her predecessor a Bangladesh parliamentary delegation called on the Chinese President, Yang Shanghan in Beijing on 21 September 1992. The leader of the delegation referred to the existing bilateral relations between Bangladesh and China and hoped that these would grow further to the mutual benefit of the two countries.[14]

CHINESE ARMS ASSISTANCE TO BANGLADESH

The security has been the most valued and important area of Bangla-China relations. China is the single largest supplier of arms and ammunition to Bangladesh Army, Air Force and Navy. During 1988- 1992 Bangladesh purchased arms worth $ 1104 million of which $ 900 million were purchased from China.[15] China gets dual benefit by supplying arms to Bangladesh and other developing countries. Economically it is valuable as a source of foreign exchange earning which is needed for Chinese defence modernisation. Politically it gives in return influence over these states. The ruling elites of Bangladesh view China as 'friend in need', a trusted friend[16]. Apart from supplying arms, ammunition and spare parts to the Bangladesh Army, Air force and Navy it provides training to defence personnel who go to China regularly for this purpose. Some of the arms supplied by China are second hand. The terms and conditions of the arms supplied by China are easier than any other supplier. Table-1 describes the arms supplied by China to Bangladesh.

Table-1

Supply of Chinese Weapons to Bangladesh

Year of order	Qty. ordered	Weapons designation	Weapons description	Year of delivery	Qty. delivered
1976	50	F-6	Fighter	1972	14
				1978	36
1978	36	F-6	Fighter	1979	24
1979	12	BT-12	Trainer	1979	12
1980	48	F-7	Fighter	N/A	N/A
1980	36	T-59	MBT	1980	18
				1981	18
1980	48	F-7	Fighter	1981	48
1981	4	Hainan class	FAC	1982	1
1982	4	P-4 Class	FAC	1983	4
1983	20	Type-54 122mm	SPH	1984	20
1983	6	Romeo class	Submarine	1984	1

1984	3	Hainan class	FAC	1984	3
1985	36	F-6	Fighter	N/A	N/A
1988	2	Jiang class	Fast Frigate	1989	1
1988	24	Hai Ying 2L	Sh Sh M	1989	16
1988	2	Hai Ying 2	Sh Sh M Launcher	1989	1
1989	16	F-7	Fighter	1989	16
1992	21	F-7 MA Airguard	Fighter aircraft	N/A	N/A
1992	40	F-6	"	1992	40
1992	2	Huang fen Class	Fast attack craft	N/A	N/a
1992	8	Hai Ying 2	Sh Sh M Launcher	N/A	N/A
1992	2	"	"	N/A	N/A

Source: Muhammad Tajuddin, '*Foreign Policy of Bangladesh*', (New Delhi, 2001), pp.197-198.

It is true that after the visit of Rajiv Gandhi to Beijing in December 1988 which was a watershed in the Sino-India normalisation process,China became indifferent to India's policies towards its neighbours. Contrary to the earlier practice of exploiting bilateral disputes of India with the regional states, China advised them to resolve the disputes through bilateral negotiations. In spite of this consideration of India, it continued to supply arms to Bangladesh and still is committed to always stand by Bangladesh in its struggle for protecting national independence and sovereignty and to achieve economic progress.[17]

REGIME OF SHEIKH HASINA AND BANGLADESH-CHINA RELATIONS

The Awami League government under Sheikh Hasina (1996-2001) revised the India and Pakistan policies of the preceeding government, but followed the China policy as developed by her predecessor Begum Zia. China was the second foreign country after Saudi Arabia to which Sheikh Hasina paid a visit in September 1996 when she became Prime Minister.[18] She had also visited China in September 1993 as the leader of the opposition. The only irritant in the relations of the two countries was the negative balance of payment, which was increased progressively. China took initiatives to minimise the gap through more imports from Bangladesh and also through joint investment in Bangladesh. China also gave $ 131 million in aid to Bangladesh from 1975 to 1996. Most of aid was given for the Chinese funded projects. The two countries signed a protocol in January 1998 for the construction of the fifth Bangladesh-China friendship bridge on the Barisal- Jhalakhanti-Bhandaria- Pirojpur road.

SHEIKH HASINA'S VISIT TO CHINA

The first official visit of Prime Minister Sheikh Hasina was made to China after her assumption of office as Prime

Minister at the invitation of Chinese Prime Minister Li Peng on 12 September 1996. On her arrival she was given a hearty reception. She was accompanied by Abdus Samad Azad, Foreign Minister and Motia Chowdhury, Minister of Agriculture and Food. In the official talks Sheikh Hasina and Li Peng reviewed the entire gamut of bilateral relations and discussed regional and international issues of common concern. The talk focussed on economic investment, trade and defence matters. Hasina requested China to increase its imports from Bangladesh to narrow the trade gap and invest in Bangladesh in the new investment environment created after her government's coming to power. She sought increased Chinese assistance for Bangladesh's infrastructure building effort. She also discussed Bangladesh-China defence relations.[19]

Initiating the talks the Chinese Prime Minister Li Peng cordially welcomed the Bangladesh Prime Minister and her entourage members to his country and said, as *the Awami League is in power, we are ready to strengthen our cooperation with the present government of Bangladesh to the mutual benefit of both the governments and the peoples. We are glad over the victory of the Awami League in the election and the party assumption* of *power.*[20]

Reciprocating the feelings of Li Peng, Prime Minister Sheikh Hasina described the Bangladesh-China relations as historic and recalled with respect the proud visits of the father of the nation, Bangabandu Sheikh Mujibur Rahman to China in 1952 and 1957. She also referred to the visit of late Chinese Premier Zhon Enlai to the then East Pakistan when the late Hossain Shahid Suhrawardy was the Prime Minister of Pakistan and Sheikh Mujibur Rahman was a minister of the provincial cabinet.[21] She recalled that she had welcomed the late Chinese Premier Zhou Enlai in Dhaka with a banquet in 1957. She referred to her party's relentless struggle for the last 21 years and said that it had finally come to power through free and fair elections observed by over 200 foreign observers. Sheikh Hasina further said that Bangladesh would welcome Chinese investment in joint ventures like agro-based industries.[22] Bangladesh would also welcome China's infrastructural aid to develop technology in Bangladesh's agriculture sector including livestock and fisheries.

Li Peng said that the Chinese government believed in good neighbouring countries and described Bangladesh as a good neighbouring country.[23] On 12 September 1996 Bangladesh and China signed four agreements on avoiding double taxation, investment, Chinese grants and loans for Bangladesh. The agreements were signed in the presence of the visiting Bangladesh Prime Minister Sheikh Hasina and Chinese Prime Minister Li Peng.

The major agreements were, 30 million yuan Chinese grant; 100 million yuan Chinese soft loan for Bangladesh; promotion and protection of each other's investment agreements and avoidance of double taxation. The Bangladesh Ambassador to China, Mustafijur Rahman signed the agreements on behalf of Bangladesh while Chinese Vice-Minister for Foreign Trade signed the first treaty on behalf of China and the double taxation treaty was signed by the Chinese Commissioner of Taxation. At the request of the Prime Minister of Bangladesh Li Peng agreed to visit Bangladesh.

On 13 September 1996 Sheikh Hasina had a meeting with Chinese President Jiang Zemin at the presidential villa in Diaonyutal State Guest House. She appraised the Chinese President of her government's poverty alleviation programme. She again stressed up on strengthening economic cooperation between the two countries. She urged the Chinese government for further bolstering the mutual relations between the two governments. The Chinese President Zemin, while talking with Sheikh Hasina, assured reduction of the trade deficit between the two countries.[24]

The Bangladesh students studying in various universities of China gave letters of memorandum to the Prime Minister. In their letters, they mentioned inadequate stipend money. The Prime Minister announced the grant of 50 US dollars per head in addition to the monthly stipend provided by the Chinese government.[25]

BANGLADESH-CHINA RELATIONS UNDER BEGUM KHALEDA ZIA

China conveyed through its Ambassador in Dhaka, greetings of the Chinese President Jiang Zemin and Prime Minister Zhu Rongji as well as deep appreciation of his government to Prime Minister Khaleda Zia on 21 October 2001 for the landslide victory of BNP at the general election. Describing the bilateral ties as 'excellent', China expressed its strong determination to work with Bangladesh not only for strengthening bilateral relations but also in the international fora, including UN to establish global peace and security. Both the governments showed their eagerness to identify areas of cooperation and extend possible economic assistance to those fields.[26] Both the countries decided to welcome economic cooperation between state-owned companies as well as prominent private-sector companies.

CHINESE PREMIER'S VISIT TO DHAKA

Prime Minister of China Zhu Rongji arrived in Dhaka on 1 1 January 2002 for a three-day official visit to Bangladesh. Both Bangladesh and China assumed that Sino-Bangladesh friendship had not only conformed to the common aspiration and the fundamental interests of the two countries and peoples, but also conduced to peace, stability and development in the region. Bangladesh and China are close neighbour and both countries established an equal, cooperative and mutually beneficial relationship since they established diplomatic ties in 1975.[27]

A seven-point memorandum of understanding (MOU) including a $650 million grant assistance for Bangladesh was signed between Chinese Prime Minister Zhu Rongji and Bangladesh Prime Minister Begum Zia. Bangladesh and China agreed to boost economic cooperation between the two countries taking further measures for reducing huge trade imbalance against Dhaka. China appreciated economic development; improved livelihood of the people and remarkable progress in all areas that Bangladesh had achieved in recent years. Referring to the construction of the Bangladesh-China Friendship Centre and the Sixth Bangladesh-China Friendship Bridge and project Chinese government assistance, were the new monuments of friendship between the two countries. The Conference Centre was built at a cost of 100 million yuan. China provided the interest free assistance for this purpose. The Chinese Prime Minister remarked during his talks with Khaleda Zia that China regards all countries as equal irrespective of size and power.[28]

BEGUM ZIA'S VISIT TO CHINA

Prime Minister of Bangladesh Begum Khaleda Zia visited China from 23 to 27 December 2002. The visit of Khaleda Zia proved to be beneficial for further consolidation of the cordial relations between the two Asian nations. Her visit was considered as very important for strengthening economic, cultural, political and defence relations with China. During the visit Bangladesh signed three protocols related to economic and defence cooperation with China. While holding talks on increasing the areas of mutual cooperation, the area of trade, particularly of the prospects of the entry of Bangladesh's products into Chinese market figured prominently.[29] The visit of Begum Zia was proved as one of the high points in her administration efforts to further open the eastern horizon for Bangladesh entrepreneurs.

During the Chinese visit, the Bangladesh Prime Minister not only had the opportunity to hold talks with Chinese Prime Minster Zhu Rongji and Chinese President Xiang Zemin, but she also met the Secretary General of Chinese Communist Party Hu Jin Tao. This was important because at that time sixteenth Congress of the Communist Party of China was just concluded with a smooth and meaningful transition of leaderships from one generation to another. In a way, the visit enabled Bangladesh to convey its thanks to the 'old guards' and welcome the new leadership.[30] This renewal of high level contacts also gained particular significance given the fact that Begum Zia was paying a return visit within twelve months of Chinese Prime Minister Zhu Rongji's visit to Dhaka.

It was expected that the leaders of both sides exchanged views on regional and international issues of common interest. They apparently also agreed to strengthen and intensify the special bilateral ties in different fields between the two countries. In this context-many accords were signed between the two sides. China provided Bangladesh with a grant of US $7.25 million for construction of the sixth Bangladesh-China Friendship Bridge over the Dhaleswari river. China also provided a soft loan of over $6.04 million and the conversion of a $3.02 million credit into grant.[31] The Chinese government demonstrated their goodwill for the peoples of Bangladesh by announcing that the new Conference Centre in Sher-e□Bangla Nagar, Dhaka built with Chinese assistance of $24 million would be a gift from the Chinese people.[32]

Another important aspect of the visit was the signing of an umbrella defence cooperation agreement aimed at integrating piece-meal accords. The agreement maximised the cooperation in defence training, maintenance and also in some areas of production. The defence agreement facilitated the supply of Chinese armaments, military hardware and special equipment to Bangladesh. The agreement provided assistance in the modernization of the armed forces in Bangladesh. The defence agreement was made for five years in the first stage, with the provision of further extension if both parties so agree. Supporters of the Khaleda Zia's government in Bangladesh hailed the signing of this agreement as a turning point in foreign policy of Bangladesh.

On I March, 2004 Bangladesh-China relations were strained due to Bangladesh decision to allow Tiwan Trade Office in Bangladesh. Actually, the Board of Investment (BOI) of Bangladesh gave permission to Taiwan to open the trade office in Dhaka and the office was promptly registered under the BOI act. The Chinese Ambassador in Dhaka made sharp reactions on the issue and said that his government wanted Bangladesh to shut down the Taiwan office in Dhaka. Chinese officials made it clear that they would not object to any country's exchange of business and cultural delegations with Taiwan as long as these are on an unofficial level. But such ties could only be acceptable to Beijing when the countries strictly adhere to one China policy.[33]

As expected, on 30 March 2004 Prime Minister Begum Khaleda Zia reaffirmed Bangladesh's one-China policy. Further she added that Bangladesh has been following the principle of one-China policy and will always remain firm in this stand.[34] Meanwhile, on 19 May 2004 Bangladesh formally informed the China government that it had decided to closed down Taiwan Trade Office in Dhaka.

THE YEAR OF BANGLADESH-CHINA FRIENDSHIP

The year 2005 has been declared as the 'Year of China-Bangladesh Friendship' marking the 30th anniversary of diplomatic relationship between the two countries. This declaration was made by both sides while Chinese Prime Minister Wen Jiabao was in Dhaka on a two-day state visit to Bangladesh on 7 April 2005.[35] Bangladesh and China have agreed to establish a comprehensive partnership of cooperation based on equality for a long-term friendship to reap equal benefits in all sectors.

The Chinese Prime Minister said, 'It is my deep conviction that as we both work still harder, our traditional friendship and mutually beneficial cooperation are bound to get stronger.' The Chinese leader further said that the official establishment of diplomatic relations between China and Bangladesh 30 years ago turned over a new page in the friendship and bilateral cooperation.[36]

Expressing his gesture that the Bangladesh-China friendly relations and cooperation were based on Five Principles of Peaceful Coexistence, the Chinese leader mentioned that China always pursues her independent foreign policy of peace, advocating that "all countries, big or small, rich or poor, strong or weak, are equals.[37] Prime Minister Khaleda Zia sought new and imaginative approaches to the cooperation between Bangladesh and China for further improving the bilateral ties through interaction in all mutually beneficial fields. The 11 session of Bangladesh-China Joint Commission as scheduled to be held in Dhaka soon, would explore these prospects, she said, adding that cooperation in defence, education and culture and deepening of regional initiative and contacts, however, continue apace.[38]

The Chinese Prime Minister led a 102 member delegation including four important cabinet ministers, four state ministers and high officials to facilitate discussions on the whole gamut of bilateral ties and cooperation. 'It would be a curtain unveiling event of our co-celebrating activities marking the 30th anniversary of diplomatic relations with

Bangladesh," said Chai Xi, the Chinese Ambassador in Bangladesh on the eve of Jiabao's visit to Dhaka. [39] This visit of Chinese Premier was seen as a milestone in the 'time-tested' brotherly relations between the two counties since they establish diplomatic ties in 1975.

A joint communique issued on 8 April 2005 prior to the departure of Chinese Premier carried two county's pledge to continue efforts to further strengthen cooperation in the field of economy, trade, investment in industrial and agricultural sector, transportation, tourism, education and culture which would promote mutual benefit. Power plants, fertilizer factories, marine fisheries, infrastructural development, including six Friendship Bridges and Bangladesh□China Friendship Centre remain milestones in bilateral relationship of constructive engagement.[40] The short but eventful visit of the Chinese Prime Minister may be considered as a successful one, in view of the emphasis laid on specific areas of cooperation between the two countries.

The 13-point communique released simultaneously from Dhaka and Beijing spelt out extensive cooperation in matters related to bilateral, regional and international issues.[41] Reading out the salient features on the eve of departure of the visiting Chinese Premier, Bangladesh Foreign Minister M. Morshed Khan billed the Prime Minister Wen Jiabao's official tour as a 'great success' as it raised the bilateral relations to new heights. He noted that the visit would enhance cooperation in various sectors, including agriculture, human resource development, peaceful use of nuclear energy and defence.[42] The joint declaration carried an agreement to promote development of multidimensional and multi-level trade, and economic cooperation and allow joint Economic and Trade Commission to develop potential and expand bilateral trade.

The areas that are offered by the China to assist Bangladesh include among others, water management, nuclear energy, trade and investment, training of security and defence personnel, infrastructure development, technical assistance, tourism, construction and communication. Regarding investment, the two countries agreed to improve their investment environment and fulfill the commitments defined in the existing investment agreement. China would actively support Chinese enterprises in expanding investment in Bangladesh to scale down the trade imbalance. As a gesture of goodwill, China would take steps to promote Chinese enterprises' investment in textile sector of Bangladesh. This appears to be quite significant that tends to suggest serious commitment of the Chinese side to promote development of multi-level trade and economic cooperation.

Bangladesh and China have also signed nine accords to develop bilateral cooperation in various sectors particularly in economic and social fields, nuclear energy and the public security. The agreements, memorandum of understanding and exchange of letters were signed capping official talks between the two governments led by Bangladesh Prime Minister Khaleda Zia and visiting Chinese Premier Wen Jiabao. The four agreements signed by the two sides were, the agreement on cooperation in social and economic sectors, the agreement on framework for concessional loans, the agreement on peaceful use of nuclear energy and the agreement on cooperation in the public security. The three Memorandum of Understanding (MOU) signed were, cooperation in the field of agriculture, digital telephone projects for the capital, districts and upazilas and management of the Barapukuria coal mine. After the talks between the two Prime Minister, two letters on the subjects-cooperation on the use of water resources and direct air link had been exchanged between the two countries.

Two of the nine agreements signed by Bangladesh and China, are politically significant and may have raised some eyebrows outside the country, searching to find some special meanings to it. One of the agreements is to help development of nuclear power generation capacity, nuclear medicine and biotechnology in Bangladesh by China. And the other agreement is for cooperation in the field of water resources, utilization and protection of water resources of the trans-boundary rivers in the region, on the basis of equality and fairness. It may be mentioned here that Bangladesh as a signatory to the Nuclear Non-Proliferation Treaty (NPT) is committed to use nuclear power only for peaceful purpose. On terrorism, both Bangladesh and China reaffirmed their commitment to fight against terrorism and transnational crimes. The both countries also agreed to share information, exchange intelligence and cooperation in law enforcement to ensure peace and stability in the region.[43]

Since the establishment of diplomatic relations in 1975, China has become one of the important development partners of Bangladesh. Bangladesh has so far received 181 million US dollar as interest free loan, 75 million US dollar as interest subsidized preferential loan and 764 million US dollar as supplier's credit and 33 million US dollar as grant.[44] Six bridges have been constructed under the grant and interest free loan from China. The entire loan for construction of Bangladesh-China Friendship Conference Centre has also been converted to grant. Barapukuria coal mine project and Dhaka power project are also being implemented with supplier's credit from China.

The huge imbalance in trade with Bangladesh is the most important area where Bangladesh expects to reach better understanding with China. The volume of import from China has been increasing rapidly every year, as China has got a large economy with enormous production and supply of goods. The import of Bangladesh which was worth nearly 222 million US dollar in the fiscal year 1993-94 rose to 739 million US dollar in the fiscal year 2002-03. On the other hand Bangladesh exported goods worth 18 million US dollar to China in the fiscal year 2002-03 as against only 13 million US dollar in the fiscal year 1993□94.[45]

China is a global economic power. America and China together account for almost half of global economic growth over the year 2004. The year 2005 might well see that America, China and India contributing to two-thirds of the global economic growth. China has much to do for reducing the imbalance in trade with Bangladesh. It is a great pleasure for Bangladesh that China has recognized the imbalance in trade with Bangladesh and would take 'active steps' to increase imports from Bangladesh.

The Chinese Prime Minister Wen Jiabao said that his government would give subsidy to their business people to increase import of Bangladeshi goods. The two other steps Wen Jiabao spelt out, were reducing tariffs and increasing understanding between the business communities of Dhaka and Beijing, especially through holding more trade fairs.[46]

Bangladesh imports over a billion dollars worth of goods from China annually and most likely it will be increased much with establishment of direct road and air links between Bangladesh and Kunming in southern China. But Bangladesh-China economic relation suffers much from the huge trade imbalance for Bangladesh. Increasing high trade imbalance is a cause of great concern as well as of frustration for Bangladesh. China is now likely to grab the American market of readymade garments in the post MFA regime. Bangladesh may also seek help from China for transfer of its cheap technology for manufacturing in the fields of readymade garments and electronics. Viewed in the context of good relationship, it can be said that China will also be considerably benefited from such measures.

BEGUM KHALEDA ZIA'S VISIT TO CHINA

It is true that Beijing and Dhaka had agreed to boost cooperation in a wide range of fields as a part of greater economic interaction between the two countries. The convergence of trade and economic priorities of China and Bangladesh was visible in the six accords signed during the Bangladesh Prime Minister's trip to Beijing from 17 August to 21 August 2005. There were significant developments like China's offer of 300 million yuan for the North Dhaka Water Treatment Plant and Sewerage Plant- a crucially important project for Dhaka city.[47] China has also agreed to extend cooperation to peaceful use of nuclear energy in Bangladesh, which Bangladesh needs due to the mounting energy shortage.

The accords and MOUs signed cover various sectors and should lead to greater cooperation between China and Bangladesh based on a pragmatic assessment of Bangladesh needs. China has shown keen interest in investing in Bangladesh's developing economy which has certain strong points. Bangladesh has a large domestic consumer base which could turn any foreign investment into a lucrative proposition. Bangladesh has duty free access to some rich countries which is a big advantage that investors can always exploit. Bangladesh incentive package compares favourably to other competitors in the field. Of course low labour and production costs are also a plus point that prospective investors should be interested in. Finally, China has huge potential to invest in any EPZ in Bangladesh, designed and operated to cater to the needs of foreign investors.

One of the major developments of Begum Zia's visit was that China has agreed to import readymade garments from Bangladesh. It is Bangladesh's competitor in this field, but here are many complementarities that the two sides could take advantage of. China and Bangladesh can have mutually beneficial trade relations in many areas because of these complementarities.

Begum Zia assured the Chinese investors of all cooperation from the Bangladesh side and also proposed that the two countries may develop "strategic" trade ties in order to reap maximum benefits from the joint ventures.[48] Bangladesh believes China will favourably examine Khaleda proposal.

If the agreements and the memorandum of understandings (MOUs) signed between Bangladesh and China during Prime Minister Khaleda Zia's visit are faithfully pursued and implemented one can expect to reap immense benefits. China is not Bangladesh's immediate neighbour but a neighbour nevertheless. Not only China is the second largest economy of Asia, experts believe that in another few decades this country of more than a billion people would be only second to the United States.[49] Taking everything into consideration a good, friendly and businesslike relationship with China would help Bangladesh in many ways.

Precisely what agreements and MOUs have been signed are not that important. What is important is upgrading the existing relations. It is believed that the mandarins of Bangladesh Ministry of Foreign Affairs are quite aware of the geo-political realities of South and South-East Asia and would act with wisdom. In international relations there are no permanent friends or foes, only national interests are permanent. As a small and under-developed country Bangladesh need the goodwill of all, especially Bangladesh neighbours.

The agreement to boost trade and investment, if handled judiciously, can have a favourable impact on Bangladesh economy. As of now the biggest problem is the huge trade gap. Beijing's allowing duty-free access of some selected items from Bangladesh is unlikely to have any impact on this gap because Bangladesh basket of exports is small. The two sides shall have to find other ways and means to reduce this gap. The co-operation promised in electricity generation and nuclear energy is also welcome. Electricity generation is a capital intensive affair. Therefore, in this crucial area China's co-operation can ease the situation for Bangladesh.

The visit of the Prime Minister of Bangladesh has opened the door. Now it will be for the government to translate the warmth thus generated into fruitful cooperation in all mutually agreed field. The Prime Minister of Bangladesh Begum Khaleda Zia may order a small but high-powered task force to handle things.

CONCLUSION

It is evident that Bangladesh values its friendship with China and views it as a positive factor in maintaining peace and stability in South Asia. Bangladesh has viewed China as a dependable political, strategic and economic ally. The relations developed by Bangladesh with China during Zia regime have been further expanded and intensified by the following regimes in Bangladesh. The frequent exchange of official and unofficial delegations enabled the exploration of new areas of cooperation between the two countries. The economic and technological interaction between them on the basis of mutual cooperation is viewed as a modal of South-South Cooperation. China has expressed its political support to Bangladesh in its disputes with India. They interact with each other to explore possibilities of a common stand on international problems. The post-Mujib regimes in Bangladesh have tried to follow identical perception with China about most of the international problems and issues.

REFERENCES

1. Muhammad Tajuddin, *Foreign Policy of Bangladesh,* (New Delhi: 2001), p.9.
2. Ibid, p.11.
3. J.N. Mahanty, China and the Emergence of Bangladesh : Role of Great Power Global Perceptions, *India Quarterly* (New Delhi), Vol. 39, No. 2, April-June 1983, p.146.

4. *Hindustan Standard,* 19 February 1973.
5. *Bangladesh Observer* (Dhaka) 5 and 20 May 1975.
6. Muhammad Tajuddin, China and South Asia : A Perspective for the Study of Bangla-China Relation, *Azad Institute, Paper-5* (Calcutta, 1996), pp.21□26.
7. Raunaq Jahan, Banglabandhu and After : Conflict and Change in Bangladesh, *Round Table* (London), No. 261, January 1976, p.81.
8. V.P. Puchkov, *Political Development of Bangladesh 1975-1985* (New Delhi, 1988), p.188.
9. *Asian Recorder* (New Delhi), Vol. XXXVI, No.37, p.2133, 10-16 September 1990.
10. *Ibid,* p.2134.
11. *Ibid,* p.2136.
12. *Bangladesh Observer,* 7 November 1996.
13. *Asian Recorder* (New Delhi), Vol. XXXVII, No.30, p.21827, 22-25 January 1991.
14. *Bangladesh Times* , 22 April 1992, quoted in P.O.T., Vol. XVII, No.221, 28 September 1992.
15. *SIPRI Year Book: Armament and Disarmament* (New York, 1992), p.208.
16. *Bangladesh Observer,* 15 April 1995.
17. *Bangladesh in International Affairs* (Dhaka), Vol. 12, No. 11, November 1989, p.440.
18. *Bangladesh Foreign Policy Survey, Vol.* 2, No. 3, July-September 1996, *p.10.*
19. *Bangladesh Observer,* 17 September 1996.
20. *The Statesman* (Calcutta), 13 September 1996.
21. *Daily Star,* 15 September 1996.
22. *The Telegraph* (Calcutta), 16 September 1996.
23. *Bangladesh Observer,* 16 September 1996.
24. Sirajuddin Ahmed, *Sheikh Hasina . Prime Minister of Bangladesh,* (New Delhi, 1998), p.266.
25. *Ibid,* p.265.
26. *Daily Star,* 22 October 2001.
27. P.O. T., Vol. XXVII, No. 65, 5 March 2002.

28. *Bangladesh Observer, 14* January 2002.
29. *The Bangladesh Times,* 28 December 2002.
30. P.O.T., Vol. XXVIII, No. 30, 30 January 2003.
31. *Bangladesh Observer, 29* December *2002.*
32. P.O. T, Vol. XXVIII, No. 31, *31* January *2003.*
33. *Bangladesh Observer, 5* March *2004.*
34. *The Bangladesh Times, 31* March *2004.*
35. *Bangladesh Observer, 9* April *2005.*
36. *P.O.* T, Vol. XXX, No. *88, 14* April *2005.*
37. A.N.M. Narul Haque, China-Bangladesh Relations in *Bangladesh Observer, 14* April, *2005.*
38. *New Age, 15* April *2005.*
39. *The Bangladesh Times, 9* April *2005.*
40. *Bangladesh Observer, 9* April *2005.*
41. *Bangladesh Observer, 12* April *2005.*
42. *Bangladesh Observer, 10* April *2005.*
43. *P.O. T, Vol.,* XXX, No. *92, 19* April *2005.*
44. *P.O. T,* Vol. XXX, No. *97,24* April *2005.*
45. *Bangladesh Observer, 27* April *2005.*
46. *Bangladesh Observer, 25* April *2005.*
47. *P.O. T, Vol.* XXX, No. *210, 25* August *2005.*
48. *Bangladesh Observer, 23* August *2005.*
49. *P.O. T, Vol. XXX,* No. *215, 30* August *2005.*

CHAPTER-5

Bangladesh Relations with India

In South Asia India is the most important neighbour of Bangladesh, whether seen in terms of its political, security, strategic or economic considerations. The perceptions of India towards Bangladesh may change with the change in the nature of regime in Bangladesh and the vice-versa, but the geo- strategic and economic importance of India for Bangladesh, is a permanent factor towards which every regime remains conscious. The chapter would focus upon various dimensions of Bangladesh's relations with India.

India-Bangladesh relations since 1971 to the present time can be studied by dividing it into five phases. The first phase begins with the Liberation War of Bangladesh, which was fought with all out Indian support to the exile government led by Tajuddin Ahmed and to the *Mukti Bahini,* fighting the Pakistani armed forces. The last phase of the Liberation War was fought under the joint command of India and Bangladesh. Pakistan surrendered before India on 16 December 1971 at Dhaka and Bangladesh emerged as an independent country. The Mujib regime represents the second phase in the bilateral relation between Bangladesh and India. Under his regime the relations were based on sovereign equality. Bangladesh and India followed common national ideology and a similar world view. The period between 1975-1996 may be taken as third phase in Indo-

Bangla relations due to the common nature of the perceptions of Bangladesh about India and similar Indian policy of the regimes, which were in power in Dhaka during this period. The state ideology and world view of Bangladesh were different from India during the regimes of Zia, Ershad and Khaleda Zia. The fourth phase started when Awami League again came to power in March 1996 under Sheikh Hasina. The political understanding returned during her regime. The fifth and final phase of Bangladesh-India relations began in October 2001, when Begum Khaleda Zia sworn in as Prime Minister of Bangladesh for the second time. During the regime of Begum Zia, both Bangladesh and India have tried to resolve their disputes through exchange of visits of their leaders and by mutual dialogues.

Sheikh Mujibur Rahman maintained cordial political, economic and security relations with India. The security relationship with India was formalised by Sheikh Mujib in the friendship treaty signed in March 1972 when Indian Prime Minister Indira Gandhi visited Dhaka. Mujib organised Jatio Rakhi Bahini (JRB), a para military force from among his loyal youths as a counterbalance to army in case of any coup move by the army. The officers of the force were trained in Indian Military Academy, Dehra Dun.

After 15 August 1975 both the countries maintained political and diplomatic relations which appeared to be normal but the actual relations were based on deep suspicion and mistrust.[1] The image of India as a liberator was proved to be short lived. Due to different political, economic and security reasons the new image of India which emerged in Bangladesh, was that of an 'exploiter' and 'enemy'.[2]

In Bangladesh, the post-Mujib regimes perceived that Bangladesh was a junior partner in its bilateral reations with India. Bangladesh's interests were subservient to the Indian interests and Dhaka was under the policy control

Table-1
Details of Weapons Supplied by India to Bangladesh

Qty. Required	*Weapons designation*	*Weapons description*	*Year of order*	*Year of delivery*	*Qty. delivered*
3	An-12	Transport	1971	1971	3
4	DHC-3 Otter		Dec. 1971	Dec. 1971	4
1	DHC-4	-	-	-	1
4	Chetak	Helicopter	1972	1973	4
30	Model 56 105 mm	TH	-	-	30
2	Abhay Class Petrol boat Disp.	DC	1972	1972-73	2

Source: Muhammad Tajuddin, *'Foreign Policy of Bangladesh'* (New Delhi, 2001) pp. 186-187.

and guidance of India. They considered India as an important neighbour, and endeavoured to have good relations with New Delhi on the basis of sovereign equality. They resented to deal with New Delhi with a feeling of obligation for the role India had played in its liberation.

The post-Mujib Bangladesh maintained people to people and government to government level contacts with New Delhi. Through diplomacy Dhaka wanted to resolve the bilateral disputes between Bangladesh and India, to increase cooperation in different fields for the maximum utilisation of its resources and to deter the potential threats from India to be converted into actual danger. All the heads of governments of the non-Awami League governments had utilized all opportunities at different multilateral and regional summits to discuss their bilateral problems with New Delhi at the highest level and established personal rapport with the Indian Prime Ministers.[3] One objective of these interactions was to ward off Indian susceptivity of any alignment of Bangladesh with China and Pakistan against India.

Ziaur Rahman, Ershad and Begum Zia had generally avoided any hostile public statement against India despite strong public resentment against the later, particularly during the floods in Bangladesh. After 1988 flood which was most devastative till that time, Ershad refused to accept the Indian help which was an unfriendly act. Later Ershad clarified his intention to assuage the Indian feelings. Bangladesh maintained a restrained behaviour towards the bilateral problems of India and Pakistan and India and China. Bangladesh patiently continued negotiating with the Indian government to peacefully resolve the bilateral disputes and seek her cooperations.

The diplomacy of Bangladesh with India in the post-Mujib regimes reveals that its success depended upon the positive attitude of the then regimes in India. During the regime of Janata Party government in India, Zia succeeded in convincing Prime Minister Morarji Desai about the need of a watersharing agreement between the two countries. The result was the first Ganga Water Sharing Agreement signed in September 1977. On the other disputes also New Delhi listened to Dhaka's version sympathetically. The next water sharing agreement was signed in 1982 for two years by Ershad and Indira Gandhi which was perceived in Bangladesh as less favourable to Dhaka and expired in 1984. But the third water sharing agreement was signed only after one year in 1985 for three years. The delay was caused because Bangladesh wanted to make the water sharing arrangement permanent and negotiate separately to augment water flow but India wanted to decide both the issues concurrently.[4] After the expiry of the third water sharing agreement in 1988 Dhaka failed to convince New Delhi to sign the next agreement during the earlier regime of Khaleda.[5]

Knowing the limitations of the geo-political realities the regimes in Dhaka in the post-Mujib era were satisfied to get whatever they could achieve through diplomacy with New Delhi without compromising their sense of independence, sovereignty and equality. Without loosing hope and patience inspite of its diplomatic failure in getting resolved the water dispute with New Delhi, all the post-Mujib regimes had continued negotiations through all possible means like the mechanism of Joint River Commission (JRC)[6] and Joint Economic Commission (JEC)[7], visits of officials, Foreign Ministers and Presidents[8] to India. The objective was to achieve whatever limited could be achieved in the disputed areas and increase cooperation in the non- disputed areas in the prevailing situation.

BANGLADESH-INDIA RELATIONS UNDER BEGUM KHALEDA ZIA

The important achievement of Khaleda's regime (1991-96) in Bangladesh-India relations was the signing of a lease agreement between the two countries about the Teen Bigha corridor i. e. a strip of land connecting Bangladeshi mainland with its enclaves within Indian territory. The agreement was signed during her visit to New Delhi in May 1992.[9] In the joint communique issued at the time Bangladesh indirectly recognised the issue of illegal Bangladeshi migrants in India. The Indian push back action of some allegedly Bangladeshis from Delhi slums in the same year marred the goodwill created by the solution of the Teen Bigha corridor problem.

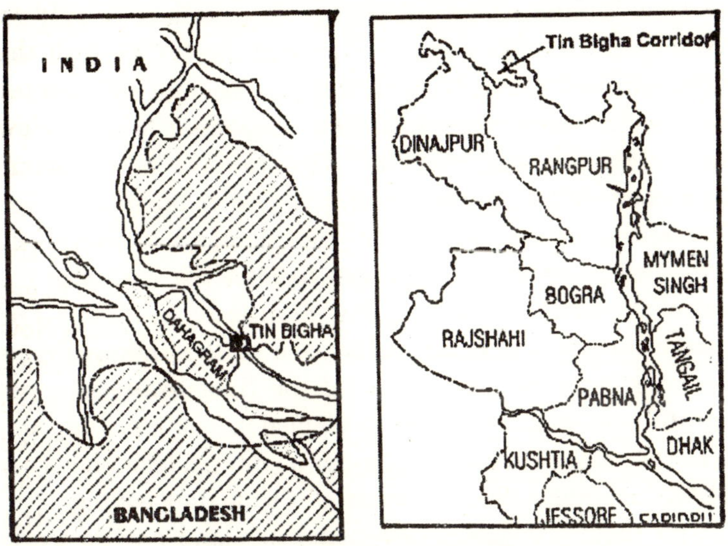

Map -1 Tin Bigha Corridor

THE FALL OF BABRI MOSQUE AND BANGLADESH-INDIA RELATIONS

Attitudes were hardened and the situation was worsened after the demolition of the Babri Mosque in Ayodhya in India on 6 December 1992. Bangladesh expressed its deep shock and intense concern at the demolition of this mosque describing it as "an outrageous act of desecration unprecedented in the annals of history[10].

Khaleda Zia conceded on 10 December 1992, that Ayodhya was certainly India's internal problem, but hastened to emphasise its regional and international consequences.[11] The situation arising out of the demolition of the Babri Mosque made an adverse impact on India-Bangladesh relations. Leaders of the Bangladesh Nationalist Party (BNP) at a rally in Dhaka on 9 December 1992 called upon the people, irrespective of caste and creed, to uphold the heritage of communal harmony in the country and resist the trouble-mongers indulging in terrorism, violence and anarchy.[12] Jamaat Islam Secretary General and Chief of its parliamentary party, Mumbu Rahman Nizami called upon the muslim world to boycott India economically unless the Babri Mosque was rebuilt.[13] The Jamaat Islam on 10 December 1992 submitted a memorandum to the Indian High Commission containing a five-point demand as part of its three-day programme in protest against the razing of the Babri Mosque.[14] Among the demands made in the memorandum which was addressed to the Indian Prime Minister, were reconstruction of the Babri Mosque at its rightful site, and on the previous model. *The Morning Sun* of 11 December 1992 added, "as far as Bangladesh and other SAARC members are concerned, it is time they got together, put all their grievances down on paper and let the world know how the Indians have behaved to crush each of them culturally, economically and politically."[15] In a devastating statement, it said, "India, the bully of the sub continent has at last exposed itself to be nothing but a crude Hindu state." The Bengali daily Dainik *Meillat* in an editorial observed,[16] "Lt has been proved without any doubt that there was a secret blessing and evil conspiracy of the Indian ruling quarters in connection with the ultra Hindu organisation BJP's demolition of the historic Babri Mosque and the construction of a temple there. Even a child can understand that the Indian government could have saved the Babri Mosque from destruction if it so wished."

On 10 February 1993 the Bangladesh Parliament adopted a unanimous resolution condemning the razing of the Babri Mosque in India and the outbreak of communal violence there. Decrying India's rejection of the resolution on the mosque issue Salaq Khan in an article in the weekly *Holiday* of 29 January 1993 said, "According to some reports India is shelving dialogue on bilateral issues by saying that there is no scope to initiate any discussion at the moment.[17]

The government of India rejected the resolution adopted by the Bangladesh Parliament relating to the disputed structure at Ayodhya. It described the resolution as "a totally unacceptable interference in our internal affairs".[18] This was a marked departure from the traditional position adopted by Pandit Nehru and ostensibly maintained by successive Congress governments, namely that vulnerable communities are a common heritage, scattered around South Asia, and matters of neighbourly concern through historical reality.[19] The government of India also took strong exception to the fact that the Bangladesh Parliament completely ignored the tragic but widely known facts about the violent reactions in Bangladesh in the aftermath of the demolition of the Babri Mosque.

The prevailing political tension in India worsened its relations with Bangladesh. Though the seventh SAARC meeting held in 1993 raised hopes of improving relations between the two countries, these were belied. Since 1975, that is, since the assassination of Sheikh Mujibur Rahman, relations between the two big Asian neighbours have been constantly under stress and strain. The breaking point was reached after the collapse of the Babri Mosque at Ayodhya on 6 December 1992.[20]

BANGLADESH-INDIA RELATIONS UNDER SHEIKH HASINA

Change of regimes in India and Bangladesh in 1996 was a positive development for their bilateral relations. Sheikh Hasina led Awami League had different perception about India than the preceding regimes. Indian leadership under a coalition government in which Indian left was a partner and I. K. Gujral as its Foreign Minister, was very considerate and responsive to the bilateral problems of the small neighbours. The determination to settle the water sharing problem and the sincere negotiations at different levels resulted in the signing of the Ganga Water Sharing Agreement in December 1996 for thirty years when H.D. Deve Gowda was the Indian Prime Minister.[21] Awami League government signed a peace treaty with the leaders of the ethnic communities of the CHT in December 1997. India's help for the settlement of the dispute and the repatriation of the Chakma refugees from Indian territory was very important. In the bilateral border conference held in Delhi in May 1998, the two states agreed to expedite the process of border demarcation. The Oil and Natural Gas Commission (ONGC) was awarded contracts in June 1998 for drilling nine gas wells and developing six other wells in three gas fields in Bangladesh. India and Bangladesh signed an accord in June 1998 to start a Calcutta-Dhaka to and fro bus service and finally bus service was started in 1999. India was the most important aid donor to Bangladesh in 1971 to 1972, when the flow of the international aid was meagre. The total Indian aid to Bangladesh from 1971 to 1996 was $368 million.[22]

Bangladesh recognised India's security concerns. The government of Sheikh Hasina assured India that Bangladeshi territory would not be allowed for anti-India activities. She did not criticized India's nuclear explosion in May 1998. She visited New Delhi after the explosion and stated that every country has sovereign right to perceive its security threats and take suitable measures to remove it. She also expressed her acceptance of the Indian policy of bilateralism to resolve bilateral disputes among the regional states.[23] The reciprocal friendly attitude was not changed even after coming to power of Bharatiya Janata Party (BJP) led coalition in New Delhi in March 1998. Both the governments sincerely tried to settle problems related with bilateral trade and transit facilities and expanded cooperation in new areas.

BANGLADESH-INDIA TREATY ON GANGES WATERS

Bangladesh and India share 54 trans-boundary rivers draining through Bangladesh. The Ganges is one of the most important of these, and the largest trans-boundary river flowing through the South Asian region, with its basin spreading over China, Nepal, India and Bangladesh. The Ganges originates from the southern slopes (at around 23,000-ft) of the Himalayas. It flows through Nepal into India, coursing through seven States (Provinces) of India before entering Bangladesh. It traverses a total distance of 1,570 miles before emptying into the Bay of Bengal.

The Ganges has three trans-Himalayan tributaries, namely the Karnali, Sapt Kosi and Sapt Gandaki emanating from Nepal which provide 71% of the total dry season flows and 41% of the annual flows of the Ganges at Farakka. Farakka is of relevance in this reckoning because this was the place, 11 miles upstream of the Bangladesh border, situated in the province of West Bengal in India, where India constructed a Barrage for diverting waters to the Hooghly River, thus affecting Bangladesh's traditional of apportionment of the share of the Ganges waters.

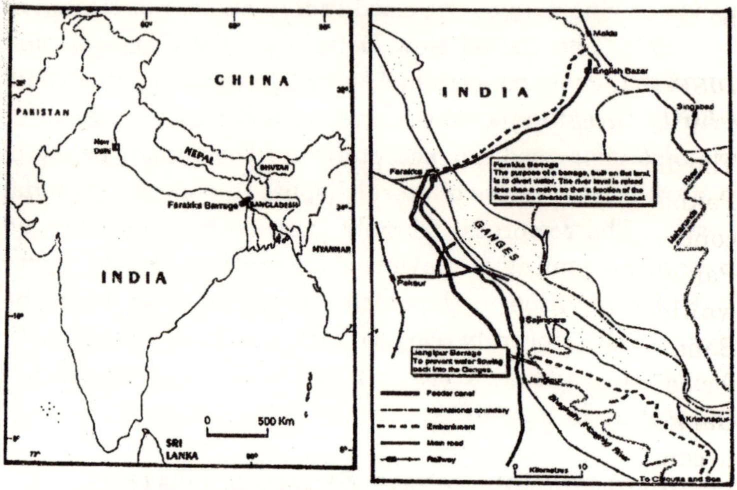

Map-2 Location of the Farakka Barrage

The precipitation over the Ganges Basin is mainly due to the South West Monsoon. The average rainfall in India varies from 350 mm in the western part to about 1000 mm in the middle course and between 1,500 mm to 2,200 mm near the delta. Glaciers in the Himalayas are also an important source of water for the Ganges, with probably 3500 glaciers draining part of their waters into the Ganges (by way of comparison, the Indus Basin in India-Pakistan also has 3500 glaciers draining into it, while the Teesta and Brahmaputra basins have only 600 glaciers draining into them).[24]

The flows of the Ganges are highly seasonal. Floods during the monsoon and scarcity during the dry season are the two extreme characteristics of its flows. The total availability of the Ganges water at Farakka during peak monsoon floods often exceeds 2.5 million cubic feet per second (cusecs). In stark contrast, during the driest months (March-April for Bangladesh) total availability at Farakka before the commissioning of the Farakka Barrage by India, used to be between 55 and 65 thousand cusecs.

DISPUTE OVER GANGES AND A BRIEF HISTORY OF NEGOTIATIONS 1947-71

The dispute over Ganges emerged soon after the creation of Pakistan as an independent state. Pakistan expressed its concern over the Indian project on the river Hoogly.[25] Pakistan believed that the proposed barrage at Farakka would have ruinous effects on East Pakistan (now Bangladesh).[26] India did not agree to it but expressed desire for cooperative development of the water resources of the Ganges with Pakistan.[27] It did not happen and India decided to construct a barrage at Farakka.

NEGOTIATIONS BETWEEN 1971-1975

The government of Bangladesh took up the matter on a priority basis with India. Sheikh Mujibur Rahman raised the matter with the Indian Prime Minister, Indira Gandhi during his stop-over at Delhi on his way back to Bangladesh in January 1972 after his long incarceration in Pakistan. In March 1972, the Prime Ministers of Bangladesh and India in a Joint Declaration announced the establishment of the Indo-Bangladesh Joint Rivers Commission (JRC).

The two Prime Ministers met once again in New Delhi in May 1974 and discussed among others, the Ganges issue. Following their meeting, a Joint Declaration after the meeting was issued on May 16, 1974. This Declaration observed that during the periods of minimum flow in the Ganges, there might not be enough water and therefore the fair weather flow of the Ganges in the lean months would have to be augmented to meet the needs of Calcutta Port and the full requirements of Bangladesh. The two Prime Ministers also mandated the JRC to study the best means of augmentation through optimum utilization of the water resources of the region available to the two countries.[28] The two sides expressed their determination that before the Farakka Project was commissioned they would arrive at a mutually acceptable allocation of water available during the periods of minimum flow in the Ganges. The original mandate of the JRC was thus expanded.

The question of augmentation of water during the off season and the construction of reservoir raised controversy. Two Ministerial level meetings in February and April 1975 failed to break the impasse. Given this situation the Indian side proposed that while discussions on allocation of waters in terms of the Prime Ministers Declaration of May 1974 continued, a test run of the Feeder Canal of the Farakka Barrage was necessary in view of the advent of the lean period of the dry season that year. The Bangladesh side agreed to the proposal. The two sides further agreed that India would carry out varying discharges ranging from 11,000 cusecs to 16,000 cusecs in 10-day periods from 21 April to 31 May while ensuring continuance of remaining flows for Bangladesh.[29] But due to the assassination of Sheikh Mujibur Rahman in 1975, relations between the two countries plunged sharply into a tail-spin and all meaningful communication on important issues including the question of sharing of the Ganges Waters, effectively ceased.[30]

NEGOTIATIONS BETWEEN 1976-1990

India continued with-unilateral withdrawals throughout the next dry season in 1976, resulting in a drastic drop in the flows at Hardinge Bridge (the point within Bangladesh where flows were monitored). In the continuing political stalemate, President Ziaur Rahman of Bangladesh decided to take the issue to the United Nations in November 1976.

On 24 November, 1976 the Special Political Committee of the UNGA devised a compromise in a consensus statement wherein both parties agreed that the situation called for an urgent solution and to this end the parties have decided to meet urgently in Dhaka at Ministerial level for negotiations with a view to arriving at a fair and expeditious settlement.[31]

This was followed by several rounds of talks that led to the two sides signing an Agreement on S November 1977 for sharing the dry season flows of the Ganges available at Farakka for a period of five years (1978-82). The sharing was apportioned according to a schedule of 10-day flows from January I to May 31. Under this arrangement, roughly 60% of the Ganges flows as available at Farakka were allocated for Bangladesh. The flows at Farakka were reckoned at 75% availability of waters as per observed data of flows from 1948-73.[32]

Furthermore, a side letter to the Agreement incorporated a Guarantee Clause under which, during the leanest period (from April 21 to May 31) in case of exceptionally low flows (below 55,000 cusecs), Bangladesh was to be guaranteed at least 80% (27,600 cusecs) of her stipulated share for the concerned 10-day period.

The tenure of sharing of the 1977 Agreement expired on 31 May 1982. In order to avoid another agreement vacuum period, the Foreign Ministers of the two countries signed a Memorandum of Understanding (MOU) in October 1982, basically extending the terms of the 1977 Agreement for a further period of 2 years (until 31 May 1984), or effectively for two more dry seasons. An important departure was the dropping of the Minimum Guarantee Clause. Another important departure in the 1982 MOU was the adoption of what became known as the "burden sharing" clause for exceptionally low flows. Under this clause, if the lowest flow at Farakka fell below 75% of the standard flow which governed the schedule, the difference between that and the standard flow was to be shared on 50:50 basis by the two sides. The 1982 MOU also enjoined upon the JRC to come up with a mutually acceptable augmentation solution.

The 1985 dry season was an agreement vacuum period as no instrument now existed for apportioning the share of the waters. Under the circumstances, the two sides once more signed a MOU, this time renewing the terms of the MOU of 1982 (i.e. the 1977 Agreement without the Guarantee Clause but incorporating the burden sharing clause), for three more dry seasons of 1986, 1987 and 1988. This MOU also provided for the two sides to arrive at a mutually acceptable solution for augmentation but this time the task was entrusted to a Joint Committee of Experts. Essentially, this turned out to be the same body of experts who had previously dealt with this thorny question but in a new incarnation. Their 24-month deliberations were as void of a solution as in the past.

Following the expiry of the 1985 MOU on 31 May 1988 a long period of agreement vacuum followed. Reflecting the slump in political relations, meaningful dialogue on the subject ceased altogether for the next five years until the end of 1990, when the government of President Ershad (in power since 1982) was forced to step down, following a mass movement led by an alliance of all the opposition parties. A neutral caretaker government took over with a mandate to conduct free and fair elections. In the meantime, the water situation in Bangladesh worsened with continuing unilateral withdrawals by India in the absence of any sharing instrument.

NEGOTIATIONS BETWEEN 1991-95

In March 1991, the new government of Prime Minister Khaleda Zia initiated discussions on the subject once again with India. The matter was discussed at summit levels in

May 1992, 1993 and 1995. Prime Minister Khaleda Zia, like her late husband had during his time in power, also decided to raise the issue at the UNGA in October 1993 but to no avail. Two rounds of JCE meetings were also frustrating to the extent that Bangladesh suspended all contacts at the JRC level.[33]

During the SAARC Summit at New Delhi in May 1995, the then Prime Ministers of Bangladesh and India during their bilateral meetings directed their respective Foreign Secretaries to immediately commence talks and try to break the logjam in the resolution of long festering problem. The two Foreign Secretaries held one round of talks immediately and agreed to follow up further on these talks at Dhaka.

Foreign Secretary of India Salman Haidar visited Bangladesh during 23-25 June 1995. Following were agreed upon in principle at the Foreign Secretary level meeting:

1. to arrive at a permanent sharing arrangement on the basis of existing dry season flow in the Ganges without linking it to the augmentation question. This marked a very important departure from the previous Indian position;
2. to revive the Joint River Commission expeditiously to work out the modalities for water sharing. JRC among other things should exchange information on projects like the Tipaimukh, Ganges barrage, Kanpur project etc. on both sides;
3. to jointly monitor the flow of Ganges at selected points; and
4. to arrive at a sharing arrangement of other common rivers on long term predictable basis.

However, no further progress was made thereafter in the wake of the political uncertainties in both countries and a period of stalemate ensued with practically no high level contacts between the two countries.

FINAL STAGE OF NEGOTIATIONS BETWEEN JULY 1996 - DECEMBER 1996

Serious discussions for arriving at a solution to the problem began only after the change of governments in both Bangladesh and India, taking place more or less around the same time. In May 1996 the United Front-led coalition government came to power in India with H.D. Deve Gowda as Prime Minister and Inder Kumar Gujral as External Affairs Minister. In Bangladesh a month later the Awami League was voted back to power again after 21 years. Sheikh Hasina, as Leader of the Party her late father had led until his assassination in 17/J, assumed once as Prime Minister. These two developments happend almost at the same time marked a turning point for both the countries. Both the sides realized the urgency of the matter and also conveyed to each other their address and resolve the

The Bangladesh Foreign Secretary visited India during 6-10 August 1996 to prepare the ground work in earnest. Indian Prime Minister Deve Gowda while receiving the Foreign Secretary said that his government was very keen to see that the issue was resolved within the shortest possible time and added that if the problem was solved the two countries could move in other areas quickly.[34] Between July 1996-December 1996 a number of visits at the bureau political level took place to discuss the Ganges water issue and prepared a for a settlement of the issue through the bilateral negotiations.

While negotiations were going on at the level of the political leadersh the Joint Committee met several times to look into the technicalities involve and worked toward arriving at an agreed draft agreement to be placed before

Bangladesh leading the Bangladesh side and the Indian Foreign Secretary leading the Indian side. It was during this final round of negotiations that the nature of the instrument to be drawn up (Treaty instead of Agreement) and the duration (30 years) were agreed upon. All that remained now was for the two Prime Ministers to sign the Treaty.

THE TREATY

Finally, the Prime Minister of Bangladesh Sheikh Hasina and Prime Minister of India H.D. Deve Gowda signed the historic Treaty on the sharing of the Ganges Waters in New Delhi on 12 December 1996 during the Prime Minister Sheikh Hasina's 3-day state visit to India during December 10-12, 1996

IMPORTANCE OF THE TREATY

The signing of the Treaty on the sharing of the Ganges waters in Delhi on the eve of the Silver Jubilee anniversary of Bangladesh Liberation Day, resolved the most vexing issue between Bangladesh and India which had been at the core of Bangladesh-India problems and held up forward movement in all other areas. The Treaty does indeed, mark a watershed in Bangladesh-India bilateral relations. It has paved the way for fruitful and mutually beneficial cooperation in other areas of common concern. The Treaty with a thirty-year validity marks a sea-change from the short duration MOUs whose renewals remained so precariously contingent upon political mood-swings.

The treaty was a landmark event in Bangladesh-India relations. It symbolizes that given political commitment and goodwill, Bangladesh and India can resolve even the most intractable of problems between them. The Treaty also sent a salutary signal to other South Asian countries that despite asymmetry between India and its smaller neighbours, given the political will, determination, a positive attitude and goodwill, other neighbours of India could also strive to resolve differences with their large neighbour amicably.

BANGLADESH–INDIA RELATIONS UNDER KHALEDA ZIA

Begum Khaleda Zia became Prime Minister of Bangladesh after 1 October 2001 elections for second time. On 26 October 2001, Indian Prime Minister Atal Behari Vajpayee sent his National Security Adviser and Principal Secretary Brajesh Mishra to Dhaka as a special envoy on a goodwill mission. During his visit Brajesh Mishra discussed the issue of Bangladeshi products gaining free access to the Indian market, gas export to India and Ganges water treaty with Prime Minister Khaleda Zia and Foreign Minister Prof. A.Q.M. Badruddoza Chowdhury.[35]

On 10 April 2002 India agreed to provide duty-free access to 40 Bangladeshi items of 16 categories at the end of the three day Commerce Secretary level Bangladesh-India trade talks. But in real terms Bangladesh was not happy as it demanded duty free access of 191 items, within 25 categories.[36]

The Foreign Minister of Bangladesh M. Morshed Khan arrived in New Delhi on 16 June 2002, for a day's visit, the first since Begum Khaleda Zia government took over. He met Prime Minister Atal Bihari Vajpayee and Foreign Minister Jaswant Singh and discussed bilateral and trade issues. He also had detailed discussion with National Security Advisor Brajesh Mishra. India raised with Bangladesh the issue of trans-border terrorism and the use of Bangladesh as a base by Pakistan's ISI. Morshed Khan demanded the duly free access of 191 items of 25 categories to the Indian markets.[37]

The visit of Foreign Minister of Bangladesh to India provided the opportunities for the two countries to review the gamut of their bilateral relations. The two sides discussed, ways to remove impediments to the path of increasing trade and bilateral cooperation. It is worth mentioning here that the discussions between the Commerce

Secretaries of the two countries that were held in Dhaka in April, 2002 raised doubts over the real intensions of foot dragging about redeeming the earlier Indian commitments, even at the highest political level, to allowing duty-free access for the mutually agreed□upon Bangladesh export items to the Indian market. For obvious reasons, the bilateral trade issue comes on the top of the agenda in matters of Bangladesh India relations. This is because of the huge and widening trade imbalance between the two countries.

Foreign Minister of India Yashwant Sinha made a high profile goodwill visit to Dhaka during 24-25 August 2002, first such high level visit made by any Indian Minister since Begum Khaleda Zia came to power. Yashwant Sinha discussed the issues like cross border terrorism, concern over the treatment of minority, illegal migration, gas export and other related issues like trade imbalance, border incidents, ratification of the 1974 Land Boundary Agreement, transit and transshipment with the Bangladesh government. Bangladesh side demanded duty-free status to remove the trade imbalance. The Indian side took positive note of Bangladesh demand and informed that notification of duty-free access of 40 Bangladeshi products under 16 categories had already been issued and is effective from 25 August 2002. Besides, the luxury tax imposed by the West Bengal government on Bangladeshi products was also removed.[38]

But in November 2002 Bangladesh-India relations turned to frozen. Actually it happened due to a much publicised statement made by Deputy Prime Minister and Home Minister of India L.K. Advani about the increase in the activities of ISI and Al-Qaeda after the change of government in Bangladesh. The Indian government claimed that there were some 99 training camps located in Bangladesh where the anti-Indian miscreants and insurgents got trained to operate against India. The Foreign

Office of Bangladesh reacted sharply on the matter. The Foreign Office on 10 November 2002 summoned Indian High Commissioner Mani Lal Tripathi to convey its serious reservation about Advani's comment. Bangladesh government declared Advani's statement as baseless, incorrect and motivated.[39]

The relations between Bangladesh and India got further deteriorated because Bangladesh banned the import of Indian yarn through land ports in November 2002. The Indian High Commissioner in Dhaka wrote a letter to the Finance Minister Saifur Rahman in which he vigorously objected to the ban.[40] The Bangladesh government took the letter very seriously because it considered the contents to be highly objectionable. Just after the ban was imposed there was a meeting between the two countries at the Commerce Secretary level where the Indian government demanded the lifting of the ban. But the meeting almost broke down on several occasions and was fruitless. This issue, along with General Pervez Musharrafs visit to Bangladesh, the change of the route of the Asian Highway by Bangladesh, the Bangladeshi government's indecision on the export of gas to India and India's resentment at what it perceived to be Bangladesh foreign policy leaning towards China-Pakistan axis made Bangladesh India relations further embittered.

However, Bangladesh Foreign Minister M. Morshed Khan arrived in Delhi on 14 February 2003 to cool down the situation. He discussed bilateral relations with Prime Minister Atal Behari Vajpayee, Deputy Prime Minister Lal Krishna Advani and Foreign Minister Yashwant Sinha. Both the countries talked about the sharing of the Ganges waters, the insurgency in the Chittagang Hill Tracts, the many instances of border problems and a whole lot more. But what had been of considerably more significance was the ability of the two nations to work around their problems in order to move on.[41]

Finance Minister of Bangladesh Saifur Rahman visited India from 19 to 22 May 2003 and discussed bilateral and trade ties with Indian Prime Minister Vajpayee, Finance Minister Jaswant Singh and Commerce Minister Arun Jaitly. During the meetings, Saifur Rahman advocated that without trade liberalization and a quantum jump in Bangladesh's export to India it would be very difficult for Bangladesh to sustain high level of imports from India.[42] Bangladesh proposed to the Indian government to sign a free-trade accord on an experimental basis for six months. The two countries also agreed on some other measures to help improve bilateral trade and movement of people across the border like toning up storage facilities at trading points on both sides of the border, quick introduction of bus service between Agartala and Dhaka and movement of people by train.

After a long six year gap, the sixth meeting of the Joint Economic Commission (JEC) between Bangladesh and India was held on 14-15 July 2003 in Dhaka. The India-Bangladesh JEC was formed in 1982 and the last meeting of JEC was held in 1997. At JEC Foreign Minister of Bangladesh and India discussed issues like Indian zero tariff to Bangladeshi products, free trade agreement (FTA), road transit, Dhaka Shealdah train communication and opening of the Dhaka-Agartala bus service. Most of the time discussions centred on zero tariff and FTA. The Indian side initially stuck to its position not to continue commodity wise discussion other than the FTA. On the other hand, Bangladesh made it clear that it would not be possible to discuss the FTA without the product wise discussion on zero tariff. At one stage there was a serious stalement. Finally good sense prevailed. Bangladesh formally agreed to discuss the FTA and the Indian side agreed to consider the zero tariff for more than 100 items including the garment products.[43]

India also insisted on the transit issue but Bangladesh made it clear that at this stage it would not possible to discuss the road transit issue. An Indian credit worth $150 million for the implementation of the six different railway projects also came up for discussion. Bangladesh was interested to discuss the issue but India wanted to integrate the road development issue with the railway projects. Dhaka was not agree to integrate the road development issue with the railway project. India offered to develop different roads for smooth sailing of land transit facility. Bangladesh urged India to reduce the huge trade gap. Both the countries were happy and remarked that the JEC meeting made a good progress unlocking doors to different new areas of cooperation, including science and technology, IT, agriculture and natural disaster.[44]

Finally, the long awaited Dhaka-Agartala bus service was flagged off on 19 September 2003 with state owned buses from two neighbouring countries crossing into each other's, territory at around the same time. It was the second direct bus service after the one between Dhaka and Kolkata which was commissioned in 1999. The bus services between Dhaka-Kolkata and Dhaka-Agartala are the most convenient form of inter-country transportation for the common people. And with exchange of visits between more of the middle class citizenry, closer economic, political and socio□cultural relations become inevitable. The inauguration of Dhaka-Agartala bus service was a further step forward in Bangladesh-India relations. Indeed, Dhaka-Kolkata and Dhaka-Agartala bus services were the positive achievements in Bangladesh-India relations during Atal Bihari Vajpayee regime in India.

RECENT PHASE OF BANGLADESH-INDIA RELATIONS

Foreign Minister of Bangladesh M. Morshed Khan arrived in Delhi on 31 May 2004 on a four-day goodwill visit to discuss bilateral issues with the newly formed Congress government in India. He met new Indian Prime Minister Manmohan

Singh, External Affairs Minister K. Natwar Singh and officials. The government of Bangladesh expressed we a mutually beneficial relationship wan India, based on sensitivity to each other's core concerns. Indian government was also agree to work closely with Bangladesh to further intensify the Dhaka-Delhi bilateral cooperation and promote regional cooperation. Both the countries discussed problems like non-tariff barriers, transit questions, issuance of visa which was about five lakh annually, insurgency, arms seizure in Chittagong and interlinkine of rivers.[45]

Bangladesh and India agreed to resolve all outstanding bilateral issues, including security concerns of both the countries through free and frank dialogue. This agreement was reached at a meeting held in Bangkok between Prime Minister Khaleda Zia and Manmohan Singh on the sideline of the BIMSTEC Summit that concluded in the Thai capital on 31 July 2004. Both Khaleda and M. Singh agreed on holding regular expert level dialogue on water management. Both the countries observed that dialogue on management of joint rivers and flood control would be a continuous process.[46] This was the first meeting between Begum Khaleda Zia and Manmohan Singh after the Congress-led UPA government ascended to power in New Delhi in May 2004. Actually, the Bangkok Summit of the BIMSTEC provided the Prime Ministers of both countries an opportunity to get acquainted with one another.

The devasting floods of July 2004 sweeped eastern India and most of Bangladesh once again underscored the urgency of the two sides for cooperation in finding a long-term solution. Manmohan Singh assured Dhaka that India would not do anything without taking Dhaka into confidence was a gesture that was appreciated by Dhaka during the meeting.[47]

But unfortunately, once again relations between Bangladesh and India became strained. This was happened due to Bangladesh Foreign Minister M. Morshed Khan's swipe at India for its unreasonable accusations. Clearly, his anti-Indian outburst came at a wrong time and a wrong place. He was speaking at a seminar for young journalist from India and Bangladesh on 7 September 2004. The Foreign Minister countered the charges of harbouring insurgents in Bangladesh territory and assed for proof, if any. He then accused the Indian government of talking to the media instead of talking up the issues directly with Bangladesh government.[48] The minister clearly committed the same mistake of which he accused the Indians. Indeed, it was him to talk tough. This whole episode took place in iian High Commissioner to Bangladesh Veena Sikri However, in December 2004, Bangladesh and India once again initiated positive steps to improve bilateral relations and foster economic cooperation. Finance Minister of Bangladesh M. Saifur Rahman visited India during 4-8 December 2004. Saifur met Indian Ministers for Finance. Defence, Commerce, Agriculture and Petroleum, the National Security Adviser to Prime Minister, as well as business magnates including Tata Group Chairman Ratan Tata. The agenda of Saifur's discussion with Indian leaders included a trans-national gas pipeline, bilateral trade barriers and trade deficit, land transit for Bangladesh through India connecting Nepal and other economic issues.

On transit issue, Bangladesh offered rail transit for India and did not offer road transit. India wanted transit for all modes of transportation. On the trans-national gas pipeline issue connecting Bangladesh, India and Myanmar, both the government could not make concrete decision. Both the government were agreed to resolve all problems through discussion. Bangladesh also emphasised the need for accelerating execution of the SAFTA agreement instead of FTA.[49]

The two-day meeting of the Foreign Secretary-level between Bangladesh and India took place in New Delhi on 21-22 June 2005 after a gap of two years. It was the right step to sort out pending issues that have put bilateral relations on strains.

Such meetings are always welcome and constitute a part of confidence-building measures. The two-day meeting in New Delhi was held in the backdrop of deterioration of relations between the two countries for sometime.[50] Dhaka and Delhi agreed to cooperate in security, peaceful border management, sharing of waters of common rivers and economic exchange. The statement reported in the media contains 26-agreed plan of action that needs to be implemented.[51]

NATWAR SINGH'S VISIT TO DHAKA

It may not have resulted in a spectacular breakthrough but signs of inching forward towards a better understanding between India and Bangladesh were visible following the three-day visit of K. Natwar Singh, Minister of External Affairs of India to Dhaka from 6 to 8 August 2005. It was the first ever visit of a senior member of the Manmohan Singh cabinet to Bangladesh. The visit, during which Natwar Singh had discussion with his counterpart in Dhaka, Morshed Khan and also called Prime Minister Begum Khaleda Zia to hand over a letter from Prime Minister Manmohan Singh, did break the ice in almost chilled relations between the two countries. The visit also opened windows for further discussions and negotiations between New Delhi and Dhaka to help initiate a confidence-building process

The Indian Foreign Minister was also accompanied by the Foreign Secretary Shyam Saran, which gave additional seriousness of purpose to this visit and raised hopes about a multi-pronged and multilevel confidence-building process being pursued.

Whatever other dimensions of this Indian initiative might be a tangible outcome visible was the willingness of Begum Khalida Zia to visit India on an invitation from Mamnohan Singh. She reciprocated the gesture by inviting the Indian Prime Minister to pay a bilateral visit to Bangladesh in addition to his trip for the SAARC summit, scheduled for 12-13 November 2005 in Dhaka.

While Natwar Singh described his visit as "a part of confidence -building measures", he said that discussions at various levels during the three days at Dhaka were "fruitful, useful, successful and constructive."[52] The Bangladesh Foreign Secretary Hemayatuddin said that the Indian minister was going home with a very good impression and would discuss at appropriate levels the matters of resolving the outstanding issues between the two countries.[53] As the influential Indian daily *The Hindu,* commented, "India's relations with Bangladesh were so problematical that there were no expectations of breakthrough during Natwar Singh's visit to Dhaka.[54]

Among the issues which had cast shadows over the relations of New Delhi and Dhaka were India's perceptions and concerns about the illegal migration of Bangladeshis to its North-Eastern states. The impression in New Delhi was that this illegal infiltration was encouraged by Dhaka. India was also worried that Bangladesh was providing safe haven to insurgents from the North East. Bangladesh denied this.Bangladesh also opposed the Indian initiative at raising 4000 kilometer long fencing to check such infiltration on the argument that it could be "military construction".[55]

Bangladesh too had its own perceptions and concerns and fears. Dhaka was worried at the trade imbalance between the two countries, heavily tilted against Bangladesh and the proposal being mooted in India about the linking of river waters, which it feared would have adverse consequences for Bangladesh.

MUTUAL ISSUES

There were several mutual issues which had hung fire for several years perhaps because the leadership of both the countries was pre-occupied with serious problems of economic development and internal security. Even though in this first initiative by the Indian Minister, only a modest inching forward might be visible, one could entertain the hope that at least such inching forward will continue.[56] Although immediate response form Dhaka might not be forthcoming for a mutual extradition treaty between the two countries and for the proposal to construct a pipeline to bring gas from Myanmar through Bangladesh, at least these issues were raised at the Dhaka discussions and both the sides put forward their respective positions. From the Dhaka parleys one can at least derive some satisfaction that the two countries have taken a step to restore the high level mutual contacts which had been steadily dwindling during the last few years.

Foreign Secretary Shyam Saran and Foreign Minister of India Natwar Singh was reported to have said that India had solicited the support of Bangladesh to its candidature for permanent membership of an expanded U. N. Security Council, as also for the G-4 proposal and the Bangladesh side had promised active and friendly consideration.[57] Saran had emphasized that the two countries had to join hands to effectively deal with the terrorist activities, particularly misuse of border areas by elements which are inimical to interests of both the countries.[58]

Natwar Singh's meeting with the Bangladesh Finance Minister, Saifur Rahman had also raised expectations of future interaction on economic and trade cooperation between the two countries. As the daily *Tribune* commented editorially, External Affairs Minister Natwar Singh's visit to Bangladesh has been fruitful to the extent that the two countries have agreed to remove some of the irritants coming in the way of improving their relations.[59] Dhaka is going to do its utmost to prevent illegal cross-border activities. This means Dhaka would not allow North-East insurgent to use Bangladesh territory to create trouble in India. There will be coordinated patrolling covering more areas along the 4000 km long border between the two countries. Dhaka has expressed its readiness to allow the gas pipeline from Myanmar to India via Bangladesh. All this indicates that India and Bangladesh are moving forward for better bilateral relations.[60]

This, however, does not mean that the mistrust and suspicion between the two neighbours has come to an end. The conciliatory attitude of Bangladesh should be seen against the backdrop of the coming meeting of the South Asian Association for Regional Cooperation (SAARC) on 12-13 November 2005 in Dhaka. The Khaleda Zia government wants to ensure that the rescheduled SAARC session is a success, which is not possible without India's cooperation.

OUTCOME OF THE VISIT

- India and Bangladesh agreed to move closer by removing the irritants during Natwar Singh's visit.
- During the talks, the two Foreign Ministers agreed to establish more land custom stations to facilitate economic exchanges and people to people contact
- While acknowledging their differences on 1975 Border Guidelines, both sides agreed to maintain a peaceful border, free of illegal movements and troubles.
- India sought multi entrv visas for Indian travelers through the Dhaka-Agartala bu

- India also offered 500 more scholarships to Bangladeshi school students and 100 scholarships to undergraduate students as a part of technical and economic cooperation.
- Natwar Singh also expressed his government's desire for signing the Trade Agreement and concluding bilateral Free Trade Agreement, improvement of road, rail and air links for augmenting trade and investment, signing Bilateral Investment Protection and Promotion Agreement and keeping aside politics.[61]
- Natwar Singh reiterated the offer of US $ 150 million credit for infrastructure projects, especially in railway sector
- He said as far as economic and commercial relations are concerned India would not expect strict reciprocity from Bangladesh.[62]
- "As a bigger country and a country with a larger industrial base, we are ready to offer Bangladesh asymmetric benefits and early harvest," he said, adding "failure to avoid available synergies and complementarities will adversely impact on not just India but also Bangladesh.[63]
- Morshed Khan, Bangladeshi Foreign Minister, however, said his talks with Natwar did not cover the tri-nation gas pipeline from Myanmar to India through Bangladesh.[64]
- But, he added, not only the gas pipeline, the issues of Bangladesh's export to Nepal through India and proposal for the import of energy from Bhutan are also economic issues which need to be worked out.[65]
- Responding to Singh's remarks about India's wish for a secular Bangladesh and joint fight against terrorism and fundamentalism, Khan said, "It would not be right to consider Bangladesh as non-secular. India can see whatever way they like-we are guided by our own thoughts and culture." Bangladesh, he said, has never tolerated, does not tolerate and will not tolerate international terrorism. "We are against international terrorism and against blind fundamentalism of any religion."[66]
- Political analysts observed these issues and differences of views and concerns are not new to any side. The ball started rolling perhaps on the right track. A number of ministerial meetings

on varied subjects are in the offing. A Summit meeting between Manmohan Singh and Khaleda Zia will take place in November 2005 on the sidelines of the 13th SAARC summit in Dhaka.

MAJOR IRRITANTS IN BANGLADESH AND INDIA

1. 'Push- in' and 'pushback' of Bangladeshi nationals.
2. Frequent exchange of fire between the border guards.
3. New Delhi's allegation against Dhaka of sponsoring the northeastern insurgents.
4. Dhaka's complaint against sheltering Bangladesh's criminals and anti-Bangladesh campaigns in India.
5. "War of words" between the two countries.
6. Trade imbalance against Dhaka.
7. Undemocratic 6.5-km border.
8. Sharing of the waters of Teesta and other common rivers.
9. Border fencing.
10. Security concerns.

No doubt the Dhaka visit of K. Natwar Singh did raise some hopes for the future of the long stalled Bangladesh-India ties. That no Indian Prime Minister had the inclination and the opportunity to visit an important neighbour like Bangladesh, told the sad story of the deterioration of the bilateral relationship. Even though the Indian Foreign Minister's Dhaka visit appeared to have broken the mould, a lot of hard thinking, hard talk and hard work will have to be done to make the visit of the Prime Ministers of the two countries to Dhaka and New Delhi worthwhile.

BANGLADESH–INDIA ECONOMIC RELATIONS: AN OVERVIEW

India is the biggest trade partner of Bangladesh surrounded by that country on three sides. India's market interest in Bangladesh is magnified with geo-political interest. Economic relations between the two countries are in favour of India to the proportion of 15:1. But the economic interests of each other are mutually vital. Bangladesh depends on India in areas like raw industrial materials, all kinds of motor vehicles, food- stuff of different varieties and cosmetics etc.

EARLY STAGE OF BANGLADESH-INDIA ECONOMIC RELATIONS

After the liberation of Bangladesh in 1971, India contributed to the shaping up of the economy of the newly emerged state. During Seikh Mujibur Rahman's regime (1971-75), the effect of Indo-Bangla political relations markedly influenced economic relations of two countries. India's contribution to Bangladesh's economy was substantial. Bangladesh received US $ 275.27 million as grants from India from 1971-76. An India-Bangladesh Trade Agreement was signed on 28 March 1972, based on a friendly and cooperative environment. Following this, a new Trade Agreement (for a period of three years) was signed on 5 July 1972. After the killing of Bangabandhu Sheikh Mujibur Rahman in August 1975, Bangladesh-India relations deteriorated seriously, so did economic activities.

In the year 1980, the two countries reached a decision to develop their economic relations with a new spirit. In the same year a new trade agreement was signed on the basis of the previous agreement signed by the Mujib government. To strengthen economic relations, a new Joint Economic Commission (JEC) was set up in 1982. Up to 2005 this commission met very infrequently. A Memorandum of Understanding (MOU) was signed during the JEC meeting held in Delhi in 1997. The agreement promised cooperation among the signatories and covered sectors like industry, education and culture, science and technology, agriculture, border trade, transport cooperation and telecommunication etc. The sixth JEC meeting was held between Bangladesh and India at Dhaka during 14-15 July, 2003. Both countries agreed to start talks about FTA (Free Trade Agreement) between the two countries. The FTA talks started in mid October, 2003, but some issues like tariff and para-tariff barriers remained unresolved and the agreement left unsigned.

PROBLEM OF TRADE IMBALANCE

Bangladesh-India economic relation suffer from trade imbalance for Bangladesh. Increasing high trade imbalance is a cause of concern and frustration. In the year 1996-97 the deficit was US $ 891.30 million. In the year 1998 the total amount of deficit reached 21248 crore, 585 lakh. This excludes illegal trade or smuggling .[67] In the year 2002-2003 the deficit reached a record high of US $1270.86 million. Bangladeshi products cannot enter India due to policy barriers like tariff, para-tariff, dumping, anti-dumping, etc. Bangladeshi jute carpet, industrial and vehicle battery, melamine, etc. have a good demand in Indian market. But the Indian authorities are imposing high taxes on these items. As a result these products cannot enter India as cheap imported items. On the other hand, Bangladesh has reduced its taxes imposed on Indian products. In the year 1993-94, Indian products had to face 300 per cent import tax while entering the Bangladeshi market. It was reduced in 1994-95 up to 60 percent.[68]

In the year 2001-02, Bangladesh pushed India to narrow down the huge trade imbalance. Bangladesh requested India to remove tariff barriers from 191 items, of which India agreed to 40. But the duty-free access to 40 items did not make much difference considering the size of the trade imbalance and the demand for those categories of product in Indian market. In the Sixth JEC meeting held at Dhaka in July, 2003, Bangladesh had demanded dutyfree entry of 180 items to India. India had reviewed it but no final promise was expressed. The three-day Bangladesh-India Joint Secretary level trade talks ended in Dhaka on October 22,

Table 2

India's Exports of Principal Commodities to Bangladesh (1995-02) (Million US $)

Commodities	*1995-96*	*1996-97*	*1997-98*	*1998-99*	*1999-2000*	*2000-01*	*2001-02*
All Commodities	1050.63	869.69	787.41	996.37	636.92	874.41	945.52
Cotton yarn fabric made-ups, etc.	277.41	337.19	273.6	123.4	157.2	175.99	145.16
Wheat	22.87	9.67	0	0	0	25.26	86.27
Transport equipments	86.69	66.68	34.67	25	25	60.81	74.24
Machinery and equipments	45.62	55.89	47.29	36.03	36.03	57.46	72.06
Coal	23.4	14.88	18.94	27.24	27.24	29.95	39.79
Sugar	0	4.69	0.03	0.02	0.02	10.94	37.87
Manufacturers of metal	11.25	12.15	13.17	12.7	12.7	31.32	31.79
Oil meals	0.65	0.28	1.44	1.79	1.79	21.78	31.36
Paper/wood products	25.32	21.62	10.97	7.98	7.98	20.94	28.18
Drugs, pharm and fine chemicals	13.95	16.15	21.52	23.86	23.86	29.85	26.55
Prim and semi-tin iron and steel	31.4	39.08	34.49	16.5	16.5	26.03	25.52
Electronic goods	19.44	16.8	17.7	80.17	8.17	8.74	24.28
Fresh fruits	9.63	11.45	11.08	7.81	7.81	15.41	22.18
Pulses	0	0.18	1.12	0.1	0.1	18.01	21.34
Glass/glassware/ceramics/cement	29.91	33.53	41.35	24.21	24.21	38.32	20.56
Inorg/org/agro chemicals	11.94	6.83	6.44	5.62	5.62	22.04	18.48
Plastic and linoleum	3.94	5.37	9.43	7.87	7.87	9.22	17.26
Other ores and minerals	15.96	24.23	9.07	6.35	6.35	11.18	17.04

Source: *Economic and Political Weekly*, 27 November 2004

Table 3: India's Imports of Principal Commodities from Bangladesh (1997-02) (Rs. lakh)

Commodities	1997-98	1998-99	1999-2000	2000-01	2001-02
Jute raw	5053.63	9163.46	13922.82	7929.35	8781.43
Inorganic chemicals	4548.00	3331.27	7433.48	9102.4	7175.68
Clothing and readymade garments	2928.78	3896.97	2841.85	10973.4	5326.06
Textile yarn, fibre, made u articles	2925.78	5896.97	2102.93	209.7	1514.69
Fertilisers manufactured	1195.06	0	1130.43	0	861.55
Read made garments (woven and knit)	-	-	141.8	549.1	805.07
Leather	412.34	407.18	354.1	505.14	669.71
Electrical machinery except electronic	18.79	71.42	273.27	105.37	289.63
Fruits and nuts excluding cashew nuts	0	0	10.5	200.63	210.31
Non ferrous metals	0	2.84	529.85	0	182.66
Silk raw	0	0	0	0	151.8
Machinery except electrical and electronic	12.68	68.78	293.08	154.76	110.01
Textile am and fibres	0	0	298.82	139.03	183.38
Electronic goods	30.31	45.1	8.05	16.46	84.38
Non-metallic mineral manufactured excluding earls	9.4	60.14	143.88	69.51	80.37
Other cereals	0	0	0	0	34.37
Wheat	0	0	0	0	33.65
Raw hides and skins	29.25	11.19	44.88	95.04	20.24
Manufactures of'metals	0.33	12.84	1.04	2.3	15.34
Total	17164.35	22968.16	29530.78	30052.19	26530.33
Percentage of the total	90.89	85.81	87.20	84.05	94.10
Grand Total	18884.54	26765.02	33865.95	35753.41	28194.05

Source: Economic and Political Weekly, 27 November 2004

2003. In that meeting, the Indian side did not respond clearly to the issue of removal of non-tariff barriers imposed by India. Indian negotiators expressed that India could not frame special rules for the interest of Bangladeshi exporters. On the basis of this condition Bangladesh has to think carefully about FTA and its outcomes.

South Asian Preferential Trade Arrangement (SAPTA), which was signed in 1995 by the seven member countries of SAARC could be a filter by using which Bangladesh might reduce trade gap with India. SAPTA allowed its member countries to import merchandise from each other at 10 percent lower tariff than those imposed on similar goods from non-SAARC countries. Under the SAPTA arrangement India agreed to reduce tariff on 106 items. Among them Bangladesh is able to produce only 13 items. Moreover, in reality, India has not reduced tariffs and eventually Bangladeshi products like jute carpet, vehicle battery, melamine etc. are facing 20 percent tariff while entering India.

Table - 4

Trade position between Bangladesh and India (Million $)

Year	*Export*	*Import*	*Trade-Balance*
1990-91	31.06	180.65	(-) 149.59
1991-92	2.07	231.32	(-) 229.25
1992-93	9.85	341.97	(-) 332.12
1993-94	16.81	413.37	(-) 396.56
1994-95	45.16	687.69	(-) 642.53
1995-96	72.35	1100.05	(-) 1027.70
1996-97	46.26	921.75	(-) 875.49
1997-98	65.58	933.74	(-)868.16
1998-99	59.72	1228.28	(-) 168.56
1999-2000	64.88	836.13	(-) 771.25
2000-2001	62.28	1174.41	(-) 1112.13
2001-2002	50.18	1018.80	(-) 068.52

Source: P.O. T., Vol., XXVIII, No.35, 10 February 2003.

CREDIT ARRANGEMENT AND JOINT VENTURES

Bangladesh does not have a good record in spending credits with due timeframe. Bangladesh gets a broader timeline to utilize credits from other donors compared to India. However, some Indian credit arrangements are there for Bangladesh. India entered into an agreement with Bangladesh to extend a credit line of Rs. 200 crore to Bangladesh in June 1999. This credit line is being utilised to import double-decker buses, railway locomotives and other related item. There are 28 Indian joint ventures in Bangladesh with an equity participation of US $ 16.6 million and 7 wholly owned subsidiaries with an equity of US $ 0.6 million in various areas such as textiles, building industry, chemicals, IT, automobile sector etc.

India's business giant Tata Group signed an Expression of Interest (EOI) with the Board of Investment of Bangladesh (1301) on 13 October 2004. Tata's interest is expressed mainly in three proposals- setting up namely-a steel industry to produce hot rolled coil and other basic steel products, 1000MW gas-fired power station in two phases, and a million-ton capacity fertilizer factory. All these three proposals would entail investment of a total of US $2 billion in Bangladesh. If this investment takes place it will be the single largest investment in the history of Bangladesh. And it will eventually influence various other important things like future investment prospects in Bangladesh, employment opportunities for Bangladeshis and Bangladesh-India relations.[69]

The World Bank committed $ 2 million for a study on the investment proposals and preparing terms and conditions for Bangladesh. Donors have promised to provide technical support and assist the largest single investment plan in Bangladesh. The deputy country representative of the ADB in Bangladesh Hua Du assured support for infrastructure development.[70] B. Muthuraman, MD of Tata Steel pointed out that the proposed investment would create 8000 employment directly and 60,000 indirectly.[71] Bangladesh is suffering from unemployment problem and the proposed projects would undoubtedly create job opportunities.

Like Tata group other Indian industrialists can also invest in Bangladesh. Bangladesh government should renew and formulate an enhanced business policy to protect foreign private investment.

CONCLUSION

In inter-state relations, political and economic relations cannot be eparated because they are intertwined. Most often good political relations lead to and economic relations. What to be recognised is that suspicious relations have their own momentum to the detriment of interests of both countries, unless intervened. Continuing good relations are not taken for granted and need to be sustained constantly. Relations are compared to nurturing a plant that needs regular attention and if left unattended, it will either not grow or wither away.

It is not understood why a long interval of two years has elapsed before the senior officials met at Foreign Secretary-level meeting in June 2005. Whatever the state of relations, good or strained between neighbouring countries at least annual if not six monthly meeting at Foreign Secretary level ought to be utinely held. In Europe, the frequent meetings of the heads of state of government are routine, despite their major differences on many issues. Likewise, the need of the regularity of meetings between Bangladesh and India at a Foreign Secretary level is imperative.

Indian Prime Minister Manmohan Singh, while talking with foreign journalists said on 30 May 2005 that India has "emotional ties" with Bangladesh and reiterated his desire to work out solutions to all outstanding bilateral issues.[72] By referring to "emotional ties", it is believed that he was referring to India's material and diplomatic support to the 1971 Liberation War of Bangladesh. If there exists good will at the highest political level, why have relations worsened at a time when India's profile in the world is on the rise? Given the changed global political and economic environment, whatever "local difficulties" in the region exist need to be resolved and there is no adequate reason why Indo-Bangladesh relations cannot but be friendly, given the common platform of raising quality of life of vast majority of people of both countries.

India has certain strategic and security interests in South Asia and wants that all the smaller neighbours should not only appreciate but also share India's perception. The difficulty is that India perceives China's military power as a threat to its security while other smaller neighbours of India do not share the same perception. In fact India's position is so central and dominant in South Asia, that some of the neighbouring states perceive China as a counter-weight to India in the region. India is a rising regional, if not a global power within decades. India thinks that Bangladesh has not been playing a constructive role in maintaining their security interests within South Asia. India holds the view that to maintain cooperative and mutually supportive bilateral relations, Bangladesh needs to be anchored within a broad framework of strategic and security relationship with India.

On 14 February 2005, India's Foreign Secretary was candid about India's security perception while addressing at the India International Centre. He said, "The countries of South Asia, while occupying the same geographical space, do not have a shared security perception and hence a common security doctrine....... In security, at least some of the states perceive security threats as arising from within the region ... Do countries in our neighbourhood envisage their own security and development in cooperation with India or hostility to India or by seeking to isolate themselves from India against the logic to our geography?[73] Although the Foreign Secretary did not name the countries of South Asia but it is not difficult to say that reference to "some states" certainly means Pakistan and may possibly include Bangladesh. This implies that Bangladesh does not have the same security perception as that of India. Unless the big picture is sorted out, it seems Bangladesh's relations with India are likely to be difficult.

Another factor in bilateral relations appears to be that India wants to link various bilateral issues with one another. This means, for example, that if Bangladesh wants sharing of waters of common rivers, in return Bangladesh should provide transit facilities to northeastern states. This is based on India's doctrine of reciprocity. That implies if Bangladesh wants anything from India, India should receive in return something. Bangladesh does not perceive in the way India chooses to link bilateral issues. The sharing of waters of common rivers, according to Bangladesh, stands on its own legitimate right not only under rules of international law but also in terms of the 1996 Indo-Bangladesh Ganges Water Treaty (Article 9 of the Treaty). Furthermore Bangladesh perceives linking issues as an unfair and unequal bargain advantage on the part of India.

Although India expressed satisfaction over the commencement of coordinated patrolling by the border forces of the two countries. India suspects presence of anti-Indian militant groups in Bangladesh territory, increased suspected activities of Pakistani intelligence on border area and smuggling of weapons across common borders to northeastern states.

While Bangladesh has consistently denied presence of anti-Indian militants in the country and other allegations, India is not impressed by the denials. Bangladesh on the other hand complained about providing "safe haven" to criminals from Bangladesh and not returning them to Bangladesh authorities. It is hoped that allegations and counter-allegations will now stop in future between the two countries.

It has to be recognised that Indo-Bangladesh -bilateral relations are essentially of asymmetrical nature because they involve between a large country and a small country. Furthermore, Bangladesh is surrounded by India on three sides and on the fourth open side to the Bay of Bengal, Bangladesh faces a strong and powerful India Navy. It requires any small country in such geographical situation to make efforts in developing stable bilateral relations unless the big neighbour appreciates the reality of situation of small neighbours. Bangladesh perceives that India with its dominant position tends to extract unfair concessions from Bangladesh. Whether the perception is right or wrong that may be a debatable proposition.

India needs to recognise that reciprocity is not always possible for a small country and as a big neighbour it has certain responsibility towards its smaller neighbours. Power and responsibility go together. It is in the interests of both countries outstanding relations need to be resolved with fairness and justice. Good relations cannot be imposed because they are based on principles of mutual respect and equality.

Former Indian Prime Minister I.K. Gujral appeared to have recognised the sensitivity of small countries when he stated that, *"First with neighbours like Bangladesh, Bhutan, Maldives, Nepal and Sri Lanka, we do not ask for reciprocity but give what we can in good faith."*[74] India still adheres to this point of view.

It may lastly be concluded that Bangladesh and India are neighbours and they are destined to live as neighbours.

No one can change the fundamental reality. If Bangladesh is prosperous, it is good for India as it provides good market for India. Bangladesh has no competition with India but at the same time no country including Bangladesh appreciates being pushed around by a big neighbour.

Another question that looms large is-why security concern should be overblown by India with its sizeable military power when economic cooperation may open a new vista in Indo-Bangladesh relations?. At the dawn of the 21st century, the prime consideration for India is to build regional economic blocs within South Asia to enhance their economic gains in the competitive globalised world.

REFERENCES

1. Abul Kalam, Bangladesh and India: A Perspective of Cooperative Relationship in a Regional Strategic Environment in Muzaffar Ahmad and Abul Kalam (eds.), *Bangladesh Foreign Relations . Changes and Direction* (Dhaka, 1989), p. 101.
2. Moudud Ahmed, *Bangladesh . Era of Sheikh Mujibur Rahman* (Dhaka, 1983), pp. 182-93.
3. Zia negotiated the first Ganga water sharing agreement with Desai at the London Commonwealth summit in 1977. Ershad reached the second Ganga water sharing agreement with Indira at the Nasau Commonwealth summit in 1982.
4. Khurshida Begum, *Tension over the Farakka Barrage: A Techno-Political Tangle in South Asia* (Dhaka, 1987).
5. Ishtiaque Hossain, Bangladesh-India Relations : Issues and Problems, in Emajuddin Ahmed (ed.), *Foreign Policy of Bangladesh: A Small State's Imperative* (Dhaka, 1984).
6. JRC was established in March 1972 after Mrs. Gandhi's visit to Dhaka to settle bilateral river disputes between the two countries and to increase bilateral cooperation for improving the utilisation of the regional water resources on an equitable basis.
7. JEC was established in October 1982 after Lt. Gen. Ershad's first visit to New Delhi as the Chief Executive of Bangladesh.

The purpose of the JEC is to increase bilateral economic cooperation in different economic fields.

8. President Ziaur Rahman visited New Delhi in December 1977, January 1980 and September 1980, President Ershad visited New Delhi in October 1982, November 1984, July 1986 and after the flood of 1988 in Bangladesh.
9. India Bangladesh signed the land border agreement in 1974 which included the settlement of the enclaves issue in the reciprocal territory. A fresh agreement exclusively about the enclaves was signed in 1982. The constitution of India debar the government to secede or lease any Indian territory to other state. The Supreme Court's verdict of May 1990 about the lease of the Teen Bigha cleared all hurdles and the territory was leased.
10. P.O. T, Vol. XVII, No. 284,23 December 1992, p. 3733.
11. *Bangladesh Observer,* 13 December 1992
12. P.O. T, Vol. XVII. No. 284, 23 December 1992, p.3828.
13. *Daily Star,* 12 December 1992.
14. *Bangladesh Observer,* 11 December 1992
15. *The Morning Sun,* 11 December 1992.
16. *Daily Meillat,* 10 December 1991.
17. *Daily Star,* 17 November 1993.
18. P.O. T, Vol. XVIII, No. 30, 12 February 1993.
19. *Ibid.*
20. *Kersing's Record of World Events,* News Digest for October 1992, Vol. 38, No. 10, pp. 39148-39149.
21. Muhammad Tajuddin, India-Bangladesh : A New Era in *Newsletter, M.A.K.A. Institute* of Asian Studies (Calcutta), Vol. *3, No. 2-3,* February *1997, pp. 28-31.*
22. *The Statesman, 15* June *1997.*
23. *Asian Age* (Calcutta), *17 June 1998.*
24. Ahmad Tariq Karim, *The* Bangladesh-India Treaty on Sharing of Ganges Waters, *BIISS Journal* (Dhaka), Vol. *19, No.2, 1998.*
25. Ibid, p.218.
26. *J.N.* Dixit, India's Foreign Policy, *Strategic Analysis* (New Delhi), Vol. *123,* No. *12,* March *1991, p.1409.*
27. *The Bangladesh Times, 14* April *1994.*

28. B.M. Abbas, Bangladesh-India Negotiations on Ganges Water, in Muzaffar Ahmad and Abdul Kalam, (eds.), *Bangladesh Foreign Relations :Changes and Direction* (Dhaka, *1989), p.32*
29. *Ibid, p.38.*
30. *Ibid, p.44.*
31. Narul Momen, *Bangladesh in the United Nations: A Study in Diplomacy,* (Dhaka, *1987), p.21.*
32. Ibid., p.23.
33. James J. Novak, *Bangladesh . Reflections on the Water* (Dhaka *1994), pp. 4-5.*
34. *The Times of India, 17* August *1996.*
35. *Bangladesh Observer, 28* October *2001.*
36. *The Independent, 11* April *2002.*
37. *P.O. T, Vol.* XXVII, No. *131, 18* August *2002.*
38. M. Sakhawat Hussain, Yashwant Sinha's visit : Balancing Act, *Bangladesh Today, 26* August *2002.*
39. *Bangladesh Observer, 14* November *2002.*
40. *The Hindu, 12* January *2003.*
41. *News Today, 15* February *2003.*
42. *The Times of India, 26* May *2003.*
43. *Financial Express, 17* July *2003.*
44. *P.O. T, Vol. XXVIII,* No. *208, 2* September *2003.*
45. *The Hindu, 5* June *2004.*
46. *P.O. T, Vol. XXIX,* No. *186, 11* August *2004.*
47. *The Times of India, 9* August *2004.*
48. *Bangladesh Observer, 9* September *2004.*
49. P. O. T . Vol. XXIX, No. *287, 9* December *2004.*
50. *Bangladesh Observer, 23* June *2004.*
51. *The Hindu, 25* June *2005.*
52. *The Times of India, 9* August *2005.*
53. *Daily Star, 9* August *2005.*
54. *The Hindu, 9* August *2005.*
55. *Bangladesh Observer, 11* August *2005.*
56. *P.N.* Khera, New Delhi and Dhaka Inching Forward Towards Better Understanding, *South Asia Politics,* Vol.4, No. 5, September 2005, pp. 35□36.

57. *Ibid.,* p.39
58. *Ibid.,* p.37
59. *The Tribune,* 9 August 2005.
60. *Ibid*
61. *The Bangladesh Times, 1 l* August 2005.
62. Jojo Mathews, Indian Bilateral Relations, *Competition Wizard, Vol. XIV,* No. 10, October 2005.
63. *Ibid.,* p. 75.
64. *Ibid.*
65. *Ibid.,* p. 76.
66. *Ibid.*
67. *Bangladesh Observer,* 15 July 2004.
68. *Ibid.*
69. *Bangladesh Observer,* 15 October 2004.
70. *The Bangladesh Times,* 15 November 2004.
71. *Bangladesh Observer,* 21 November 2004.
72. *The Daily Star,* 31 May 2005.
73. *The Hindu,* 15 February 2005.
74. P.O. T, Vol. XXX, No. 166, 12 July 2005

CHAPTER-6

Bangladesh Relations with Neighbouring Countries

Bangladesh is located at the south-eastern edge of the mainland of the Indian sub-continent. Its geographical, historical and cultural relations with the sub-continent are of permanent nature. The political, security and economic interests of Bangladesh are strongly attached with the region. Therefore, a cardinal principle of Bangladesh's foreign policy is to seek the closest possible relations with its immediate neighbours to attain the path of progress.

Bangladesh has cordial relations with its smaller neighbours like Myanmar, Bhutan, Nepal, Sri Lanka and Pakistan. The bilateral and multilateral relations of Bangladesh with these neighbouring countries are playing an important role at international and regional level. These countries have supported Bangladesh in different international fora on the issues in which Bangladesh has a stake. These countries are also economically significant for Bangladesh. Good bilateral relations with these neighbouring countries are essential for Bangladesh to achieve its political and economic objectives. This chapter discusses the bilateral relations of Bangladesh with individual country separately.

BANGLADESH-MYANMAR RELATIONS

Bangladesh shares a common border of 271 km with Myanmar and maintain traditional, commercial and cultural ties with that country.[1] Bangladesh-Myanmar relations officially began on 13 January 1972 with Myanmar's recognition to Bangladesh as a sovereign state. Immediately after independence, Bangladesh moved to set up diplomatic relations with Myanmar (then Burma) and appointed a senior diplomat as its Ambassador to Yangon (former Rangon). Since then, officials and leader of the two governments exchanged visits at the top level a number of times. Two countries have signed many agreements on different subjects including boundary demarcation, general trade, air transport, repatriation agreements, border trade and agreement on prevention of trafficking of narcotics etc.[2]

Meanwhile, some issues have cropped up as irritants to bilateral relations between the two countries. The most prominent has been the inflow of Rohingya refugees in 1978 and again in 1991-92 into Bangladesh and so the question of their repatriation to Myanmar. While repatriation of the Rohingya refugees was accomplished in 1978 amicably and a major portion in the 1990's also has been repatriated, the issue of repatriation of the remaining refugees is rather complicated. However, both sides have taken steps to promote bilateral trade cooperation. But as the overall political relations remain somewhat murky, full-blown economic cooperation is yet to take shape. Myanmar could offer a huge market for Bangladeshi goods and both countries could go for joint venture investments in exclusive export processing zone in Taknaf-Cox's Bazar area on fishing, cement, paper etc. Similarly, Bangladesh could also provide essential goods and services to Myanmar and at the sametime buy Myanmar's commodities at cheaper rates.

DEVELOPMENT OF POLITICAL RELATIONS

Political relations between Bangladesh and Myanmar started with a positive note. In May 1972, Foreign Minister of Bangladesh Abdus Samad Azad undertook an official visit to Myanmar. A Joint communique issued simultaneously from Dhaka and Yangon on 28 may 1972 emphasized closer ties and development of bilateral relations on the basis of peaceful co-existence, non-alignment as well us mutual respect for sovereignty and national dignity.[3] Soon after independence, Bangladesh sought international support both political and economic to re-construct the war-ravaged country. So Bangladesh decided to import rice from Myanmar to meet food deficit. Afterwards, Bangladesh Foreign Minister visited Myanmar for the second time in July 1972. The then Foreign Secretary of Bangladesh also led a team of officials to Yangon in early 1973 to finalize a deal for the purchase of rice from Myanmar. Sheikh Mujibur Rahman sent special envoy, Shamsul Haque, to Myanmar in May 1973 to muster support of the Burmese government for the young state of Bangladesh. These visits enhance the warm political relations between the two countries in early phases.

In such pleasant environment, the then Burmese President Ne Win visited Bangladesh as the first Asian Head of state on 26 April 1974. President Ne Win emphasized that Bangladesh and Burma were "close neighbours, linked together by geography, history and culture" and added that their "friendship would be everlasting.[4] Considering the importance of politico-economic relations with Bangladesh, President Ne Win again visited Bangladesh in May 1979 and November 1982. Prior to these visits, the then Bangladesh President General Ziaur Rahman paid a state visit to Burma in July 1977. This was the first visit of a Bangladesh Head of State to Burma.[5] The whole gamut of Bangladesh-Burma relations came up for review at the summit talks between General Zia and President Ne Win. It resulted in broad agreement on all issues of common concern to Bangladesh and Burma.[6] During his visit in May 1979, the Burmese President emphasized on preservation and promotion of the existing congenial relations in future.[7] At the official talks, an agreement was signed on the demarcation of 197 km land boundary between the two countries.[8] The Bangladesh Foreign Minister described the agreement as another milestone in the friendly relations between the two countries.[9]

In February 1982, during President Abdus Sattar's visit to Burma, he emphasized the need for further augmenting and diversifying trade and strengthening of economic cooperation between the two countries.[10] On 19 May 1983, former President of Bangladesh Lt. Gen. H.M. Ershad also visited Yangon. The Burmese Foreign Minister, who visited Bangladesh in May 1984, urged increased cooperation between the two countries in the fields of trade and commerce. In August 1985, Dhaka-Yangon further strengthened their ties with the authentication of clear-cut demarcation of 197 kms of common land boundary jointly finalized by the Survey Departments of the two countries.[11] This formal demarcation concerned land boundary stretching from the southern end of the Naaf river to the tri junction of Bangladesh-India-Burma boundaries. The final work of demarcation with 53 boundary pillars and preparation of the strip maps were taken up under the Land Boundary Demarcation Accord signed between the two countries on 23 May 1979.

As other issues like the Rohingya refugees cropped up in Bangladesh–Myanmar relations, the border issue remained dormant for many years. To resolve the outstanding problem on border demarcation, a meeting between survey delegation of Bangladesh and Maynmar was held on 17 January 1997 at the Department of Survey in Yangon. The meeting decided that a joint survey team will visit the bordering Taungbro town on 21 January 1997 and would determine the seven undetermined pillars (no. 31, 34, 35, 36, 38 and 39) while the related field works will be finished by 31 January 1997. Bangladesh delegation submitted a proposal for a draft treaty at the meeting and the Myanmar side agreed to submit their observation on the draft treaty by 15 February 1997.[12]

At last the long awaited Land Boundary Treaty between the two countries was signed in Yangon on 12 November 1998.[13] The conclusion of the treaty was the outcome of a series of negotiations and field trips by officials of the two countries since signing of the Land Boundary Agreement in 1977.

ROHINGYA ISSUE

The first major crisis in Bang ladesh-Myanmar relations erupted in 1978 when Myanmar's military regime drove out about 2 lakh people of muslim minority community, known as Rohingya, living in its Arakan state into Bangladesh. Bangladesh was not prepared to bear the adverse socio-political consequences of such huge refugee exodus from Myanmar. Together with efforts aimed at resolving the dispute bilaterally, Bangladesh also brought the issue to the international forums, including the United Nations. Under pressure from international community, particularly China, Rangoon finally signed an agreement in July 1978 on the repatriation of Rohingya refugees to Myanmar. Repatriation started on 6 of October 1979 and was completed within a record time by December 24, 1979. The agreement was acclaimed as an example of good neighbourliness. However, ground for another round of refugees was being prepared again in the late 1980s.

The persecution of Rohingyas found a legal basis following the introduction of a new Citizenship Act in 1982 by Burmese President Ne Win which stipulated that those who had migrated after 1824 would lose their citizenship.[14] The Ne Win regime enforced in 1984 the new Citizenship Act which required a person to have up to 200 years of family tree in Burma to become a citizen. This was aimed at the Chinese, Indian and Bengalee immigrants. With fueling the segregation feeling, Ne Win planned to utilize religion and ethnicity as a weapon to remain in power.[15] Since then, the Rohingyas became victim of systematic repression of Yangon authorities. But Bangladesh asserted with concrete historical evidence that the Rohingya muslims are a distinct group who have lived in Rakhine for more than a thousand years and that there was no ground to throw them out of Myanmar. In early 1991, the authoritarian Yangon military ruler dominated by Burman ethnic group initiated a well-planned border offensive against a dozen ethnic minority insurgent groups which continued until 1992 and beyond. The government forces were fighting Karen rebels along the Thai border around Manerplaw, Kachin rebels in the north west, Naga rebels near the border with India and the Rohingyas near the border with Bangladesh. They were also fighting a number of other ethnic groups like Mon, Shan and Wa.

Cracks were developed in the bilateral relations between the two countries following an attack on 21 December 1991 by the Myanmar Border Forces on a Bangladesh Rifles (BDR) camp at Rajupara under Naikhongchari thana in Bandarban district. Again in early 1992, due to an army crack down on civilians of the state of Arakan, over 2.65 lakh Rohingya fled across the border into Bangladesh. Furthermore, during the attack, Myanmar forces killed a member of the BDR personnel, injured seven others and looted arms and ammunition from the camp.[16] The influx of Rohingya refugees and other related developments created severe problems for

Bangladesh. These were of security, humanitarian, socio-economic, political, ecological as well as diplomatic in nature. Bangladesh tried to convince the world leaders, the UN and Myanmar for an amicable settlement of the Rohingya issue. In this connection, Myanmar Foreign Minister U Ohn Gyaw visited Bangladesh during 24-29 April 1992 and signed an agreement on repatriation. Accordingly, the Myanmar government agreed to take all necessary measures that would halt the outflow of Myanmar residents to Bangladesh and encourage those who had left Myanmar to return voluntarily to their homes. According to the agreement, the repatriation was started on 15 May 1992 for the limited time of six months.[17] However, the process of repatriation was very slow and stopped many times. The repatriation process picked up in 1994-95 and till 2004 the total number of Myanmar refugees repatriated was about 201,599.[18]

Repatriation process was slowed down from the end of May 1995 due to Myanmar authority's dilly-dallying in clearing the refugee's list. To expedite the repatriation process, the then Foreign Minister of Bangladesh Abdus Samad Azad visited Myanmar during 3-5 September 1996. During the visit, Bangladesh and Myanmar officials discussed matters of mutual interest including the exchange of visits of high defence personnel, repatriation of Myanmar citizens from Bangladesh and cooperation in various fields, especially in the economic sector.

The repatriation process again stopped as the UN High Commissioner for Refugees (UNHCR) complained that Bangladesh was using force to send the Rohingyas back home. The alleged forcible deportations on 20 July 1997 sparked violence in refugee camps and protest lodged on 23 July 1997 from the UNHCR to Bangladesh Foreign Minister Abdus Samad Azad. This has forced Bangladesh authorities to postpone the repatriation once again. But the State

Minister for Foreign Affairs of Bangladesh, Abul Hasan Chowdhury, assured UNHCR that Rohingya refugees, residing in two camps in Cox's Bazar, would not be repatriated forcibly.[19] In a press briefing on 1 August 1997 Foreign Minister of Bangladesh Abdus Samad Azad declared that Bangladesh would not allow remaining 21,000 refugees to settle in the country. He added that "lot of vested interests has been created centering the refugees," the Minister said without elaborating.[20] But Bangladesh cannot allow such permanent settlement.

There was another view that in the name of relief distribution, some beneficiary NGOs and even high-paid UNHCR officials were trying to delay the repatriation process for their own interests. Some western countries were also trying to keep the Rohingya problem alive with a view to using it against the present government of Myanmar.[21] Myanrnar's Foreign Minister's visit during 15-17 April 1998 did not make it clear when the Myanmar government would take back the rest of the Rohingya refugees. The Foreign Minister of Myanmar said that he had not come to Bangladesh with specific issues except bilateral discussion on various issues.[22]

The second push in 1991 saw more refugees flowing than the first one. The process of refugee repatriation in the second round seemed to be very complicated as there was growing reluctance of the refugees to go back to Arakan. Uninterrupted supply of food and shelter in camps by different humanitarian agencies and UNHCR also lured the refugees to stay back in Arakan. Secondly, "some fundamentalist Islamic groups were fanning the no return sentiment among the refugees to try to create an independent Arakan state for the Rohingyas through insurgency. The discussion on repatriation of the remaining 21,000 refugees is still going on at the bilateral level.[23]

The stranded refugees had given rise to situations related to the conflict, tension and insecurity in the border areas, both in relation to internal as well as external security. Regarding internal security, the presence of thousands refugees created conditions of destabilisation and disruption of political, economic, social and ecological systems in the border areas. The refugees found various ways to strained the law and order conditions in Cox's Bazar. Refugees have also shown the tendency to indulge crimes inside and outside the camps and created conflict with the local people. The refugees might have link with fundamentalist groups to gain petty political interest and with local underworld in trafficking drugs, arms and women. Renegade Burmese communists and Arakan Liberation Army engaged in cultivating heroin in the remote areas of Thanchi thana of Bandarban district since 1980. Drug lords killed farmers and abducted a Thana Nirbahi Officer who went against their interest.[24] The refugees might had link with the drug barons and pose severe security threat.

It can be said that political relations have suffered due to Rohingya issue. Bangladesh has always been emphasizing to resolve the issue peacefully. However, Myanmar has not given encouraging postures.[25]

ECONOMIC RELATIONS

A huge potential exists between Bangladesh and Myanmar to enhance trade and economic cooperation between the two countries. There is no denying the fact that Rohingya issue affected the economic relations. But it could not affect the overall economic cooperation between the two countries. However, the trade between the two countries did not develop to its desired level. It is due to Myanmar's severe shortage of foreign exchange and pattern of trade between the two countries developed on the basis of a single commodity exchange - Myanmar's rice for Bangladesh's jute. Bangladesh was dependent on Burma for rice to meet the country's food deficit while, Bangladesh exported jute products, newsprint and paper to Myanmar. The two countries concluded a trade agreement on 23 March 1972 under which Bangladesh imported rice from Burma and exported jute products, newsprint and paper. For expansion of trade relations, a general Trade Agreement was also signed on 3 August 1973 during the visit of Bangladesh trade delegation led by the then Commerce Minister AHM Kamruzzaman to Myanmar. The Agreement provided the general basis for trade between the two countries in any convertible currency.[26] Both countries agreed to treat each other as most favoured nation with regard to custom procedures, tariff, taxes and charges.

Table - 1
Bangladesh- Myanmar Trade (Million US $)

Year	*Export*	*Import*	*Balance*
1990-91	0.19	0.30	(-) 0.11
1991-92	0.58	0.13	(+) 0.45
1992-93	6.73	2.48	(+) 4.25
1993-94	10.36	6.67	(+) 3.69
1994-95	4.24	8.98	(-) 4.74
1995-96	3.33	3.37	(-) 0.04
1996-97	3.45	3.8	(+) 0.37
1997-98	1.39	12.39	(-) 11
Total	30.27	38.12	(-) 7.85

***Source*:**. Yunus Ali Sheikh, 'Bangladesh-Myanmar Relations', BIISS *Journal, Vol.* 19, No. 4,1998.

The table-1 gives a comparative picture of trade relations between Bangladesh and Myanmar. Between 1990 to 1998, the aggregate export figure from Bangladesh to Myanmar was US$ 30.27 million. During the same period, the import was US$ 38.12 million. Thus Myanmar enjoyed a relative trade surplus during this period. Looking at the year-wise trade figure, the table shows that in the first four years export increased in absolute terms. Similarly during the last four years, it declined in the same manner. On the other hand, during the first four years import has increased in absolute terms and declined in the same manner during the last four years. The cause of the trend may be attributed to the political relations between the two countries. It is clear from the table that overall export-import between Bangladesh and Myanmar did not give any steady picture. It may be noted that the export trade in the year 1997-98 did not include border trade.

BORDER TRADE

The post-independence trade agreement shows Bangladesh's eagerness to develop close relations with Myanmar. A Border Trade Agreement was signed in Dhaka on 18 May 1994 as both the governments agreed to develop trade in border areas on the basis of equality and mutual benefit. The agreement was signed between the then Bangladesh Commerce Minister M. Shamsul Islam and Myanmar's Trade Minister Lt. Gen. Tun Kyi. The formal opening of border trade between Myanmar and Bangladesh was inaugurated on 5 September 1995 at Teknaf and Maungdaw. The opening was jubilantly welcomed by local inhabitants of both sides of the Naaf river.

There were nine Articles in the agreement which provided the general basis for border trade between the two countries. In connection with implementation of Border Trade Agreement between the two countries, a Bangladesh trade delegation led by Commerce Secretary visited Myanmar during 2-5 July 1995. To implement the Border Trade Agreement, a banking arrangement was signed between the Sonali Bank of Bangladesh and the Myanmar Investment and Commercial Bank of Myanmar on 31 May 1995.[27] Bangladesh also made an arrangement with Myanmar regarding the opening of representative offices of the National Bank and the Arab Bangladesh Bank in Yangon.

During the visit in Yangon on 28-30 October 1996, Industry and Commerce Minister of Bangladesh , Tofael Ahmed, said that with the opening of the offices of the representatives of these three banks, the border trade between the two countries would gain momentum. Myanmar is a country of huge mineral resources and forestry, the Minister said adding that there was ample opportunity to develop bilateral economic cooperation between the two countries.[28] The Myanmar government had shown interest in importing fertilizer, pesticides, leather goods, jute goods, pharmaceutical, cosmetics, ceramics and textiles. For their part, they were willing to export bamboo and limestone for paper mills and cement factories.

In order to increase volume of trade between the two countries, the first Bangladesh Single Country Trade Exhibition was held in Myanmar in March 1995 and second Exhibition was held on 24 May 1996. In March 1995, Minister for Commerce of Bangladesh paid a visit to Myanmar in connection with First

Bangladesh Trade Exhibition. Products displayed in the fair were pharmaceutical, artificial flower, specialized leathers, electric cables, copper wire, toiletries (cosmetics), ceramic (melamine) products, tooth brush, different types of bags and other handicrafts, sanitary ware (fittings), artificial leather, grameen check, tea, biscuits etc. Many businessmen from Bangladesh took part in the Exhibition and displayed their products. Myanmar importers were made aware of the diversified exportable products of Bangladesh that they had been ignorant. Many trade enquiries were received and importers of Myanmar showed keen interest in melamine products, tea, sanitary ware, biscuit, cosmetics, handicrafts, ball pen, tooth brush etc. In the interest of expanding trade, Bangladeshi traders should be encouraged to utilize the new avenue for purchasing goods from Myanmar and selling goods to Myanmar as Myanmar government prefers to deal with private parties in the field of trade.

RECENT TRENDS IN BANGLADESH-MYANMAR RELATIONS

Bangladesh and Myanmar on 17 December 2002 agreed to set up two committees to study feasibility of establishing a direct road link between the two countries. The agreement was reached at formal talks between Prime Minister of Bangladesh Begum Khaleda Zia and visiting Head of State of Myanmar Senior General Than Shwe at the Prime Minister's Office in Dhaka. At the end of the talks, the two sides signed an MOU stipulating meetings alternately in the two capitals between their Foreign Ministers and Foreign Ministry officials for quicker decisions on urgent issues. They also signed a protocol to strengthen bilateral cultural cooperation. The two sides agreed to increase bilateral trade, simplify border trade and hold negotiations to develop coastal shipping to facilitate bilateral trade promotion.

Such visits and talks, held in cordial and frank atmosphere and "laid the foundation for a new era of cooperation" between the two neighbours. The Myanmar leaders also emphasised to simplify visa formalities for Bangladeshi traders and also to facilitate their stay in Myanmar for the purpose at least for six months. They also agreed to consider the request to allow Bangladeshi businessmen to go up to Sitte.[29] General Than Shwe, Chairman of Myanmar Peace and Development Council and Prime Minister, responded positively to Begum Zia's request to take back remaining Rohingya refugees through negotiations between officials of the two sides. The Myanmar leader assured that the refugee issue would be settled as soon as possible. The refugee issue, he said, was not "a key issue" but an issue as could be between any two neighbouring countries now focused more on boosting economic, cultural, diplomatic and political ties.[30] Bangladesh described the talks "very fruitful," and a new course of cooperation for mutual benefits.

Prime Minister of Bangladesh Begum Khaleda Zia visited Myanmar during 19-20 March 2003 to discuss bilateral and economic relations with Myanmar. During the visit, both countries agreed to talk directly over telephone for easy official communication, whenever needed to maintain good and cordial relations. Both Bangladesh and Myanmar agreed on the direct diplomacy for welfare of the people of the two countries.[31]

They agreed on 19 March 2003 to establish road link between Dhaka and Yangon for easy communications and strengthening people-to-people contact in a landmark development in the relations between the two next-door neighbours. The road was to be named as "Bangladesh - Myanmar Friendship Road".[32] This major decision was reached at the official talks between Prime Minister of Bangladesh Begum Khaleda Zia and Myanmar Prime Minister and SPDC Chairman Than Shwe. At the talks the two sides also approved the signing of two MOUs on Account, Trade and establishment of Joint Trade Commission aimed at bolstering bilateral economic cooperation. The MOUs were signed by Bangladesh Commerce Minister Amir Khosru Mahmud Chowdhury and Myanmar's Commerce Minister Brigadier General Pyi Sone, in presence of the two Premiers at the parliament building Pyithu Hiuttaw. Another MOU on Coastal Shipping was signed on 20 March 2003. Both leaders discussed "entire gamut" of bilateral relations, with economic cooperation figuring high. During the talks, the Myanmar Prime Minister billed Bangladesh leader Begum Khaleda Zia's visit as a milestone and said that it would open a new chapter in Bangladesh-Myanmar bilateral relations.[33]

The three-day Dhaka Conference of the Border Security Forces of Myanmar and Bangladesh concluded on 22 May 2003 with the signing of a Joint Record of Discussions. During the meeting at top-level, BDR tabled various important issues relating to border problems with their counterpart the Immigration Headquarters of Myanmar. BDR chief Major General Jahangir Alam Chowdhury and Director General of Myanmar Immigration Headquarters U Maung Htay led the respective side in the talks. During the meeting, the two sides signed the JRD paving the way for holding such conferemce in every six months to resolve the border problems. The issues of cross-border smuggling, Bangladesh fishermen's problems while fishing in the Bay of Bengal and holding of commander-level flag meetings between the two border forces came up in their discussions. They also discussed the issues of repatriation of innocent trespassers, exchanging lists of detained citizens and other bilateral problems of two countries.

Bangladesh and Myanmar on 25 September 2005 agreed to enhance bilateral trade, including ensuring adequate supply of onion from Myanmar to Bangladesh ahead of the holy month of Ramzan.[34] The agreement was reached when the visiting Member of Myanmar State Peace and Development Council (SPDC) and Chief of General Staff General Thura Shwe Mann called on Prime Minister Begum Khaleda Zia at her office in Dhaka on 25 September 2005. General Thura, who was leading a 31-member high-powered official delegation to Bangladesh, assured Begum Zia that the on-going repatriation of the remaining 21,000 Rohingya refugees in Cox's Bazar would be expedited. The two sides laid stress on completing construction of the road on Asian highway along the Bangladesh-Myanmar border soon. Bangladesh will construct 23-kilometre road from Gundam to Buthidong. The Prime Minister of Bangladesh and the

Myanmar SPDC member also agreed to enhance trade and commerce between the two next door neighbors along with improving the road communication system.

Begum Zia said Bangladesh and Myanmar are close neighbours and good friends. Bangladesh gives importance to its relations with Myanmar, and Myanmar can import quality consumer goods, including ceramics and medicines from Bangladesh. Zia referred to natural resources of the two neighbouring countries and said that the people of both countries would be benefited if they can work together.[35] Gen. Thura appreciated Bangladesh success in various sectors, including making Dhaka city pollution free, green and clear. He also lauded the quality of education and training in the institutions of Bangladesh armed forces and performance of Bangladeshi soldiers in the UN peace missions.[36] The Myanmar SPDC member further apprised the Prime Minister of Bangladesh to reestablish democracy in his country.

BANGLADESH-BHUTAN RELATIONS

Bangladesh and Bhutan, two of the South Asian countries, became active members of the international community in the beginning of 1970s. In 1971, Bangladesh emerged as an independent state. The same year, Bhutan became a member of the United Nations. Both, Bangladesh and Bhutan, are situated in the East-North-eastern part of South Asia. They are close neighbours, but separated by a strip of Indian territory.

Cordial and stable relations between Bangladesh and Bhutan are of recent origin. Historically, there has hardly been any long-standing or meaningful contact between the peoples of the two countries. However, the developments of 1971 served as the turning point in the history of relations between them. Bhutan had extended wholehearted support to Bangladesh during her War of Liberation in 1971. Bhutan was the second country after India to officially recognised Bangladesh on 7 December 1971 -at the most critical juncture of Bangladesh's history. Since then, cordial relations between Bangladesh and Bhutan have always been considered by them to be mutually beneficial, both politically and economically.

POLITICAL RELATIONS

In some respects, Bangladesh and Bhutan are asymmetrical partners. Bangladesh is a large country with an area of 147570 sq. km. and a population of about 141 million.[37] As comparison to Bangladesh, Bhutan is a much smaller country with an area of 47 thousand sq. km. and a population of only 697 thousand according to 2004 estimates.[38] The asymmetry is not confined only to size and population. For centuries, the inward-looking people of Bhutan were living in isolation on their land. Their exposure to the outside world was limited to Tibet and adjacent Indian territories. Even after 1971, when Bhutan became a member of the United Nations, its external relations were virtually confined to India alone. On the other hand, Bangladesh's exposure to the outside world in terms of political contacts, trade relations, cultural exchange and demographic movement covers a period that spread over several millennia.

The relations between Bangladesh and Bhutan developed steadily and rather rapidly, particularly by Bhutanese standard. While Bangladesh's interest in gaining Bhutan's support is understandable, Bhutan's interest in supporting the cause of Bangladesh needs some elaboration. As it appears, Bhutan's decision to recognise Bangladesh during the critical time of December 1971 was not simply motivated by its treaty obligations with India that require Bhutan to closely coordinate its foreign policy on the basis of New Delhi's foreign policy preferences. Bhutan's decision was also prompted by the consideration of its own long-standing interests. Bhutan could realise that the emergence of Bangladesh was inevitable and the new country would play an important role in South Asia, its strategic location, size, population and economy being significant factors. It perceived that a friendly Bangladesh, in addition to a friendly India, would be of great help to it in developing trade and commerce. As a landlocked country, it saw the advantage of an other outlet.[39]

In more concrete terms, a closer association with Bangladesh would strengthen Bhutan's political and diplomatic position and add significant leverage in exercising her independence. Economic calculations also played an important role in Bhutan's decision. In this regard, expectations for the development of trade relations were a significant point. While trade would be on a modest scale initially, potential for further expansion was considered. Bangladesh was seen as an alternative and easily accessible market and a source of supply that would allow the country to diversify its trade relations which were exclusively with India. Bangladesh was also viewed as a possible outlet of trade with the rest of the world through its two major seaports-Chittagong and Mongla. Thus, Bhutan came to consider her prospective relationship with Bangladesh as being important politically, economically and psychological ly.[40] It is in this backdrop that Bangladesh became a logical choice as the second country after India with which Bhutan established formal diplomatic relations.

The Foreign Minister of Bhutan, Lyonpo Dawa Tsering, paid an official visit to Bangladesh during 15-20 April 1972. Shamsul Huq, the then Minister for Local Government, Rural Development and Cooperatives of Bangladesh, led a delegation to Bhutan in August 1972. In early 1973, formal diplomatic relations were established between Bangladesh and Bhutan with the exchange of diplomatic representatives.

The then President of Bangladesh, Muhammadullah, paid an official visit to Thimpu during 1-5 June 1974 to attend the coronation of the King of Bhutan, Jigme Singye Wangchuck.[41]

Bangladesh-Bhutan relations made a qualitative shift towards closer contacts in January 1980 when both the countries decided to set up diplomatic missions in each other's capitals and exchange resident Ambassadors. It was a significant move, particularly on the part of Bhutan. Because, apart from its mission in New Delhi, Bhutan's mission in Dhaka was the second one. It reflected the importance that Bhutan accorded to its relations with Bangladesh. Subsequently, exchange of visits between the two countries, including at the highest levels, became a regular feature of bilateral relations between the two neighbours. During the period following the formation of SAARC, contacts between the two countries became more frequent and more purposeful.

ECONOMIC RELATIONS

The development of closer economic cooperation between Bangladesh and Bhutan has been one of the major goals that both the countries intended to pursue in their bilateral relations. As early as in April 1972, during the visit of Bhutanese Foreign Minister to Bangladesh, the leaders of both the countries expressed their desire to develop bilateral trade. They also thought of developing water resources through joint ventures.[42] In practice, however, the initiation of economic cooperation between the two countries proved to be a highly difficult undertaking. Its development remains still quite problematic with vast unused potentials.

TRADE AND TRANSIT ISSUES

On 8 September 1980, two agreements on trade and transit were signed between Bangladesh and Bhutan in Thimpu.

Initially valid for ten years, the trade agreement would be renewed for a period of another ten years. Both the countries agreed to accord to each other the most favoured nations (MFN) treatment in respect of trade.[43] According to the agreement, Bhutan could export to Bangladesh dolomite, gypsum, dust coal, slate, graphite, copper and timber products, cardamom, gum, resin, ginger and dry chillies, orange and apple. The list of goods for Bangladesh to export to Bhutan included items such as, newsprint, jute products, leather and leather products, chemicals and detergents, betel leaves, tea, tobacco, pharmaceuticals and medicine.[44] The terms of the trade agreement were quite liberal and mutually beneficial.

The trade agreement, however, remained ineffective for a rather long time because of India's lack of preparedness to provide overland transit facilities. Bhutan made persistent attempts to secure the transit facility through India in order to develop trade relations with Bangladesh. New Delhi took the position that it had some technical difficulties in providing the transit facility to Bhutan.[45] The policy continued even after India's signing of two agreements, one with Bhutan in December 1983 and the other with Bangladesh in January 1984, which provided transit facility. India provided transit route through its territory for the conduct of Bangladesh-Bhutan trade in 1987.

Trade between Bangladesh and Bhutan had been very slow in picking up and the problem of transit was not the only hurdle. Though close neighbours, Bangladesh and Bhutan were unfamiliar with each other. However, they continued their efforts with a view to developing the trade relations. During the visit of King Jigme Singye Wangchuck of Bhutan to Bangladesh in February 1984, two accords were signed between the two countries. These were: (a) The Protocol on Expansion and Regulation of Trade; and (b)

Agreement on Economic and Cultural Co-operation.[46] The officials of the two countries met in January 1985. After reviewing the latest status and implementation of the trade agreement of 1980, both sides agreed to increase the number of items that could be traded.[47] Again in March 1985, the Bhutanese Minister for Trade, Industry and Forest, Prince Namgyel Wangchuck, met Air Vice-Marshal Sultan Mahmud, Bangladesh Minister for Industry, Commerce, Jute and Textile, in Dhaka. The meeting reviewed the whole gamut of trade relationship between the two countries. Both the sides agreed that the existing friendly relations between the two countries had not been reflected in the sphere of trade and commerce, and stressed the need for increased cooperation.[48] Nonetheless, the trade relations between Bangladesh and Bhutan continued to remain one of exploratory nature.

However, there was a rather radical change during the late 1980s. Mainly two factors could be identified as the driving force behind this transformation. First, in 1986, both the countries decided to exempt all taxes, levies and duties on the goods to be traded between the two countries. Second, India, at last, decided to permit Bhutan to use the most convenient Burimari-Chengrabandha route for its trade with Bangladesh with effect from January 1988. With the opening of the Burimari-Chengrabandha route, Bangladesh- Bhutan trade increased more than fifty times just in one year. Bhutan's export to Bangladesh increased from Tk.2.10 million in 1986-87 to Tk.105.80 million in 1987-88. In 1988-89, it stood at Tk. 248.90 million. Despite some fluctuations and decline in Bhutan's export to Bangladesh, in 1993-94, it stood at Tk.327.60 million. Against this, Bangladesh's export to Bhutan remained stagnant in between Tk.3.26 million and Tk.8.92 million during the whole period since 1988-89 to 1995-96 (Table-2). In other words, Bangladesh-Bhutan trade became a one-way traffic. Only Bhutanese export to Bangladesh has increased dramatically, while Bangladeshi export to Bhutan remained stagnant at a meargre amount.

Bangladesh has time and again emphasised to the Bhutanese side the need for boosting its imports from Bangladesh with a view to bridging the existing imbalance in bilateral trade. Bhutan is very much aware of the fact that it earns foreign exchange from tourism and her exports to Bangladesh alone. So, Thimpu's stakes in the continuation of its trade relations with Bangladesh are quite high. While the Bhutanese side has repeatedly expressed its keen desire to remove the trade imbalance with Bangladesh, Thimpu still remains far from initiating any serious and effective measure in this regard. Persisting severe imbalance in trade between Bangladesh and Bhutan has grossly undermined the mutuality of interests in bilateral cooperation. It remains the single-most important obstacle in the way of further development of trade.

Table-2
Bangladesh-Bhutan Trade (Millions US $)

Year	*Export from Bangladesh*	*Import into Bangladesh*
1986-1987	-	.30
1987-88	-	2.10
1988-89	3.26	105.80
1989-90	5.16	248.90
1990-91	5.54	167.50
1991-92	8.15	165.00
1992-93	8.92	88.30
1993-94	4.50	327.60
1994-95	8.60	88.90
1995-1996	7.87	211.80

Source : A.K.M. Abdus Sabur, 'Bangladesh-Bhutan Relations, *BIISS Journal, Vol.* 19, No. 1, 1998

TECHNICAL AND CULTURAL COOPERATION

Bangladesh has always been keen to develop technical and cultural cooperation with Bhutan. In this regard, a commitment was made to Bhutan that Bangladesh would provide, within its limited resources, whatever assistance needed by Bhutan in the field of education and technical training. Even without any formal agreement, a modest technical cooperation with Bhutan was initiated by Bangladesh during the early 1980s. Accordingly, some Bhutanese students came to study in Bangladesh on Bangladesh government's scholarship.[49] In February 1984, during the visit of the King of Bhutan to Bangladesh, an agreement on Economic and Technical Cooperation was signed between the two countries. A good number of students received education regularly in Bangladesh. Bangladesh offers every year a total of 34 seats to the Bhutanese students in different institutions in a variety of fields, including medicine and engineering.

The Air Service Agreement between Bangladesh and Bhutan was signed on 4 June 1986. The agreement provided for air services between and beyond the respective territories of the two countries. From October 1987, the Druk Air had started operation between Paro and Dhaka.

An agreement on Cultural Cooperation was signed between Bangladesh and Bhutan on 4 June 1986. However, cultural exchange between the two countries remained a very rare incident. Bhutanese Minister for Cultural Affairs visited Bangladesh at the invitation of his Bangladeshi counterpart in November 1993 during the Sixth Asian Biennial Art Exhibition.

COOPERATION IN THE DEVELOPMENT OF WATER RESOURCES AND JOINT VENTURES IN INDUSTRY

Bangladesh and Bhutan considered cooperation in the field of the development of water resources through joint ventures as an objective even in 1972. However, for a quite long time, they undertook no initiative to this direction. Only in October 1988, during the visit of the then President of Bangladesh, H.M. Ershad to Bhutan, an initiative aimed at cooperation in the field of water resources development, flood control in particular, was undertaken. Accordingly, a Joint Team of Officials on Flood Control was established. The Joint Team of Officials met three times - in January 1989 (Dhaka), in August 1989 (Thimpu) and in December 1989, again in Dhaka - and finalised the report for submission to the governments of the two countries. The Team recommended, *inter-alia,* co-operation in flood forecasting and warning, in hydrometeorology and setting up of an institutional framework for follow-up of the recommendations. As it appears, there had been no progress in the matter. More importantly, the vast potential for the joint management and development of water resources could not even be considered by the two sides.

Bhutan possesses huge quantities of untapped mineral and forest resources suitable for joint ventures in cement, railway sleepers, paper and pulp and a host of other mineral based and agro-based industries. In this regard, mutually beneficial joint venture between the two countries is feasible. It is particularly because of the fact that there exist remarkable complementarities between the two countries in terms of the supply of raw materials and manpower, production as well as marketing, in the regions as well as outside. Bhutan also has vast potentials for generating hydro-electricity. Increasing demand for electricity in Bangladesh and India, and the financial and ecological cost involved with the production of electricity using fossil fuel in these countries, are also creating a vast market for the product. As a mater of fact, Bhutanis potential for generating hydro-electricity as well as its demand in India and

Bangladesh would be so vast that it could make Bhutan what oil made Kuwait.

RECENT TRENDS IN BANGLADESH-BHUTAN RELATIONS

During the meeting between Prime Minister of Bangladesh Begum Khaleda Zia and Bhutanese Prime Minister Lyonpo Khandu Wangchuck at 11th SAARC Summit in the Napalese capital Kathmandu in January 2002, the two leaders termed the existing relationship between the two countries as excellent. On the issue of trade, Bangladesh Prime Minister urged Bhutan to import more products from Bangladesh, including pharmaceuticals to reduce trade imbalance which is presently in favour of Bhutan. The Bhutanese Prime Minister urged his Bangladeshi counterpart to give more tariff concession for his country's products. He also urged Begum Zia to create scope for the study of more Bhutanese students in Bangladesh.[50]

The government of Bangladesh approved a proposal to renew the trade agreement with amendments to the previous one and the related protocol on 28 April 2003.[51] The two countries had signed a trade agreement in 1980 and the protocol in 1984, both of which expired in September 2000. But export and import between the two sides continued on the basis of mutual understanding. However, a Commerce Secretary-level meeting between the two countries in November 2002 sought renewal of the expired agreement and protocol with certain amendments. Accordingly, a draft of the agreement and the protocol was prepared with a consensus between the two countries.

The Bhutanese Ambassador to Bangladesh Dasha Jigme Tshultim and State Minister for Civil Aviation of Bangladesh Mir Mohammad Nasir Uddin in July 2005 took a decision for direct air service between Dhaka and Thimpu.[52] Both the countries also agreed to launch a direct flight operation of Druk Air between Thimpu and Chittagong, the commercial capital and port city of Bangladesh. The Bhutanese airliner will later be given the flight operation opportunity up to Cox's Bazar, the longest sea beach in the world.

BANGLADESH–NEPAL RELATIONS

It is evident that Geography played an important role in shaping Bangladesh-Nepal relations. Both Bangladesh and Nepal form part of the Indian subcontinent and are separated from each other by a seventeen mile long strip of the Indian territory. This geographical proximity with Bangladesh is important for Nepal because of the fact that Nepal is a landlocked country and India alone provides sea-route to it. Bangladesh can provide an alternative sea-route to Nepal.[53] The geographical location of the two countries has put certain limitations in their foreign policies. Both, Nepal and Bangladesh are linked with India.[54] Both smaller countries always feels closeness vis-a-vis India's much larger size, population and resources. Both, these countries have clear understanding to pressurise India.[55]

However, Nepal is surrounded on three sides by the Indian territory. Its border with India is open and without any natural barrier. Both the countries have deep socio-cultural links. Majority of Nepal's trade is with or through India. It receives a large amount of aid from India. A large chunk of Nepalese population is employed in India. Bangladesh on the other hand, is surrounded by the Indian territory from three sides. Economically and politically Bangladesh is a weak country to pose any threat to India's security. Yet, political instability and behaviour of governments in Bangladesh causes indirect economic and security problems for India. The infiltration of Bangladeshi people into the Indian territory is a serious problem. Another important problem is the distribution of water resources. It has been a major source of tension between the two countries. In the extent of geo□political conditions Bangladesh and Nepal cannot ignore India while developing their mutual relationship. In fact, they have to establish their relations within these geo-political limitations.

Need for greater economic cooperation is the other important factor which determines Bangladesh-Nepal relations. Both Bangladesh and Nepal have underdeveloped economies, largely dependent on foreign aid and not complimentary to each other. Yet, there are certain areas where they can cooperate with each other for mutual economic benefits. A large part of the Himalayan river system originates in Nepal and enter into Bangladesh after crossing India. These rivers can be tapped for the purpose of irrigation, hydro-power generation, navigation and food control through mutual cooperation.

Bangladesh also provides opportunity for Nepal's trade diversification. Before 1971 Nepal's trade with Pakistan was largely confined to the East Pakistan region. Nepal had concluded a Trade Agreement with Pakistan in 1962. The emergence of Bangladesh as an independent nation in 1971 widened prospects for increasing trade relations between the two countries. Bangladesh can also provide an alternative sea□route to Nepal for its overseas trade. The deep rooted socio-cultural connection had also been an important factor in the development of bilateral relations between Bangladesh and Nepal. The social and cultural interaction between the people of the two countries had been there much before the emergence of Bangladesh.

DEVELOPMENT OF BILATERAL RELATIONS

In January 1972, Nepal formally recognized Bangladesh. The emergence of Bangladesh was considered as an unavoidable political reality.[56] Both the countries showed keen interest in coming close to each other. Bangladesh first took steps in this regard. In June 1972, nearly after five months of Nepal's formal recognition, Bangladesh Foreign Minister paid a visit to Nepal. This indeed, marked the beginning of bilateral relations between the two countries. In a joint communique issued at the end of the visit, leaders of the two countries emphasized the need for regional cooperation .[57] It also indicated possibilities of concluding a trade treaty in order to resume trade relations.

The visit of Bangladesh Foreign Minister was reciprocated by the Foreign Minister of Nepal in January 1973. During his visit both the countries expressed their desire to strengthen friendly and neighbourly relations. Both adhered to the policy of nonalignment and peaceful coexistence. These visits not only showed that both Bangladesh and Nepal wanted to come closer to each other, but also reflected the identitv of interest of the two countries.

The coup de'at of August 1975 in Bangladesh marked a shift in Bangladesh foreign policy. Although the new regime declared continuation of the fundamental principles of foreign policy laid down by late Sheikh Mujib, yet, certain changes were apparent in its operation. Bangladesh relations started deteriorating after 1975. It was alleged that Bangladesh had become an innocent victim of a big power-India. In the wake of anti-Indian tirade in the post-coup period, Bangladesh found it an urgent necessity to strengthen relations with other smaller neighbouring countries of the region.

On the other hand, Nepal also had strained relations with India on the issue of Sikkim's merger with the Indian Union and wanted to come closer to Bangladesh. Nepal showed promptness in recognizing the new regime in Bangladesh and in March 1976 appointed its first resident Ambassador in Bangladesh.

The closeness between Bangladesh and Nepal was apparent when king Birendra proposed Nepal as a zone of peace to seek international cooperation for Nepal's security. The then President of Bangladesh Ziarur Rahman during his visit to Kathmandu in December 1977 welcomed Nepalese proposal. Again, on the occasion of King Birendra's visit to Dhaka in January 1978, President Zia stressed on the need for declaring the region as well as whole of the Indian Ocean a peace zone.[58] The government of Bangladesh reaffirmed its support to Nepal's 'peace zone' proposal during Bangladesh Foreign Minister's visit to Nepal in January 1979,[59] and King Birendra's visit to Bangladesh in March 1980. A new dimension was added to Bangladesh and Nepal relations with King Birendra's visit to Dhaka in

March 1980. The leaders of the two countries gave importance to peace and stability in the region and reaffirmed their faith in the policy of nonalignment.[60] Nepal supported Bangladesh election to non-permanent Asian seat in the Security Council, and also its membership in the other international organizations.[61] In November 1982, President Ershad of Bangladesh paid a state visit to Nepal which was reciprocated by Nepal's Prime Minister in February 1983.[62] These visits indeed, further strengthened relations between the two countries.

ECONOMIC RELATIONS

Bangladesh and Nepal have enough potential for economic cooperation particularly in the field of trade and commerce and the exploitation of water resources. As a first step towards mutual economic cooperation, Nepal agreed to supply 15,000 tones of rice in 1973, when Bangladesh was faced with acute food shortage.[63] As a goodwill gesture Bangladesh, later on agreed to supply hundred tones of paper to overcome newsprint paper shortage in Nepal.

Bangladesh and Nepal first concluded a treaty of trade and transit in 1976. Although the expansion of trade between the two countries depended on India's permission to use the intervening West Bengal territory for the two way transit, yet, it opened prospects for Bangladesh and Nepal trade.[64]

In this regards, the separate trade and transit treaties between India and Nepal further widened the scope for Nepal's trade with Bangladesh which were signed in 1978. Regarding transit facilities to Nepal, provisions were laid down in the treaty that their trade route will not depend through India but they might be explore other transit route. Soon after signed the treaty, Nepal established a transit liason office at Chittagong to handle its exports and imports from overseas countries via Bangladesh.[65] In 1980 the Nepalese government agreed to establish a telephone link between Kathmandu and Dhaka with a view to provide facilities to traders. Nepal's major exports to Bangladesh are pulses, railway sleepers and rice and imports are office equipment, stationery, paper, etc.

Bangladesh and Nepal established a Joint Economic Commission in 1978 to search out the possible areas of economic cooperation between the two countries. The need for such commission had first been realized during King Birendra's visit to Dhaka in January 1978. The commission decided for a six monthly review of the economic cooperation between the two countries in its meeting which was held in Dhaka in January 1982. It also decided to expand trade, technical and economic cooperation between the two countries. In January 1982, Nepal also concluded an agreement with Bangladesh to establish a jute mill in Nepal on joint venture basis.[66]

At the time of Nepalese Premier's visit to Dhaka in 1983, it was decided to launch a time bound programme to undertake projects in areas such as industry, agriculture, trade, telecommunication and technical cooperation. Both the countries also emphasized upon the promotion of group tourism between them. Nepal promptly endorsed Bangladesh proposal for regional cooperation in South Asia further enhanced scope for economic cooperation between the two countries.

RECENT TRENDS IN BANGLADESH-NEPAL RELATIONS

Prime Minister of Bangladesh Begum Khaleda Zia visited Kathmandu as SAARC Chairman in 1995. In the ninth JEC meeting which was held in August 1995 the two countries agreed to enhance their annual trade which was $10 million at that time. Nepal-Bangladesh to and fro transit facility granted by India through its territory in September 1997 further boosted their bilateral trade. In its trial phase of six months, India allowed transit facilities through Kakarbhita-Phulbari-Banglabandhu route for two days in a week. After expiry of the trial period, New Delhi agreed in April 1998, to simplify the transit formalities and to keep open the route for seven days a week. The tenth meeting of the Joint Economic Commission was held in March 1998 in which the two countries signed minutes for cooperation in different sectors.[67]

After the conclusion of 11 SAARC Summit in Kathmandu on 6 January 2002, Prime Minister of Bangladesh Begum Khaleda Zia and Prime Minister of Nepal Sher Bahadur Deuba held discussion on bilateral and possible regional cooperation in the fields of gas, flood control, water management and hydroelectricity. Begum Zia suggested the Nepalese Prime Minister to import more goods like jute, jute products, ceramics and melamine from Bangladesh.[68] Deuba urged Khaleda to consider tariff reduction on fruit and food items imported by Bangladesh[69] Nepal expressed gratitude for Bangladesh's cooperation in the higher education of

Nepalese students in Bangladesh and for training of Nepalese officers in Bangladesh Military Academy.

Bangladesh and Nepal signed a memorandum of understanding (MOU) on Air Service Agreement (ASA) on 23 May 2005. Chairman of Civil Aviation Authority of Bangladesh Air Commodore AKM Harun Chowdhury and Joint Secretary of the Ministry of Culture, Tourism and Civil Aviation of Nepal Yangya Prasad Goutam signed the MOU on behalf of their respective sides. Bangladesh Ambassador M Humayun Kabir and the senior government officials of Nepal, including Sushil Jang Bahadur Rana, Secretary of the Ministry of Culture, Tourism and Civil Aviation were also present during the signing ceremony.[70]

Under the MOU Bangladesh and Nepal agreed to expand frequency of air services between Bangladesh and Nepal. In order to promote the trade relations between the two countries and to facilitate third country trade, Bangladesh and Nepal have also agreed to introduce air freight services in two countries. Both sides also agreed to work together with a view to promoting economic interaction relating to air services. AKM Harun Chowdhury led the six-member Bangladesh delegation in the consultation meeting of ASA. A eight-member Nepalese delegation was led by Yangya Prasad Goutam.

BANGLADESH–SRI LANKA RELATIONS

When Bangladesh emerged as an independent state after nine months long Liberation War against the armed forces of the mother state Pakistan in 1971, with Indian help, Sri Lanka in no ambiguous terms made it known to the world that she was against the break up of Pakistan. This was amply demonstrated by her even when the struggle for liberation in the Eastern wing of Pakistan was going on. Sri Lanka had provided transit and refueling facilities to the West Pakistani military aircrafts for suppressing the revolt. She also did not vote with India on the Bangladesh issue in the United Nations.

The root cause of such a stand was Sri Lanka's own ethnic problems. If Sri Lanka supported Indian stand on Bangladesh's Liberation War, it might ignite Tamil problem in Sri Lanka. Therefore, Sri Lanka could not have adopted two standards-one for herself and another for India and Bangladesh. Consequently, Sri Lanka treated Bangladesh problem as an internal affair of Pakistan and she allowed transit facilities to Pakistan.[71]

On the other hand, the economic considerations also compelled Sri Lanka to take a stand in favour of Pakistan. By extending refuelling facilities to Pakistan war planes and allowing other PIA flights via Colombo, the country earned the much needed foreign exchange. It is on record that the turnover at the airport shops doubled during the Bangladesh war.[72] So far the trade of Sri Lanka with the undivided Pakistan was concerned, Pakistan was the largest buyer of copra. It is one of the six commonwealth countries which are Sri Lanka's biggest trading partner.[73] Obviously, Sri Lanka did not want to offend Pakistan with whom there was ample scope for enhancing tea trade. Therefore, Sri Lanka initially sided with Pakistan.

Meanwhile, Sri Lanka did not adopt a rigid and final stand on the issue of Bangladesh and offered her services to Pakistan President Yahya Khan in easing the Bangladesh crisis,[74] and later adopted strict neutrality in the Indo-Pak war of December 1971. She urged the Secretary General of the United Nations to use his good offices to end the conflict.[75] Without mincing words Bandarnaike stated, 'we are not prepared to take sides'.[76] She reiterated her stand during Indo-Pak war on 9 December 1971. In the beginning Sri Lanka refused to recognize the situation in East Pakistan as "liberation movement". Its delegates declared in the UN General Assembly that it would create a deadly precedent if

Sri Lanka recognized it as such. On 8 December 1971, Sri Lanka supported the resolution of Argentina calling for immediate ceasefire and withdrawal of troops. On this point the government faced severe criticism at home and issued a statement saying that the Sri Lankan delegates went against the government stand. Hence in the Security Council with special permission, the Sri Lankan delegates corrected his earlier statement and emphasized the need for political settlement which should precede the withdrawal of troops.[77]

After the surrender of the Pakistani troops, when Bangladesh became a reality and it was recognized by many nations, Sri Lanka did not make any haste in recognition to Bangladesh when Pakistan had threatened to sever diplomatic relations with the countries recognizing Bangladesh.[78] When the superpowers gave recognition to Bangladesh, Sri Lanka also did the same. However, till July 1978 Sri Lanka was only pondering over the question whether to open a resident mission in Bangladesh and finally in April 1979 W.A.S.E.C. Ranasinghe, a member of the ruling UNP of Sri Lanka was named as the first resident High Commissioner of Sri Lanka to Bangladesh.[79]

Meanwhile, the Sri Lankan President William Gopallawa was the first Head of state to pay an official visit to Dhaka in March 1977. Speaking on this important occasion, President Sayem of Bangladesh described the bilateral relations between Sri Lanka and Bangladesh that, "*Geographically we are neighbours, historically we are friends... ideological affinity has brought us into the fold of nonaligned movement.*[80] The Sri Lankan President expressed satisfaction on the development of "most cordial relations" between the two countries.[81]

Afterwards, both Bangladesh and Sri Lanka adopted similar stands on external affairs. There were common elements in their security perceptions. Both countries supported the issues of the Indian Ocean Peace Zone and the South Asia Nuclear Free Zone. They had similar viewpoints on Afghanistan and Kampuchea. They established resident missions in each other's capitals in the post-Mujib period. Since March 1977 when the Sri Lankan President William Gopallawa visited Dhaka there had been a number of exchanges of visits between the two countries which had further strengthened their bilateral relations. To strengthen bilateral relations, Bangladesh-Sri Lanka Joint Economic Commission (JEC) was set up in 1985.

Prime Minister of Bangladesh Begum Khaleda Zia visited Sri Lanka in 1991 to attend the SAARC Summit which was reciprocated by the Sri Lankan President Premdasa in 1992. During these visits, Bangladesh and Sri Lanka discussed the bilateral, economic and security issues of mutual interests. Begum Zia again visited Sri Lanka in January 1995 as SAARC Chairperson. Sri Lankan President Chandrika Bandaranaike Kumaratunga reciprocated the visit in March 1995.

During Kumaratunga's visit, the two states signed a three years cultural exchange programme for cultural and educational cooperation. Sri Lanka decided to increase the volume of jute goods import from Bangladesh. It expressed interest into joint ventures in fruit canning industry, vegetable and coconut plantation with Bangladesh.

RECENT TRENDS IN BANGLADESH–SRI LANKA RELATIONS

Prime Minister of Bangladesh Begum Khaleda Zia thanked Sri Lanka on 6 January 2002 at 11 SAARC Summit for keeping the process of SAARC alive despite many problems during the last three years of its chairmanship. Begum Zia praised the leadership of Sri Lankan President Chandrika Kumaratunga when she met her at hotel suite after the conclusion of 11 SAARC Summit at Kathmandu. Both leaders also discussed the gamut of bilateral and economic relations between Bangladesh and Sri Lanka. Begum Zia urged Kumaratunga to look into the possibilities of increasing imports from Bangladesh. Sri Lanka could import jute and jute goods from Bangladesh.[82] The Bangladeshi Prime Minister also requested the Sri Lankan President to take the initiative in reopening of Air Lanka flights between Colombo and Dhaka.[83]

Prime Minister of Bangladesh Khaleda Zia invited Sri Lankan entrepreneurs to avail themselves of investment opportunities and invest in different sectors of Bangladesh when she was talking to visiting Sri Lankan Foreign Minister Tyrrone Fernando on 17 April 2002 in Dhaka.[84] Sri Lanka showed interest in increasing imports of jute and jute goods from Bangladesh and discussed to improve tourism sector. Sri Lanka also wanted to participate in privatization programme of Bangladesh as Sri Lanka is opting for massive denationalization of state owned enterprises. The Sri Lankan Foreign Minister mentioned that a huge amount had invested by Sri Lankan investors in Bangladesh in various sectors, specially in jute, textile, paper and other manufacturing industries and Sri Lankan investors could utilise their experience and potential through investment in the trade sectors.[85]

CHANDRIKA KUMARATUNGA'S VISIT TO DHAKA

Sri Lankan President Chandrika Kumaratunga arrived in Dhaka on a two day official visit to Bangladesh on 19 April 2003. Kumaratunga's visit at the invitation of Prime Minister Khaleda Zia was the first official visit to Bangladesh by a Sri Lankan President since 1995. President of Bangladesh lajuddin Ahmed and Prime Minister Begum Zia received the Sri Lankan President at the airport. During the meeting, Bangladesh and Sri Lanka agreed to work more closely for the solidarity and progress of SAARC and billed it as an important event to beef up regional cooperation.[86]

Disclosing this to newsmen after the talks, Foreign Secretary of Bangladesh Sahamser Mobin Chowdhury said,[87] the two leaders held a more than hour-long official talks reviewing the entire gamut of bilateral relations and a wide range of international and regional issues including the SAARC. The issues of SAARC dominated the talks along with bilateral matters as the two leaders discussed plans for strengthening further the Dhaka-Colombo ties for mutual benefit and the South Asian cooperation for peace and progress for the region. Both leaders reaffirmed the centrality of the United Nations that constitute the bedrock of the international system in maintaining international peace and security.[88]

On the second day of the two-day visit of the Sri Lankan leader the two countries signed a protocol agreeing to hold a Foreign Secretary level meeting to be held once in Dhaka and once in Colombo as part of efforts for strengthening bilateral relations. The two leaders particularly discussed ways of economic developments through mutual cooperation keeping in mind that both Dhaka and Colombo sought foreign investments and have similar type of export basket. Begum Zia and Kumaratunga recognised the "increasingly important role being played by the private sectors of the two countries and agreed to give further impetus to their private sectors to enhance the overall volume of bilateral trade and investment".[89] The two leaders also agreed to expedite the signing of memorandum of understanding on long-term purchase of jute and jute goods by Sri Lanka from Bangladesh and encourage greater interactions between business leaders of the two countries.

Responding to a Bangladesh request, Sri Lanka agreed to reduce the existing duties on raw jute and jute goods on a unilateral and non-reciprocal basis within the SAPTA and

WTO framework and assured to simplify the registration process of Bangladesh pharmaceutical products exported to Sri Lanka.[90] Both leaders noted that significant progress could be made following the SAARC framework particularly in the work of the independent South Asian Commission on Poverty Alleviation and in finalising the Draft Treaty Framework on SAFTA. On ongoing peace process to end decades long bloody ethnic conflicts in Sri Lanka, Begum Zia said, *Bangladesh expected the solution to the prohlem keeping intact the Sri Lankan sovereignty at any cost.*[91]

Sri Lankan President Chandrika Kumaratunga on 13 April 2005 thanked the government and people of Bangladesh for the humanitarian assistance provided to the country in the aftermath of the last devasting Tsunami on 26 December 2004. Sri Lanka observed that such assistance is reflective of strength and warmth of bilateral relations between Bangladesh and Sri Lanka.[92] During Tsunami disastrous Bangladesh among other things dispatched rescue helicopters and naval ships to the affected areas of Sri Lanka. Bangladesh defence personnel took commendable part in the relief and rescue operations.

BANGLADESH–PAKISTAN RELATIONS

Bangladesh-Pakistan relations for obvious reasons have not been cordial. However, following the coup d'etat of 1975 and the establishment of military rule in Bangladesh the relationship between the two countries underwent a sea change. Pakistan viewed Bangladesh in the change context as an acceptable ally according to Pakistan's age-old policy of "brotherhood" and "special relations" with the Islamic countries. Thus a new chapter in the Bangla-Pak relationship opened. The 'special relation' and 'brotherhood' have been continuing since then despite occasional friction over the contentious issues like the 'repatriation of stranded Pakistanis' (Bihari Muslims) and the'sharing of assets'.

Both in Bangladesh and Pakistan, the restoration of democrative governments has further strengthened the continuing cordiality. Bangladesh people greeted the people of Pakistan on the successful conclusion of their movement for the restoration of democracy. The people of Pakistan also congratulated the people of Bangladesh when Banglaesh dismissed the military government of Ershad. Pakistan recognised Bangladesh during OIC Lahore Summit in February 1974. Pakistani Prime Minister Zulftkar Ali Bhutto visited Dhaka in June 1974 which could not result in the establishment of diplomatic relations due to divergent viewpoints of the two states, on the issue of the sharing of assets and the fate of the Bihari muslims who had opted for Pakistan, after the creation of Bangladesh. The succeeding government removed the condition of the settlement of the two disputes before starting diplomatic relations, and took initiative for establishing formal relations. The representatives of Bangladesh and Pakistan met in New York during the General Assembly session of UN in October 1975, and agreed to establish diplomatic relations. Bangladesh sent the first Ambassador to Pakistan in January 1976. Pakistan's Ambassador to Bangladesh reached Dhaka in the same month. Ziaur Rahman visited Islamabad in December 1977 during his tour to South Asian neighbours. During his visit he agreed to share liabilities along with assets. Pakistan agreed to repatriate 25,000 stranded Pakistanis.

Pakistani Foreign Minister Shahebzada Yaqub Khan visited Bangladesh in August 1983. He visited the national martyr's mausoleum at Savar, built in the memory of those killed by the Pakistan Army during Bangladesh Liberation war in 1971. Ziaul Haque's visit to Bangladesh was postponed due to his refusal to visit the mausoleum. He visited Bangladesh as a goodwill gesture when Bangladesh was hit by one of the worst cyclones in its history in 1985. His visit followed the visit of Rajiv Gandhi and Jayawardene. Ershad visited Pakistan in July 1986 as the first Chairman of SAARC. Pakistan agreed to complete repatriation of stranded pakistanis as soon as the fund required for rehabilitation was mobilised by Rabeta al-Alam al-Islami, a Saudi Arabia- based voluntary organization.[93] Benazir Bhutto as Prime Minister of Pakistan visited Dhaka in October 1989. She retreated from the commitment given by Ziaul Haque to take back the 'Biharis'. In 1990 the Foreign Minister of Pakistan Sahebzada Yaqub Khan and subsequently the Pakistani Chief of Staff General Aslam Baig visited Dhaka. However, these visits did not result in any remarkable progress in the bilateral relations.[94]

BANGLADESH–PAKISTAN RELATIONS UNDER H.M. ERSHAD

The President of Bangladesh Lt. General H.M. Ershad welcomed the democratically elected government of Benazir Bhutto and expressed optimism that like her predecessors, she would strive to strengthen bilateral relations. Owing to domestic pressures, specifically from her home province Sind, Benazir Bhutto discovered to her discomforts that it was not easy to resolve the issue of repatriation of 'Bihari Muslims'.[95] However, she reiterated that expeditious ameliorative steps would be taken. The assurance proved ineffective.

The issue of repatriation posed a serious domestic challenge for the Benazir government in Pakistan. On the one hand, opposition leaders and the then Punjab Chief Minister, Mian Nawaz Sharif, and the Mohajir Quami Movement (MQM) leader Altaf Hussain, criticised Benazir Bhutto for causing unnecessary delay in repatriation. On the other hand, Benazir had to face ire of various Sindhi nationalist organisations which were opposed to the repatriation of Bihari Muslims and expressed apprehensions about consequences of settling them in the Sindh province.[96]

BENAZIR'S BANGLADESH VISIT: RECIPROCITY REITERATED

During her visit to Bangladesh in October 1989, Benazir reiterated to resolve the issue of repatriation as soon as necessary financial arrangements were made and law and order were ensured in Sind province. At a banquet hosted by the Bangladesh President H.M. Ershad, she reaffirmed the resolve of the government and the people of Pakistan to consolidate cooperation and friendship with Bangladesh. She recalled the visit of her father, Zulfikar Ali Bhutto, to Bangladesh in 1974 and asserted, "Pakistan and Bangladesh were bound together by ties of religion, history and tradition. It was together that we launched a struggle for a separate Muslim identity ... over the years we have traversed a journey which at times was difficult, at times traumatic. But like two brothers who set up separate homes, we remained as members of the same family, each always caring about the future well-being and security of the other".[97]

President H.M. Ershad appreciated bold initiatives taken by Benazir and expressed satisfaction over Pakistan's reentry in the Commonwealth after a gap of seventeen years.[98] Welcoming the agreement between Pakistan and India against attack on each other's nuclear installations, Ershad hoped that this would pre-empt chances of conflict in the region. He also expressed Bangladesh's full support to Pakistan's demand for establishment of a 'nuclear-weapon free zone in South Asia.[99]

BANGLADESH-PAKISTAN RELATIONS UNDER KHALEDA ZIA (1991-1996)

The turbulence of world scenario following the Gulf crisis brought Bangladesh and Pakistan closer. Another factor to be noted was that democratically elected governments in both Bangladesh and Pakistan were in power in 1991. The Nawaz Sharif government welcomed the newly elected BNP government of Bangladesh. As Pakistan Prime Minister's special envoy, Mir Hazar Khan Bijrani, Railway Minister, was sent to Dhaka immediately after the assumption of office by the BNP Government in March 1991.

Bijrani's mission was more than a formal gesture. It was intended to be the expression of Pakistan's solidarity with Bangladesh. The message stated, "we in Pakistan immensely pleased at the conclusion of parliamentary elections in a free and fair atmosphere which has led to the establishment of a representative government in Bangladesh. This is a tribute to your courageous leadership and a vindication of the policies of late President Ziaur Rahman who was the main force of SAARC and pillar of Islamic solidarity."[100]

Bangladesh Prime Minister Begum Zia reciprocated suitably and pointed out her government's resolve to sort out various issues, namely, that of stranded Pakistanis and assets. She also assured that foreign policy priorities of late President Ziaur Rahman would continue to be pursued.

A month later, Prime Minister of Pakistan Nawaz Sharif paid a hurried visit to Dhaka on 5 May 1991 to express concern at the devastation caused by cyclone offered relief and help. The relief goods Sharif brought with him included 2,5000 tons of rice, 50,000 metres of cloth, 2,000 kg. of medicines, 5,000 tents and 97 bales of clothes. A grant of Rs. 100 million as relief for cyclone-affected people was announced and a cheque for Rs. 20 million was handed over to the Prime Minister of Bangladesh.[101] This amounted to a well thought out gesture backed by material aid and help.

Soon after, the Prime Ministers of Pakistan and Bangladesh discussed issues relating to global, regional and bilateral affairs at the Harare Commonwealth Summit on 17 October 1991 and the OIC Summit at Dakar on 10 December 1991. Begum Khaleda Zia visited Islamabad on 11 August 1992. During their meetings Khaleda Zia underscored deep concern over continued violence in Kashmir Valley and consequent escalation of tension between Pakistan and India. Just before his dismissal from power, Nawaz Sharif came to Dhaka for participating in the Seventh SAARC Summit, on April 11, 1993. The occasion was also used for strengthen bilateral, cultural, economic and trade relations between Pakistan and Bangladesh.

During his meetings with Khaleda Zia at the Commonwealth Meet at Harare and the OIC Summit at Dakar, Nawaz Sharif assured resolution of the issue of repatriation expeditiously. However, the Ordinance of 1978 (passed by General Zia ul Haque), posed a hurdle in expediting the repatriation. General Zia ul Haque had promulgated an Ordinance in 1978, inserting *Section 16-A* into the Citizenship Act, which stripped the Pakistanis stranded in Bangladesh of their citizenship rights. By the statutory injunction, the government of Pakistan deprived such erstwhile Pakistanis of citizenship who at any time before December 16, 1971, were domiciled in the territories which constituted the province of East Pakistan, or, who might have been resident abroad, or were on a visit to a foreign country at the time of separation of that province. The only exception to the rule, however, were those Pakistanis residing in erstwhile East Pakistan whose repatriation to Pakistan had been agreed to by government but who could not been repatriated. However, the list of such persons was never published.[102]

The Nawaz Sharif government did not care much for the legal hurdles posed by the 1978 Ordinance and with populist zeal, took up the repatriation issue. The government fixed 31 December 1992 as the deadline to start the "symbolic repatriation" of the first batch of 325 "stranded Pakistanis", affecting 63 families. Reflecting the over-all situation, Nawaz Sharif assured implementation of the August 1992 Accord. Out of the remaining estimated 2,50,000 stranded Biharis, only 2,38,000 were identified as genuine cases according to the census conducted by the Bangladesh government in February 1992. Nawaz Sharif government mentioned in the Accord of August 1992 that an average of 8,000 repatriates would be settled in each of the thirty-two districts of Punjab.[103] The Accord of August 1992, dealing with repatriation, was vehemently condemned by the *Sindhi* nationalists and the Saraiki speaking people of southern Punjab. On 16 October 1992, leaders of various political parties of Sindh (Sindhi nationalist groups) agreed form a "Stop Bihari Committee" (SBC) in a meeting held at Hyderabad.[104]

In view of the mounting domestic resistance against the Bihari Muslims, the government of Pakistan could not fulfill its assurance of starting the symbolic repatriation by 31 December 1992. Following his dismissal in April 1993, Nawaz Sharif was in no position to fulfil his assurances any further. This had compounded the fate of the remaining helpless Bihari Muslims. However, Bangladeshi Prime Minister Begum Khaleda Zia once again visited Islamabad as SAARC Chairman in 1995. The Joint Economic Commission of Bangladesh and Pakistan signed a long term trade agreement in 1995.

BANGLADESH–PAKISTAN RELATIONS UNDER SHEIKH HASINA

Sheikh Hasina maintained normal relations with Islamabad. But Bangladesh's attitude towards Pakistan significantly changed. In the observance of national day, Pakistan was depicted as an intruder and aggressor on government controlled media. The commonality in security concern and security strategy was also changed. The Awami League government considered India more important for bilateral relations than Pakistan, but wanted to maintain good relations with Pakistan too. Hasina was conscious of the fact that any worsening of Bangla-Pak relations would be interpreted in Bangladesh as a subservient to New Delhi, which was not good in the interest of the party. The Pakistani Foreign Secretary, Najmuddin Sheikh visited Bangladesh in August 1996. Pakistan expressed its desire to establish closest relations with Bangladesh during the visit of the Bangladeshi Foreign Minister, Abdus Samad Azad in early March 1997. Sheikh Hasina visited Pakistan in March 1997 to attend the special session of the OIC, on the eve of the Golden Jubilee celebration of Pakistan's independence. She again visited Islamabad after New Delhi in response to their nuclear explosion in May 1998, in pursuance of Bangladeshi nuclear diplomacy in the region. The Joint Economic Commission between the two countries met in Islamabad in May 1998 and decided to set up joint venture projects in Bangladesh in the fields of textile, transport equipment and 10-20 megawatt power plants. They also agreed to take measures to arrest the declining trend of bilateral trade and work for its balanced growth and to revive the cooperation committee between the two national Chambers of Commerce.[105]

THREE NATION BUSINESS SUMMIT

Bangladesh became host to the first-ever "Three-Nation Business Summit" held on 15 January 1998 at Sonargaon Hotel in Dhaka. The Summit was initiated by Sheikh Hasina, Prime Minister of Bangladesh. Three Prime Ministers-India's I.K. Gujral, Pakistan's Nawaz Sharif and Bangladesh's Sheikh Hasina-met on a common turf accompained by delegations of leading businessmen of the three countries. The Summit promised to be a turning point for the three countries of South Asia.

Official talks between the Prime Minister of Pakistan, Nawaz Sharif and Sheikh Hasina were held in the

International Conference Centre on 16 January 1998. Bangladesh and Pakistan expressed their desire to expand the scope and volume of trade between the two countries.[106] The two countries signed an agreement on promotion of cultural programmes after the official talks. During the talks, Sheikh Hasina proposed settlement of all outstanding issues between the two countries including repatriation of stranded Pakistanis and divisions of assets. Sheikh Hasina said that there was no progress on the issue of assets sharing between the two countries.[107] She requested Nawaz Sharif to take back the Pakistani citizens stranded in Bangladesh. Pakistan Prime Minister Nawaz Sharif said that Pakistan would repatriate stranded Pakistanis from Bangladesh when funds would be available for the purpose. He described repatriation of stranded Pakistanis and settlement of assets and liabilities between the two countries as outstanding issues and assured Islamabad's cooperation in this regard.[108] A meeting of the Bangladesh-Pakistan Joint Economic Commission was held in February 1998 to review the trade and economic relations between Dhaka and Islamabad.

RECENT TRENDS IN BANGLADESH–PAKISTAN RELATIONS

Perhaps no event in Bangladesh-Pakistan relations has been of greater significance as the visit of Pakistan's President Pervez Musharraf to Dhaka in 2002 as he apologised Pak army's crackdown in 1971.[109] In fact it was also the first official visit by a Pakistani head of the state to Bangladesh.

It was after the defeat of Awami League in October 2001 elections and the meeting between the Prime Minister of Bangladesh Khaleda Zia and President Musharraf on the occasion of SAARC summit held at Kathmandu in January 2002 that some betterment in Dhaka-Islamabad relations took place. In that meeting Prime Minister Khaleda Zia invited President Pervez Musharraf to visit Bangladesh.

While Musharrafs visit did not witness any major breakthrough in case of settling pending issues, it created proper conditions for ushering an era of reconciliation between Dhaka and Islamabad. As far as the progress in bilateral areas of cooperation during President Musharrafs visit to Dhaka is concerned, it proved to be substantial because of two reasons. First, institutional measures to enhance Dhaka-Islamabad cooperation were taken and second Pakistan granted duty-free access to Bangladesh jute and tea to its market. Both the leaders termed official talks successful. While giving her reaction to newsmen about talks, Prime Minister of Banglaesh Khaleda Zia said that she was fully convinced that the future of Bangladesh-Pakistan relations is extremely bright.[110] After Bangladesh-Pakistan official talks held on 30 July 2002 two Protocols were signed. The first protocol called "Cultural Exchange Programme "between Bangladesh and Pakistan, have a duration from 2003-2007. The protocol signed on "Bilateral Consultations" called for periodic consultation between the Foreign Affairs Ministries of the two countries. Another area in which Bangla-Pak cooperation took a new leaf was defence sector. Pakistan Defence Secretary Hamid Nazaw who accompanied President Musharraf held talks with his Bangladeshi counterpart and the service chiefs. Generally speaking, President Pervez Musharraf visit to Bangladesh could be analyzed as the resumption of' high level contacts and interaction at the official level between the two countries resulting in the signing of Protocols and MOU on strengthening the areas of bilateral cooperation.

BANGLADESH–PAKISTAN TRADE RELATIONS

The eighth meeting of the Bangladesh-Pakistan Joint Economic Commission (JEC) was held in Dhaka on 12 September 2005 had set a target of raising the bilateral trade volume between the two countries to US $1 billion by 2007.[111]

For two countries with a combined population of about 300 million, this should not be considered too much. However, the reality appears to be quite different. For example, according to the latest available trade figures for FY2004–05, the two-way trade stood at US$ 260 million- Dhaka imported goods worth US $ 210 million from Pakistan while its exports reached a meagre US $50 million.[112] After the meeting, Commerce Minister Altaf Hossain Chowdhury, who led the Bangladesh delegation, described the target as "ambitious, but achievable.[113] The Pakistan delegation leader Salman Shah, adviser to Pakistan Prime Minister for finance and revenue, had put it differently, *it is possible to achieve despite being ambitious.*[114] However, considering the constraints of logistics, a 400 per cent rise in trade volume in 27 months is not a practical target.

But it is also true that the Pakistan-Bangladesh JEC meeting after the gap of seven years had taken some very important decisions and their timely implementation would greatly help boosting their trade. It had agreed to meet in September 2006 in Islamabad and proposed to set up a Joint Business Council (JBC) and a Joint Chamber of Commerce to help develop an effective mechanism for boosting the bilateral trade volume. No doubt huge potentials exist for developing greater economic ties and trade volume but before that both have to try and effectively remove the existing bottlenecks for which political will is necessary to back the official level discussions.

For example, the meeting decided that JBC will meet every six months and its first meeting will he held in Dhaka before December 2005 while the second meeting is scheduled to be held before the next JEC Islamabad meeting in September 2006. Pakistan had also proposed to continue discussions on a bilateral Free Trade Agreement (FTA) with Bangladesh to facilitate increased trade between the two countries. In addition, Pakistan had offered to increase duty-free entry of Bangladesh tea from existing 10,000 tons to 15,000 tons per year and necessary government orders would be released effective from 2006.[115]

The Pakistan delegation laid stress on setting up joint ventures in textile for developing the backward linkage facilities for the readymade garment industry in Bangladesh to cash in on the existing comparative advantages. Pakistan produces cotton and cotton yarn for fabrics that could be used by such joint venture for mutual benefit. There are many other areas where effective cooperation could be developed. However, before those are undertaken the absence of a direct shipping service between Chittagong and Karachi needs to be sorted out first.

BANGLADESH AND SAARC

The South Asian region which is by now understood to mean the seven countries belonging to the South Asian Association for Regional Cooperation (SAARC), until May 1980, did not even think in terms of regional cooperation in any concrete sense. The pertinent factor which perhaps inhibited such thinking was the lack of congenial political atmosphere in the region. The two major states of the region, India and Pakistan were politically antagonistic to each other. The principle of inter-state cooperation which is basic characteristic of the present day international relations was absent in their bilateral relations.

The birth of Bangladesh in 1971 brought about a change not only in the power balance in the subcontinent but introduced a new pattern in South Asian relations. Bangladesh, the newly emerged nation state in international scene was able to create a sense of affinity among other smaller partners of the region. The initiative of Bangladesh President Ziaur Rahman regarding the formation of South

Asian Regional Cooperation in May 1980 found its way into the regional politics. Zia not only personally discussed the idea while visiting Pakistan, Nepal, India and Sri Lanka during 1977-80, but also sent personal letters and envoys to other neighbouring countries.[116] On the basis of positive response from all the capitals, Bangladesh formally submitted a working paper in November 1980, outlining the arguments for and a draft structure of such cooperation. This paper was subsequently treated as a basis for deliberation in the first meeting of Foreign Secretaries of the Seven countries. Bangladesh felt that the regional forum might performed the matters of mutual interests in economic, social, cultural and-other fields. In his letter, President Zia proposed for summit meeting as being the only authority likely to succeed in achieving a breakthrough in making regional cooperation a reality.

It may be said that when the Foreign Secretaries of the seven South Asian countries met for the first time in Colombo on 21-24 April, 1981, the first phase of Bangladesh diplomacy in initiating cooperation in the region ended.[117] In the second phase which may be said to have a span of a little more than two years, Bangladesh undertook extensive role in setting up the stage for political initiative. Though the working paper had underlined the need for a summit level meeting in the beginning, later contacts with rest of the partners changed Bangladesh's view. Accordingly she proposed for three tiered meeting before formally launching the forum, first official, then political level at two tiers, that was, Foreign Ministers and Heads of the governments. As the proposal was her brain child, Bangladesh always tried to take a leading role in different meetings. She proposed for early convening of meeting at political level simultaneously keeping in the mind that cooperation would grow at a deliberately measured pace, enabling consolidation of the gains of each stage before proceeding to the next. While supporting cooperation in selected areas, Bangladesh had urged upon her co-partners to give formal structure to the forum by proposing institutions of Summit, Council of Ministers, Standing Committee and Secretariat and adoption of a Declaration at the political level. Except the Standing Committee, the Bangladesh working paper included provision for Summit, Council and Secretariat.[118]

In the beginning, Bangladesh was aware that the proposed areas cannot be implemented, therefore she adopted cautious attempt on selection of thrust areas. In the second meeting of Foreign Secretaries in Kathmandu which was held on 2-4 November 1981, the Bangladesh supported the convening of a Foreign Ministers' level meeting at an early date and proposed some thoughts to institutional arrangements which, could evolve into an integrated association over the year.[119]

In the third Foreign Secretaries' level meeting in Islamabad which was held on 7-9 August 1982, Bangladesh once again called for Foreign Ministers meeting as a means of launching a comprehensive programme of action in the areas already identified. As she already suggested for three tiered meeting, Bangladesh now came forward with some outlines on terms of reference of each tier, 'meeting at the official level would prepared the ground work, the Ministerial level meeting would launch the actual implementation of programmes, while the Summit would consolidate and provide further impetus to the process.[120] In the fourth meeting of the Foreign Secretaries in Dhaka which was held on 28-30 March 1983, Bangladesh proposal included formation of a Standing Committee with the Foreign Secretaries and lent support to the recommendation of the Council of Ministers to be composed of Foreign Ministers.[121] She also supported Indian suggestion on its terms of reference. Bangladesh argued that an early convening of a meeting at Foreign Ministers' level was urgent, because, such meeting could maintain momentum to preclude unwarranted speculation that hesitancy on our part due to constraints that had hitherto existed among countries of the region. Bangladesh also felt a meeting at the political level could spark people's imagination and evoke response from them and ultimately involve them in this process.[122]

The Foreign Secretaries met in Delhi on 28-29 July 1983, was a preparatory meeting to finalize the convening of the Foreign Ministers' meeting which was held in the same venue on 1-2 August 1983. Bangladesh stressed in the meeting on the need for a formal document in the form of a memorandum of understanding or declaration of intent. Bangladesh Foreign Secretary felt that this document would at the same time consolidate and sum up in a comprehensive way the outcome of the last two years and give direction and future thrust to the cooperative endeavours.[123] In the Dhaka meeting a draft memorandum of understanding was circulated by Bangladesh. She urged upon the participants to consider it in the Delhi meeting. Bangladesh once again called for formation of a Council of Ministers. With the convening of the first Foreign Ministers' meeting in New Delhi, the process for South Asian Regional Cooperation entered into the political plane. Bangladesh Foreign Minister in his speech underlined two critical actions in order to maintain viability and momentum of the cooperative endeavour. First, unequivocal reaffirmation of conviction of the participants in and commitment to the concept and process of cooperation in the region and restatement of their aims and objectives in unambiguous terms. Second, gearing and harnessing of the respective government machinery to give shape to the activities envisaged and for that purpose allocating necessary financial, technical and human resources.[124] In line with the evolutionary formula the whole process had reached a very important stage.

To Bangladesh, Foreign Ministers' meeting carried significant political implication. It would not only had given the understanding that the cooperative forum would stand but at the same time enabled the people of the region to get involved in the process. Bangladesh was aware that many efforts aimed at regional cooperation in other regions failed due to lack of above actions even after some progress had been made. The launching of the Integrated Programme of Action (IPA) from the meeting was the fulfillment of the Bangladesh's role in the second phase,[125] and ultimately South Asian association for regional cooperation (SAARC) was formed in 1985 in Dhaka.

Bangladesh has played an active role in SAARC since 1985. Bangladesh has been instrumental in organising the Summit Conferences and has actively participated in its deliberations. Since Bangladesh played a major role in the formation of SAARC, it is emotionally attached to this institution. Therefore, Bangladesh is one country that would like SAARC to grow. The 13 SAARC Summit was hosted by Bangladesh on 12-13 November 2005 in Dhaka.

The summit was first scheduled in Dhaka, from January 9 to 11, 2005 but postponed by Tsunami effects on Sri Lanka, India and the Maldives. Then it was rescheduled on 6 and 7 February 2005 but was postponed again due to India's inability to attend due to political changes in Nepal, where King Gyanendra on 1 February 2005 dismissed the government. The King declared state of emergency and took over himself the power.[126]

Bangladesh is conscious of the fact that the SAARC now faces bigger and new challenges in globalisation phase where South Asia figures as important in the perception of all the big powers. This provides India an opportunity to play a role for being the biggest partner of the SAARC. In the past, India did not gain as it failed to demonstrate its wisdom in leading the South Asian forum by creating a climate of confidence among other smaller nations of the region. This image is urgently required to rank her position along with other major powers, particularly when she aspires to be a permanent member of the UN Security Council. One must enjoy favourable support in the region first before it seeks support from others in the comity of nations. The regional forum, in fact, could not make much headway without collectively under the umbrella of SAARC with a view to ensuring a better life and living of the poverty-stricken peoples of South Asia.

It would be rather futile efforts to go for maintaining such rituals like holding the mandatory annual Summit in different capitals in rotation and having picnic-like tours and retreats for the leaders and officials that hardly these poor countries of this region can afford unless some positive results are achieved for all the seven countries like a well-knit family. However, frequently meetings of leaders together at least once a year would help remove many of the misunderstandings and misgivings.

CONCLUSION

It is clear from the forgoing discussion that Bangladesh has tried to follow a policy of cordial relations with its smaller neighbours. It is true that there are limitations in its relations with the smaller neighbours yet Bangladesh has been quite enthusiastic in forming closer ties with them in order to enhance its own identity in the region and consolidate its power of bargaining against a big neighbour. Bangladesh has gradually improved its relations with Pakistan as well. It seems that Bangladesh would be interested in Pakistan more diplomatically than any thing else. Bangladesh has contentious issues with neighbours like Myanmar but she has tried to resolve the issues through bilateral negotiations. It is certain that Bangladesh would not like to strain its relations with neighbouring countries like Myanmar, Bhutan, Nepal and Pakistan to the best possible extent.

Bangladesh-Myanmar relations in bilateral, sub-regional and regional levels are yet to blossom in full-shape. At the policy level, Myanmar has not accorded much importance to develop bilateral relations as it had done with the western countries and with India and South Asia. On the Myanmar side, its authoritarian regime character may have discouraged Bangladeshi policy makers for developing a healthy bilateral relations. Despite preoccupation with domestic problem and image crisis at international level, Myanmar must continue to remain in the mainstream of the global process of cooperative development. Myanmar can be a creative partner of Bangladesh in the globalization process by redesigning its foreign and economic policies. It is evident that the relationship between the two countries has not been all that confrontational. Both the countries have taken steps to reduce its conflictual trend regarding Rohingya refugees. Appropriate directions and vision must be provided to the policy practioners, so that a mutually beneficial economic relation can be developed between Bangladesh and Myanmar. An extensive research on identifying both the existing and potential trade-investment complementarities should be undertaken by the concerned institutes of both the countries.

I

However, the end of the Cold-War and the opening of market economy have provided much room for a sound bilateral relations. The existing economic relation between the two countries must step beyond trade, towards an extensive form of joint-investment cooperation. The possible areas are-fish and timber processing industries, mining lime stone, manufacturing clinker and clinker grinding industries and establishment of hydroelectric power plant. Now Bangladesh and Myanmar have to work for the proposed EPZ in Cox's Bazar-Arakan region which will create better opportunity for foreign investment. Both sides are tied together on the basis of some overriding mutual interests. Myanmar's joining of BIMSTEC illustrates this mutuality. It is the right time for Bangladesh to proceed with an innovative approach to develop bilateral relations with Myanmar and optimise the benefit in the days ahead.

II

Over the years, the political relations between Bangladesh and Bhutan have developed steadily and consistently. It has been vividly manifested in the frequent exchange of visits, particularly at high levels, close understanding developed between the leadership of the two countries and their resolve, as expressed on many occasions to further develop and diversify the mutually beneficial relations between the two countries. However, friendly and close political relationship between the two countries could not lead to the establishment of equally meaningful economic cooperation. The prevailing status of cooperation between Bangladesh and Bhutan in the fields of trade, communications, industry, development of natural resources and so on remained far behind the requirements of the two countries. It becomes even more obvious when one takes into consideration the vast potentials of the two countries for mutually beneficial economic cooperation.

III

Bangladesh and Nepal have tried to come close to each other. Being small states in the region they wish to safeguard their interest on a joint basis. Both the countries provide vast scope for economic cooperation. Their main areas of cooperation have been increasing trade and commercial relations, exploitation of water resources, etc. Nepal's main interest in Bangladesh lies in the fact that by increasing trade with and through Bangladesh, it can reduce her dependence over India. Bangladesh, on the other hand, wants to strengthen its bargaining power against India particularly in the context of division of water resources, by coming closer to Nepal. However, one can say that whether it is the issue of trade or exploitation of water resources, both have to depend on India. None can ignore the geo-political realities of the subcontinent. India's active cooperation is indeed essential for both the countries. Therefore, the nature and pattern of Bangladesh and Nepal relationship is bound to be influenced by India's role and attitude.

IV

Though separated by sea, Bangladesh and Sri Lanka are small neighbouring countries located in the India Ocean. Geographical factors make Sri Lanka and Bangladesh subscribe to similar, if not identical views regarding the India Ocean as a zone of peace. Bangladesh and Sri Lanka are committed to support the resolutions of the United Nations on disarmament and the declaration of the Indian Ocean as a zone of peace. It is interesting to note that both in Bangladesh and Sri Lanka, there is continuity in foreign policy which remains more or less unaffected by political changes in these countries, even when such changes have been of a radical nature.

V

There is an urgent need to encourage people to people contacts by launching exchange programmes in education, culture, media, business, science and technology and other areas between Bangladesh and Pakistan. For this purpose, air and sea links between the two countries need to be made more effective so that more and more people from both the countries can visit which might promote tourism and develop better understanding of each other. It is hoped that with the passage of time, the unpleasant part of Dhaka-Islamabad relations will be replaced with positive developments.

REFERENCES

1. *Basic Facts On The Union of Myanmar,* Government of the Union of Myanmar, Public Relations and Information Division, Ministry of Foreign Affairs, September 1996.
2. Government of Bangladesh, *A Brief on Bangladesh-Myanmar Relations,* Ministry of Commerce, 1996.
3. *Bangladesh Observer,* 29 May 1972.
4. Kamal Uddin Ahmed, Bangladesh-Myanmar Relations: The Politico-Economic Dimensions, *BASS Journal, Vol.* 7, No.4, 1986, p. 445.
5. *Bangladesh Observer,* 21 July 1977.
6. *Bangladesh Times,* 22 July 1977.
7. *Bangladesh Observer* 23 May 1979.
8. *Ibid,* 24 May 1979.
9. *Ibid.*
10. *Asia Yearbook* 1983, (Hong Kong), p. 125.
11. *Bangladesh Observer,* 13 August 1985.
12. *Bangladesh Observer,* 18 January 1997.
13. *Bangladesh Observer,* 13 November 1998.
14. S.S. Bhattcharya, Relations with Neighbours, *World Focus,* No. 145, January 1992, pp. 15-16.
15. Shwe Lu Mung, *Burma Nationalism and Ideology: An Analysis of Society, Culture and Politics* (Dhaka 1989), p.66.
16. *Bangladesh Observer,* 23 December 1992.
17. *Bangladesh Observer, 29* April *1992.*
18. Government of Bangladesh, *A Brief on Bangladesh-Myanmar Relations,* Ministry of Commerce, *2004.*

19. *The New Nation 28* July *1997.*
20. *The Daily Star, 2* August *1997.*
21. *The Daily danakantha, 28* July *1997.*
22. *The Daily Star, 18* April *1988.*
23. *India Today* (New Delhi), *15* September *2005.*
24. *The Daily Ittefaq, 5* April *1998.*
25. *The Daily Sangbad, 9* September *2001.*
26. *A.K.M. Hedayetul* Huq, Bangladesh-Burma Trade, *Asian Affairs* (Dhaka), Vol. 1, No. l, Jan-June, *1980*
27. Government of Bangladesh, *Brief on Trade Matters,* Ministry of Commerce, *1996.*
28. *The Independent, 7* November *1996.*
29. *Bangladesh Observer, 19* December *2002.*
30. *The Daily News, 25* December *2002.*
31. *Bangladesh Observer, 22* March *2003.*
32. *Ibid*
33. *The Bangladesh Times, 26* March *2003.*
34. *Bangladesh Observer, 27* September *2005.*
35. *Ibid.*
36. Ibid.
37. *World Development Report* 2004, p. 188.
38. *Ibid., p.221.*
39. R.C. Misra, Bhutan-Bangladesh Relations, a paper presented in the Seminar on *Politics in Bangladesh* held during March 13-14, 1981 at South Asia Studies Centre, University of Rajasthan, Jaipur, India.
40. Kamal Uddin Ahmed, Prospects of Bangladesh-Bhutan Relations, in S.R. Chakravarty and Virendra Narain (eds.), *Bangladesh . Global Politics,* (New Delhi, 1988), Vol. III, p.171.
41. Syed Sikander Mehdi, Bhutan and its Strategic Environment, *Strategic Studies,* Vol. XII, No.2, 1988, p.80.
42. Kapileshwar Labh, Bhutan-Bangladesh Partnership in Peace and Economic Development : Commonalities and Constraints, in S.R. Chakravarty (ed.), *Foreign Policy of Bangladesh,* (New Delhi, 1994), p.237.
43. *Bangladesh Observer, 11* September, 1980.

44. *Ibid*
45. *Ibid.*
46. *The Bangladesh Times,* 26 February 1984.
47. *Bangladesh Observer,* 30 January 1985.
48. *Bangladesh Observer,* 31 March 1985.
49. *Bangladesh Observer,* 23 February 1984.
50. *Bangladesh Observer,* 24 January 2002.
51. *The Independent,* 30 April 2003.
52. *The Daily News,* 28 July 2005.
53. *Nepal News,* 25 December 1978.
54. S.R. Chakravorty and Virendra Narain, Foreign Policy of Bangladesh, Trends and Issues, *South Asian Studies,* Jaipur, January-December 1977.
55. Ramakant, Geography as a Factor in Nepal's Foreign Policy, *South Asian Studies,* Jaipur, January-July, 1973.
56. Christopher, H Bateman, National Security and Nationalism in Bangladesh, *Asian Survey, Vol. XIV,* No.8, August 1979, pp.781-82.
57. *Times of India,* 17 July 1972.
58. 'Bangladesh,' *Asia Year Book, Far Eastern Economic Review,* 1979, p. 143.
59. *Nepal News,* 2 February 1979.
60. *Nepal News,* 14 March 1980.
61. *Bangladesh Observer,* 3 March 1980.
62. *Nepal News,* 22 February 1983.
63. *The Rising Nepal,* 17 July 1974.
64. *Asian Recorder, Vol. XXII,* No. 17, 22-28 April, 1976.
65. *Holiday,* 8 April 1978.
66. *Asian Recorder,* 24-30 June 1982.
67. *Nepal News,* 28 March 1998.
68. *Holiday,* 15 January 2002.
69. *Patriot,* 16 January 2002.
70. *Bangladesh Observer,* 27 May 2005
71. A.J. Wilson, *Politics in Sri Lanka* 1947-73 (London, 1974), p.185.
72. *Ceylon Daily News,* (Colombo), 14 December 1971.

73. Ceylon Today, November-December 1974, p.11.
74. Ceylon Daily News, 24 August 1971.
75. Ibid., 16 December 1971
76. Ibid., 1 December 1971
77. The Times ofIndia (New Delhi), 17 December 1971.
78. P.O.T., 18 July 1978, p.1016.
79. SAARC (Report, Male), 10-11 July 1984, p. 24
80. P.O.T., Bangladesh series Vol. II, No. 57, 21 March 1977, p. 416.
81. Ibid
82. P.O.T. Vol. XXVII, No. 29,29 January 2002.
83. Ibid.
84. P.O.T. , Vol. XXVII, No. 127, 5 May 2002.
85. Ibid.
86. Bangladesh Observer, 22 April 2003.
87. The Bangladesh Times, 21 April, 2003.
88. The Daily News, 23 April 2003.
89. Ceylon Daily, 25 April 2003.
90. P.O.T, Vol. XXVII, No. 141, 19 May, 2003.
91. Ibid.
92. P.O.T, Vol. XXX, No. 122, 29 May 2005.
93. IDSA News and Reviews on South Asia, Vol. 18, No. 11, November, 1985, p. 814.
94. Holiday, 18 August 1991.
95. The Pakistan Times, 18 January 1989.
96. The Frontier Post, 25 January 1989.
97. The Pakistan Times, 2 October 1989.
98. Ibid.
99. *Dawn, 29* November *1989.*
100. The Pakistan Times, 9 April 1991.
101. Bangladesh Observer, 7 May, 1991.
102. *Holiday,(Dhaka) 13* December *1991.*
103. Frontier Post, 16 October 1992.
104. Bangladesh Observer, 19 October 1992.
105. *Bangladesh Observer, 6* December *1998.*

106. Bangladesh Observer, 21 January 1998.
107. Ibid.
108. Daily Star, 19 January 1998.
109. The Bangladesh Times, 15 January 2003.
110. *Ibid.*
111. *P.O.T., Vol. XXX, No. 228, 26* September *2005.*
112. *Ibid.*
113. *Ibid.*
114. *Ibid.*
115. *Bangladesh Observer, 15* September *2005.*
116. The Bangladesh Times, 12 March, 1981.
117. Bangladesh Observer, 28 April, 1982.
118. Ibid
119. *SAARC Documents,* Ministry of Foreign Affairs, Government of Bangladesh, p. *14.*
120. Ibid., p. 49.
121. Ibid., p.76.
122. Ibid., pp.137-138.
123. Ibid., p.153.
124. Ibid., p. 176.
125. Ibid., p.175.
126. P.O.T., Vol. XXX, No. 173, 22 July 2005.

CHAPTER-7

Recent Developments in Foreign Policy of Bangladesh

It is true that the foreign policy of Bangladesh is connected to its domestic and economic position. The extreme poverty limits the capability of the Bangladeshi governmental to act on the global level, as priority is that people need to be fed. However, these conditions also make it important for successive political regimes to maintain good relations with all nations and to attract economic aid from every possible source. Bangladesh has very friendly relations with global super powers such as the U.S.A and Japan, but it does not take sides as to not make enemies. Bangladesh has been key to arranging regional economic cooperation in south Asia, which has stimulated domestic economic growth. It has also been active in international organizations, especially in those designed to solve the problems of the poorest people of the world.

In fact the government of Bangladesh has provided a mission statement reflecting this, and is a guide on which its foreign policy is conducted. It is -

A. The state shall base its international relations on the principal of respect for national sovereignty and equality, non-interference in the internal affairs of other countries, peaceful settlements of international disputes and respect for international law and the principles as enunciated in the United Nations Charter , and on the basis of those principal shall-

a) Strive for the renunciation of the use of force in international and for general and complete disarmament;
b) Uphold the right of every people freely to determine and build up its own social, economic and political system by ways and means of its own free choice; and
c) Support oppressed peoples throughout the world waging a just struggle against imperialism, colonialism and racialism.

B. The state shall Endeavour to consolidate, preserve and strengthen fraternal relations among Muslim countries based on Islamic solidarity.

The constitution of Bangladesh embodies the basic principal of foreign policy; that says, *the state shall base its international relations on the principle of respect for national sovereignty and equality, non-interference in the internal affairs of other countries, peaceful settlement of international disputes and respect for international laws and principles as enunciated in the United Nations Charter.*

However, despite its vast poverty and relatively small military capability, Bangladesh has not hesitated to defend its sovereignty and to take strong stands on many international issues. Any hint that might try to intimidate Bangladesh has provoked a fiercer response. Furthermore, Bangladesh has irritated powerful nations by standing against them on various major issues, and relations with both the United States and the former Soviet Union have gone through difficult periods. Bangladesh has also looked to maintain its Islamic identity, has encouraged very friendly relations, and has attempted to build a worldwide Muslim community with other Islamic nations. These friendly relations it has enjoyed with Islamic nations have led to the receipt of economic aid from wealthy Arab countries.[1]

Furthermore, as an active participant of the UN, NAM, the OIC, the commonwealth and various international organizations, Bangladesh has been a part of global politics. Bangladesh led the formation of SAARC-a regional co-operation forum comprising seven South Asian countries – Bangladesh, Bhutan, India, Maldives, Nepal, Pakistan and Sri Lanka. Bangladesh, has also tried to enhance economic co–operation in the region, which led to the formation and implementation of SAPTA (South Asian Preferential Trading Arrangement).

RELATIONS WITH INDIA

It is also noteworthy to mention here that Bangladesh is mostly surrounded by India through a land border, which stretches 1500 miles, its relations with India is vital. At the beginning India's relations with Bangladesh were very strong because of India's support for independence of Bangladesh. During the war, India assisted refugees, intervened militarily and brought international attention to the issue through the then Prime Minister of India Mrs. Indira Gandhi's visit to Washington. Afterwards India offered relief and reconstruction aid to Bangladesh India extended recognition to Bangladesh prior to the end of the war in 1971 and then lobbied others to follow same.[2]

But after that, India-Bangladesh relations have been strained over the years on issues such as South Talpatti Island, the Farakka Barrage and water sharing, border conflicts near Tripura and the construction of a fence along most of the border by India. There are also small pieces of land along the border region that Bangladesh is diplomatically trying to reclaim. South Talpatty Island, administered under Satkhira district of Bangladesh, is still under Indian military occupation, though the Bangladesh government sent satellite images to the Indian government proving the island to be within Bangladeshi territory.

In recent years India has increasingly complained that Bangladesh does not maintain its border properly. It fears an increasing flow of poor Bangladeshis and it accuses Bangladesh of harboring Indian separatist groups like ULFA and jihadi terrorist groups. The Bangladesh government has consistently denied these accusations. India estimates that over 20 million Bangladeshis are living illegally in India. Many Bangladeshis also feel India likes to play 'big brother' to Bangladesh.[3]

However, in 1996 relations warmed as a new Bangladesh and Indian government brought in a new softer foreign policy. A 30-year water- sharing agreement for the Ganges River was also signed in December 1996 and in October 2010 some cooperation was announced on the border issues. The new Bangladeshi government has been instrumental in much of this cooperation.

It is also true that India could not hope that Bangladesh would be forever grateful to India for its liberation. However, India did hope that of Bangladesh would be a friendly and cooperative country on India's eastern borders. However it was not to be, and over the years, Bangladesh's foreign policy has been unfriendly and almost adversarial to India except the regime of Sheikh Hasina in 1996 and her present regime which got landslide victory in general elections on 29th December 2008 and took oath as Prime Minister of Bangladesh for second time on 6th January 2009.

It is also important to mention here that Prime Minister of India Dr. Manmohan Singh visited Bangladesh on 7th and 8th September 2011 after a long gap of 12 years when Mr. Atal Bihari Vajpayee visited Bangladesh in 1999. During this visit both the countries agreed to extend trading ties, with India granting Bangladesh tax concession on textile imports it receives from Bangladesh. The other major agreements were as follows:

- A comprehensive framework agreement on bilateral cooperation;
- A memorandum of understanding on renewable energy;
- To conserve the Sundarban Mangrove Forests, Home of the Royal Bengal Tigers;
- An addendum to facilitate overland transit to Nepal from Bangladesh.

Foreign Minister of Bangladesh Dipu Moni described the visit as historic, saying it would '*pave the way for a prosperous future for the whole region*'.

RELATIONS WITH PAKISTAN

Bangladesh has friendly relations with Pakistan, despite the difficult start to their relationship, including the horrible genocide committed by the Pakistan army against the people of Bangladesh during the 1971 Liberation War.[4] Pakistan was born out of the partition of India in 1947 by the outgoing British colonial regime. The British were frustrated by the violent riots unleashed by the Muslim League under Jinnah to demand a separate state of Pakistan as a homeland for Indian Muslims, which quickened India's independence by a year. Pakistan came into existence in August 1947, with two separate parts separated by over a thousand miles of Indian territory. West Pakistan was dominated by Pakistan Punjabis in terms of numbers, while East Pakistan was dominated by Bengalis, who in terms of numbers were the overwhelming dominant population of the new state of Pakistan.

Bangladesh emerged as an independent state in1971, as a partition of the new state of Pakistan. A civil war had emerged on denial of the electoral mandate to the East

Pakistani Bengali Awami party, in which the Bengali masses in Pakistan's eastern state undertook massive protests and riots. What happened after was an ethnic genocide by the Pakistan Army against the defenseless and unarmed Bengali people. Millions of refugees fled into India and the Pakistan Army massacred millions of Bengali Muslims.[5] This created a threating military and political crisis for India on its Eastern borders. India then decided to take military intervention on the invitation of a Free Bangladesh Government-in-exile and aided by the Mukti Bahini (Bangladesh Liberation Army). An independent state of Bangladesh then emerged in December 1971 from what was formally East Pakistan.

However, relations have improved drastically since those dark days; the genocide has been largely forgiven in the light of apologies by Pakistan and the decision to put the past behind them. The two countries are now linked by their religion and their cultural heritage. As both Islamic and both with minorities in neighboring India, they are brought together in their desire for more rights and protection for Indian Muslims. Bangladesh also feels threatened by India's vast military power and looks towards Pakistan for support.

It is also important to mention here that Pakistan can be the external pressure supporting Bangladesh's aggressive foreign policy stance towards India. Pakistan's strategic objective is to distract India from the Pakistan borders by creating Bangladesh as a counter-pressure point in the east. To achieve their objectives, Pakistan has roped in Bangladesh by preying on Bangladesh's contentious issues with India and projecting India as a threat to Bangladesh's security.

Now, Bangladesh's threat receptions from India are reflected in the defense cooperation agreement with China and in it providing bases to Pakistan's ISI for launching its war and terrorism against eastern India.[6] Bangladesh has close military connections with Pakistan in recent years.

RELATIONS WITH CHINA

Early relations with the China were unfriendly due to the use of China's veto at the United Nations Security Council to block Bangladesh's accession to the United Nations. Lately however China has made efforts to improve relations with many of its neighbors including Bangladesh.

China like Pakistan has a strategic objective, which is to distract India from the China front by creating Bangladesh as a counter-pressure point in the east. China's aim is also to gain a naval base at Chittagong that would support a Chinese naval presence in the Bay of Bengal to cause problems for India.

THE DILEMMA FOR BANGLADESH

The ruling and political class of Bangladesh, over the next few years, may have to make some strategic choices and decisions. For Bangladesh, the key challenge will be to determine how to position itself between China on the one hand and India on the other.[7] The USA, and probably UK too, will certainly favor a closer Indo-Bangla link as against a colder Sino-Bangla link. USA Ambassador to India Timothy Roemer's recent, and indeed mysterious, visit to Dhaka in April, 2010 was clearly an indication of that. He seemed to be over the top in his expression of love for India and the "very close and fruitful relations" between India and the present Bangladesh government. He was also most generous in his praise for "the regional leadership" of Sheikh Hasina in forming close cooperation with India on counter terrorism.

This is quite telling as Timothy Roemer is a politician, a former congressman and reported to be very close to

President Obama. His opinions could play a very decisive role in the White House forming its own position, and this in the shaping of future Obama policy towards the region, especially the eastern rim of the South Asian sub - continent. Earlier in 2009 Timothy Roemer, then a newly arrived American Ambassador to Delhi, had pledged to rope Indian political establishment for the USA (and the West) to exert pressure on the President Rajapaksa regime to implement what the West thinks is beneficial for Sri Lanka's long-term progress. Sri Lanka is astutely playing its own "China card".

However, USA Deputy Secretary of State Jim Steinberg's recent meetings with both Prime Minister Sheikh Hasina and the opposition leader Begum Khaleda Zia in April, 2010 were more equi-balanced. He was reported to have been generous in his praise for Begum Khaleda Zia's role in building up USA- Bangladesh relations, sharp improvement in areas like women empowerment, education and economic growth during her tenures in office as Prime Minister.

Thus Bangladesh has to decide, sooner than later, how effectively and sagaciously it will manage its foreign policy towards India and China. It will probably try to maintain a policy of equi-distance, but the first priority will be to further its own national interests and national strategic objectives. Putting Bangladesh first is the new foreign policy paradigm. Bangladesh cannot afford to sit on the fences anymore. As the choices and the decisions it makes now will determine the future trajectory of the country over the course of the 21st century. It has too much at stake.

Bangladesh, if it is strategic minded, and stradling South and South–East Asia, can certainly play a pivotal role, in moving the way forward for the SAARC and ASEAN countries, and their other Asian associates, to form an Asian Union of economic, political, and defense co-operation, with an eventual tariff-free trade zone and single currency. The pan- Asian dream of its National Poet Nazrul Islam, China's first President Sun Yat-Sen and many others may yet come to fruition; thought it may take another 20 or 30 years.

As the all know that the direction of foreign policy aims at maximizing national human and natural endowments in pursuing cooperative policies with countries in the region and beyond and it seems to follow the popular doctrine that there are no permanent enemies or eternal allies and what is permanent is international interest.

Sheikh Hasina visited India, China South Korea and Japan during 2010 apart from a few European countries and the UN. She visited Bhutan as well. It is speculated that she might visit Canada, Russia and other countries in coming months of 2011.

She had participated in a number of multi-lateral conferences and meetings of inter-governmental organizations and presented among others, not only Bangladesh's environmental woes due to global climate change but also attainment of a middle-income county status by 2021

The visit of the Bangladesh Prime Minister to India in January 2010 has led to a new vista of cooperation by agreeing to the regional interconnectivity with India, Nepal, and Bhutan and use of Bangladesh ports by India and other South Asian nations and China

However the main opposition party of Bangladesh (BNP) has voiced its opposition on the grant of transit rights and use of Bangladesh ports to India on the grounds that the agreements is tilted heavily in favour of India without obtaining any concrete benefits for Bangladesh.

Meanwhile in terms of the Delhi communiqué, it is reported that the government is planning to establish road and rail links with Nepal and Bhutan along with India and Myanmar as part of the move for regional connectivity. China expressed its support and assistance in establishing regional connectivity through Myanmar to Kunming (Yunnan province) from Bangladesh, first by road and then by railways. In recent times the Prime Minister of Bangladesh has underscored the direction of foreign policy towards Africa. It is timely and appropriate. The continent with 54 counties was not in the radar of foreign policy for a long time. Only five Bangladesh diplomatic missions exist in Africa, three in Arab northern Africa. Many Bangladesh diplomatic missions opened in the 1970s & 1980 in Africa have been closed, such as in Algeria, Senegal, Nigeria and Zimbabwe. Many African countries are sparsely populated and have vast agricultural farming land. Bangladesh may take the advantage of such factors in sending people for farming on lease-hold lands in African countries. Bangladesh's low-end merchandise together with pharmaceuticals may enter into large African markets. Bangladesh's private sector together with the government may take initiatives to achieve these objectives by organizing trade mission and exhibitions in African countries.

Furthermore, Bangladesh needs to engage with countries of Latin and Central Americas. The diplomatic missions of Bangladesh in the 1970s in Brazil and Argentina have been closed years ago. Now it is proper time that Bangladesh government may seriously consider opening missions in several countries in that part of the world as part of economic and cultural diplomacy.

GLOBALIZATION

Globalization is a widely contested term, but broadly describes a series of economic, social, technological, cultural and political changes that increases interaction between people in locations all over the globe. It is also the process by which economies all over the world have become increasingly integrated. This global economy is largely Influenced by trans-national corporations, companies that operates all over the globe. They have the power to export goods to markets in many different countries, import raw materials from the cheapest suppliers in poor countries and manufacture where wage rates are the lowest. TNC's now make up 70% of the world trade, with profits that can be larger than the GNP of small nations. TNC's have challenged the concept of nations being the sole players in global politics and are massively important to Bangladesh.[8]

Globalization can be seen as both positive and negative to Bangladesh. It is an opportunity which if used effectively can achieve rapid economic growth. Bangladesh has used the global economy effectively and has a predicted GDP growth of 6.7% for this current year. Trough the global market Bangladesh has found a market for goods which may not sell well nationally, and has gained vital income. Foreign investment along with foreign aid assistance is seen as key to lifting many Bangladeshis out of poverty. There is the argument hoverer, that TNC's are exploiting the poor workers. The lack of strictly enforced and expansive law means that TNC's can operate in a way that is detrimental, such as polluting the environment and imposing poor working conditions and low wages on local workers.[9]

How Bangladesh manages TNC's is crucial because TNC's have the power to withdraw if they do not see conditions in Bangladesh as favorable. This would be disastrous because many jobs and investment projects are dependent on the foreign cash provided by TNC's.[10] So therefore, it is in Bangladesh's interest to maintain a stable climate in the region to make it attractive for investment; to maintain good relations with its neighbors and to ensure a secure political situation domestically and internationally. Bangladesh also has to be mindful that most TNC's are based in the U.S.A or in Europe when conducting foreign diplomacy and to maintain friendly relations. This does not stop Bangladesh from standing up to U.S.A. when it feels strongly about a subject, but Bangladesh would never seek to anger for fear of economic consequences. Bangladesh has lot of pressure from outside forces, both from nations and from non–governmental organizations in the subject of its domestic and foreign policy.[11]

GLOBAL WARMING

Global warming is of major concern to Bangladesh, because rising sea level threatens to engulf much of its territory, and displace millions of people. Bangladesh is particularly vulnerable because much of its land is close to or at sea level, and the land is criss - crossed by many rivers.[12] The situation is very serious, and a problem that Bangladesh has not been a major contributor too. So therefore, it is relying on the rest of the world to stop this oncoming disaster, but little action in real terms is taken to solve the problem or lessen the effects. Bangladesh is using and supporting the recent mass publicity surrounding this scientific subject, and attempting to persuade the major nations of the world to take political measures to cut carbon emissions, (the main human caused contributor to global warming).[13] The chances of success that measures to combat global warming will be substantial and quick enough to have a real effect are slim unfortunately, but the consequences of this disaster are so enormous to Bangladesh that there is no option but to take every opportunity possible. Bangladesh must conduct diplomacy, and lobby the international community and international non-governmental organizations to force action.[14]

Recommendations for Bangladesh Foreign Policy

Some specific policy recommendations for Bangladesh foreign policy are as follows:

- Increasing co- operation with Indian states adjoining Bangladesh, with Nepal, and with Bhutan. Using manpower along the entire courses of the rivers addressing local wealth and expertise.
- Need to increase flexibility and innovativeness in Bangladesh internal politics. Increase autonomy in Bangladesh's government institutions. Need to venture into ideas like context of psycho geography , imagined communities, the involvement of non-actors in state policy making and thus find out their relevance in the contexts of regional and sub regional co-operation.[15]
- Proper understanding of foreign policy determinants, establish a strong consensus among political parties both in foreign policy and domestic policy making, bring about change in political culture; policy making must be proactive, not reactive. Reversing the backwater turn in foreign policy and revise asymmetric relations with major powers, having a taskforce for foreign policy , making terms of reference relevant to region and actor wise which might be comprised of ex-diplomats with exceptional qualities, civil society members, technocrats with relevant expertise. The unfair selection of foreign policy officials, who lacked required qualification, must be discouraged.[16]
- Reengineering Bangladesh's policy towards great powers, showing national strength by proving communal harmony, democracy and secularism, establishing strong international links and leverage in all geo-strategic location amongst China, India, ASEAN countries for all types of gains, strongly pursue multilateral diplomacy, establishing friendship lobbies in the parliaments of powerful states, following or getting engaged in public diplomacy and portray Bangladesh's soft power, creating an image of secularists despite being devout muslims, manage the media etc.,[17] developing good image abroad, review the

Bangladesh stance in bi- and multilateral economic forums by portraying both past and present follies of the donors.[18]

- Enhancing democratic institutions, introduce uniform system of education, building up better agencies for law enforcement, and increase regional co-operation, the Ministry of Foreign Affairs must be an active participant in forming a comprehensive counter-terrorism strategy, enhance co-operation with other states, deny safe heaven to terrorism,[19] seek material and financial assistance, exchange information, arrange training for Bangladesh forces, monitor the visitors from foreign countries who come for pilgrimage purposes, re-branding Bangladesh as a liberal democracy.
- Avoiding identification along the line of religion, develop consensus on foreign policy among political parties, institutionalizing democracy, provide freedom to diplomats from political compulsions and give them their due honour, making sure that political appointees are highly qualified and have good sense of morality.[20]
- Sending a signal to India for earning the goodwill of Bangladesh's people, and need to address India in defining what they really wanted. Establishing a multilateral framework including Nepal, Bhutan and Myanmar, larger connectivity keeping the Asian Highway and the Trans Asian Railway in mind.
- Have well qualified negotiators both in government and private sectors, raising the amount for service charge for transit, pay attention to infrastructural damages that may be caused by foreign vehicles.
- Paying attention to political problems and their implication on transit (if given), think a lot before giving transit keeping in mind their previous records.
- Provide the Chittagong Port as transit to Tripura, and then consider transshipment gradually.

- Have a well coordinated, well managed and transparent foreign policy.
- Bangladesh and India must not overreact on transit issue, need for skilled negotiators, and use worldwide cases on transit for learning purposes and not to hurry on the issue.
- Elimination of funding behind religious terrorist activities, establishing strong visa systems for checking visitors.

CONCLUSION

It is true that Bangladesh has a very pro-active foreign policy, despite its domestic problem and extreme poverty. Regionally it has been instrumental in securing economic growth and in arranging trade agreements. Globally Bangladesh has been active in its support for certain agendas, especially those that help the world's poorest people. The phenomenons of global warming and globalization are also set to have a colossal effect on Bangladesh so the nation has been adjusting its foreign policy to solve these problems.[21]

However, the Islamic identity of Bangladesh means that it has close relations with other Islamic nations, and its past as a colony of the British Empire has resulted in very close relations with Britain as well as membership of the commonwealth. Bangladesh does not accept dominance by other nations, but will aim to maintain friendly relations with the world's most powerful nations to stimulate domestic economic growth and improve the poverty stricken situation of its people. If necessary, Bangladesh will not hesitate to defend its rights, and has fiercely responded to aggression by India in the past. The genocide committed by the Pakistan army during 1971 has not been largely forgotten but mostly forgiven, and relations between Pakistan and Bangladesh are strong. Bangladesh also has good relations with China.

The main issues facing Bangladesh currently are global warming, and the security situation in the region with tensions between China, Pakistan, India and Bangladesh. The War on Terror has not bypassed Bangladesh either; the U.S. has monitored the complaints from India that there are terrorism camps in Bangladesh.[22]

Furthermore, in the realm of foreign policy, Bangladesh could be said to be having two broad aspirations – first, the search for its security and preservation of sovereignty, and second, the quest for resources for its development and economic welfare. The first required the space for the maintenance of sufficient maneuverability in policy-making, particularly as it was a weaker neighbour bordering a far more powerful state, India. As professor Hedley Bull had asserted, rightly or wrongly, 'the deepest fears of the smaller units in the global system are their larger neighbours'.[23] Bangladesh always appeared to have the felt-need to live in 'concord with' but 'distinct from' their powerful neighbour. The 'concord' was necessary largely due to Bangladesh's geography – largely 'India-locked' – and the 'distinction' was essential because Bangladesh's own identity, as separate from the Indian communities surrounding it, could only be defined by those terms. This implied the need to build a web of extra-regional linkages. The second aspiration, the quest for resources, entailed aid, trade, remittances from her expatriates and foreign investments. It also meant having to involve herself with a wide range of countries. Both aspirations, therefore, required Bangladesh to seek a high level of international interactions.

REFERENCES

1. G. Allison, *Essence of Decision* (Boston, 1971), pp. 180-183.
2. M. Halperin, *Bureaucratic Politics and Foreign Policy* (Washington D.C., 1974), p. 86.

3. William Wallace, *Foreign Policy and the Political Process* (London, 1971), pp. 99-102.
4. F.B. Weinstein, The Uses of Foreign Policy in Indonesia: An Approach to the Analysis of Foreign Policy in Less Developed Countries, *World Politics,* Vol. XXIV, No. 3, April 1972, pp. 356-381.
5. B. Korany, Foreign Policy Models and their Empirical Relevance to Third World Actors: A Critique and an Alternative, *International Social Science Journal,* Vol. 26, No. 1, 1974, pp. 70-94.
6. S.P. Cohen, *The Idea of Pakistan* (Washington D.C., 2004), pp. 86-88.
7. S.D. Muni, *India's Foreign Policy: The Democratic Dimension* (New Delhi, 2009), pp. 199-205.
8. Erling Bjol, The Small States in International Politics, in August Schou and Arne Olav (eds.), *Small States in International relations* (Stockholm, 1971), p. 33.
9. Ralph Pettman, *Small Power Politics and International Relations in South East Asia* (Sydney, 1976), p. 58.
10. A. Vandenbosch, The Small States in International Politics and Organization, *The Journal of Politics,* Vol. 26, No. 2, 1964, p. 312.
11. J.H. Broomfield, *Elite Conflict in a Plural Society: Twentieth Century Bengal* (Berkeley, 1968), pp. 5-6.
12. T.K. Oommen, Ethnic Dimensions of Security: Situating India in the Context of South Aisa, *in Comprehensive Security in South Asia: Ethnic Dimensions Seminar Proceedings* (New Delhi, 2003), pp. 1-40.
13. Amena Mohsin, The Nationalist State and the Chittagong Hill Tracts 1971-1994, *The Journal of Social Studies*, 74, No. 1, 1996, pp. 55.
14. *Ibid.*
15. Iftekhar Ahmed Chowdhury, Prehistory of Bangladeshi Nationalism and a Theory of Tripartite Balance, *Asian Affairs,* Vol. IV, No. 5, December 1982, pp. 407-433.
16. A. Wolfers, *Discord and Collaboration: Essays on international* Politics (Baltimore, 1962), p. 71.

17. A. Aron, *Peace and War: A Theory of International Relations* (London, 1966), p. 71.
18. Meghna Guhathakurta, Narratives of women in the Chittagong Hill Tracts, in Rita Manchanda (eds.) *Women War and Peace in South Asia: Beyond Victimhood to Agency,* (London, 2001), pp. 201-203.
19. Hameeda Hossain, *Human Rights in Bangladesh 2001,* (Dhaka, 2002), pp. 150-160.
20. Kalpana Chakma, *Kalpana Chakma's Diary,* Published serially in *Bhorer Kagoj,* July 24, September 29 and October 6, 1996.
21. www.chtcommission.org/wp-content/uploads/2008/11/CHTC-Memo to PM-28 June 2010.pdf, last accessed December 6, 2010.
22. CHTC Memorandum to the Prime Minister dtd. June 28, 2010 on the Commission's Visit to Khagrachhari and Rangamati, June 19-24, 2010. BDNews24, CHT Commission Submits Probe report, June 30, 2011 on http://bdnews24.com/details.php?id=166236&cid=2 accessed on September 1, 2011. Bull, *The Anarchical Society: A Study of Order in Global Politics* (London, 1977), p. 310.

CHAPTER-8

Conclusion

Foreign policy is an instrument to promote and protect a country's national interests in the arena of international order. Foreign policy provides a general framework of a country's relations with various other states and non-state actors. The strength or weaknesses of a country are reflected in its foreign policy formulations and operationalisation. Therefore, foreign policy of a country is also a reflection of its status and power. In this context foreign policy is closely related to domestic policy. In the context of the developing countries foreign policy formulation and operationalisation is a complex phenomenon as these countries are faced with numerous political and economic strains, pulls and pressures.

Foreign policy is operationalised by policy decision makers and as such it may reflect, to a certain extent, their perception, attitude and priorities. But it has to be framed in the context of a given set of factors, variables and forces, which are termed as foreign policy determinants. These determinants may differ from country to country. Hence, foreign policies also differ from country to country.

I

The present thesis is a descriptive and analytical study of the foreign policy of Bangladesh in the post- cold war phase of international relations. The major focus of the study is to understand the dynamics of the foreign policy of Bangladesh in the context of changing global scenario marked by globalization, privatization and liberalization on the one hand and the changing patterns of politics of Bangladesh marked by democracy and liberalization of the political system on the other. The study has brought out the changing patterns of foreign policy of Bangladesh in global, regional, and domestic perspectives. The basic objective of this study is to understand to what extent Bangladesh has been able to carry forward the goals of its foreign policy in the post-cold war era in tune with the changing dynamics of the international politics and the internal political dynamics of Bangladesh. To what extent Bangladesh has been able to adjust and assimilate its foreign policy in accordance to the needs of the changes taking place at both the ends. Globalization and liberalization at the global level and democratization at the domestic level were important factors in accordance, to which the new ruling elite of Bangladesh had to shape up its foreign policy. To what extent Bangladesh maintained continuity and which are the aspects of change in its foreign policy is significant.

II

The variables which determine the nature, style, objectives, instruments and strategies of Bangladesh foreign policy are of general nature. They can be applied to analyse the foreign policy of any Third World country. The tangible domestic factors like geography, population, economy and natural resources of Bangladesh have more negative aspects than positive. They act as constraints rather than capabilities of Bangladesh foreign policy. The defence establishment as a capability grew during the post-Mujib period but it is not strong enough to play an important role in the foreign policy decision making. The Constitution of Bangladesh acts as a determinant of its foreign policy because it defines the guiding principles and objectives of Bangladeshi foreign policy.

Among the intangible variables historical legacy as perceived and interpreted by the ruling elites of Bangladesh particularly modern and contemporary history, sub□consciously influence their foreign policy. The national ideology is a divisive issue among the middle classes of Bangladesh. It indirectly determines Bangladesh's attitude towards the neighbouring countries particularly India and Pakistan. Change in national ideology in the post-Mujib era influenced the change of the regime's perceptions of the neighbouring countries particularly vis-a-vis India and Pakistan. Leadership in the post-Mujib period was restored in the hands of military and civil bureaucracy as it was during Pakistan days. The section of the leadership which became more powerful was the repatriated personnel whose values, attitude and images were not drastically changed because they did not participate in the Liberation War. The biases and the images of a situation perceived by the leadership have an imprint upon the foreign policy of Bangladesh. The restoration of democracy in 1991 did not affect the national ideology and the political character of leadership. The national ideology and the nature of leadership both changed in 1996 which have its implications on Bangladesh's neighbourhood policy.

The external variables of foreign policy are very important particularly for the least developed countries including Bangladesh. The pre-eminent state in the South Asian regional sub-system is India which surrounds Bangladesh from three sides. The situation is perceived by ruling elites of Bangladesh for the purpose of foreign policy decision making as 'India factor'. The approach of the regimes of Zia, Ershad and Khaleda Zia towards India was to minimize or if possible restrain the influences of India upon the foreign policy of Bangladesh. The Indo-Bangladesh Treaty of Peace and

Friendship became redundant for all practical purposes. Common national ideology and similar world view was the basis of the bilateral treaty which changed after the violent removal of Mujib regime. Dhaka's perceptions of the international and regional issues were divergent from New Delhi in many cases during the post-Mujib era. The Bangladeshi approach towards India again became positive and its perception's on regional and international issues became similar or at least non- hostile to the Indian perceptions with the advent of the Awami League into power.

It can be said here that it is not possible to shape foreign policy of a country on the basis of one single determinant. It is always an interplay of diverse factors. Hence, one may agree that a particular factor may give more importance at a particular time due to some reasons. Nevertheless, it can be asserted in the case of Bangladesh that the geo-political considerations and developmental constraints play a dominating role in foreign policy making.

III

Bangladesh is the youngest member of the South Asian community of nations, which came into existence on 16 December 1971 after a nine month old Liberation War against Pakistan. Bangladesh is surrounded on three sides by India. Before 1947 it formed part of grater Bengal. The Bengalee culture is so predominant in Bangladesh that it has given crises of identity to the country. The Bangladeshi ruling elite has find it difficult to distinguish the cultural components of Bangladeshi nationalism. India's overwhelming presence on three sides of the country also pose challenges for Bangladesh in terms of asserting its independent identity. The border dispute, sharing of natural resources, cross border migration, etc. are contentious issues between the two countries. In the South Bangladesh opens in the Bay of Bengal. It has indeed accorded a strategic positions to the country in the Bay of Bengal.

Economically Bangladesh is among the poorest countries of the world. While, in terms of population, it is among the highly populated countries of the third world. Bangladesh does not have sufficient land to home its ever increasing population. It is a worse poor country and poverty and unemployment are rampant. The economy of the country is largely dependent on foreign assistance. It naturally put a limit on the foreign policy options of the country.

The people of Bangladesh were subject to exploitation and humiliations during the days of Pakistan. Even after independence it has not been possible to establish strong political institutions. Democracy has been fragile and the country has faced political instability and the rise of military in politics for quite some time. The weak political institutions and instability has affected its diplomatic maneuverability.

Bangladesh is an overwhelmingly muslim country. Hindus and Buddhas are in minority. Bangladesh has exhibited a mixed picture of secularism and fundamentalism. Bangladesh's major challenge has been to acquire more and more foreign economic assistance.

The socio-economic and political conditions of Bangladesh do not provide it any strength and viability so as to become a powerful actor among the comity of nations. On the contrary, Bangladesh has limited foreign policy options. How to face its ever-increasing population and sustain the economy of developmental efforts are its primary requirements. The foreign policy has to be an instrument to attain these objectives.

IV

After independence Sheikh Mujib, the father of nation, took up the task of establishing the state of Bangladesh in the community of nations. Mujib tried to establish a secular and democratic political order. It also influenced the foreign policy orientation of the country. Bangladesh established relations with all the major countries of the world. Foreign assistance was being received for the socio-economic reconstruction of the country. Bangladesh concluded a peace and friendship treaty with India and tried to come closer to Indo-Soviet axis.

The political change in Bangladesh following the assassination of Sheikh Mujib in 1975, also witnessed a change in the foreign policy of Bangladesh. The military rulers of Bangladesh did not feel to be obliged to India as their predecessors. Hence, they tried to give a new turn to foreign policy. Bangladesh followed a policy of cordial relations with the smaller neighbors, advocated the idea of regional cooperation and also advocated multilateral diplomacy in place of bilateral negotiations. Gen. Ziaur Rahman established relations with South-East, Far East, West Asian and other Islamic countries on the basis of sovereign equality.

Gen. Ershad who overtook the reigns of power after Zia followed the foreign policy laid down by Gen. Zia. Zia's initiative to form a regional organisation was persued by Ershad which was materialized by the formation of SAARC at the first Summit of South Asian States held at Dhaka in 1985. During his regime, western donors and multilateral institutions greatly influenced the foreign policy of Bangladesh.

The disintegrations of Soviet Union and the consequent end of Cold War politics on the one hand, and the emergence of a new world order characterized by globalization and liberalization on the other, influenced the foreign policies particularly of the third world countries. The globalization and liberalization necessitated reshaping and reorientation of foreign policies of the countries of the third world. Bangladesh although was not much affected by the disintegration of the Soviet Union as the military rulers of Bangladesh did not give much importance towards establishing closer relations with the Soviet Union. However, it was bound to be influenced by the forces of globalization and liberalization. These changes at the global level coincided with the changes at the domestic front. In 1990 Bangladesh once again stepped on the path of democracy.

V

Khaleda Zia who became Prime Minister of Bangladesh after the 1991 elections followed the foreign policy shaped by her late husband Gen. Zia. However, there was a shift in the attitude. Bangladesh began to follow policy of privatization. Efforts were also made to normalize relations with India. Some of the notable achievements of her foreign policy were : opening of the Teen Bigha Corridor by India on lease to connect Bangladesh enclaves with the mainland, involvement of the UNHCR in the maintenance and repatriation of Rohingya refugees, normalisation of relation with Iran, active participation in the UN peace keeping force, and to open relations with the Central Asian states.

Sheikh Hasina formed her government after the victory of her party, the Awami League, in the 1996 general elections. The Awami League came to power after remaining twenty-one years in opposition. The installation of a new government under the Awami League ended an era of politics in Bangladesh. The new government did not give any radical shift to the foreign policy of the country. The most notable change was the redefinition of the perception, attitude and approach towards India and Pakistan. As a result of the reciprocal faith and confidence shown to each other and the strong initiative taken by Bangladesh, New Delhi and Dhaka signed the Ganges Water Sharing Agreement for thirty years in December 1996. The Awami League government also resolved the insurgency problem in the CHT region and repatriated all the CHT refugees living in India to Bangladesh. To and fro bus service between Calcutta and Dhaka began in 1999, and measures were being taken to re-open the Calcutta- Kulna rail route. The routine bilateral relations with Pakistan were maintained by the government but the similarities in the perception and understanding of the political and security developments of the region was gone. There was no remarkable change in the policies of Bangladesh towards any other friendly state under the Awami League regime. The government maintained its active participation in multilateral diplomacy at regional and international organizations with which it was associated. The government took initiatives to form some new multilateral organisations at sub- regional, South and South-East Asian and Islamic Countries level.

Khaleda Zia's return to power in October 2001 underlined a shift in the foreign policy orientation as well. During the present regime of Begum Khaleda Zia, Bangladesh is following the foreign policy of Gen. Zia. Now Bangladesh's relations are correct with India, but not cordial. However, the long awaited Dhaka-Agartala bus service was flagged off on 19 September 2003 and this was a welcome step. The change of regime in New Delhi in 2004 and the visit of the Foreign Minister of India to Bangladesh in September 2005 are creating good atmosphere between Bangladesh and India. On the other hand, this regime of Khaleda Zia maintained excellent relations with developed nations especially with U.S. Bangladesh also had warm relations with China, and other neighbouring countries of South Asia including Myanmar, Bhutan, Nepal, Sri Lanka, Pakistan and

Maldivies. Khaleda Zia also maintained good relations with OIC.

Dhaka has given high importance to its politico-security diplomacy with the western developed countries particularly the United States. Any disruption in the annual aid flow from these countries and the west dominated multilateral economic institutions may create political and economic instability in Bangladesh. Dhaka always try to follow the US line or remain neutral if possible on different international issues. The diplomatic strategy of Bangladesh is to keep its foreign policy as much as possible in harmony with Washington. On some occasions it has taken euphemistically pro-west stands, in international forums like NAM and the UN General Assembly, which have been against the mainstream Third World viewpoints on the bidding of Washington. The pro- US approach in its foreign policy has gradually increased because of its increased dependency on western aid. It would not be wrong to state that gradually it has become a client state of the US.

India is the most important neighbour of Bangladesh. Bangladesh-India relations have passed through five phases from 1971 to 2005. The first phase lasted from March 1971 to March 1972. In this phase the pattern of relations was that of patron and client. Bangladesh came into existence with the total support of India. It remained heavily dependent upon New Delhi in the early months of its existence. The bilateral relations of the two countries after signing of the friendship treaty in March 1972 upto August 1975 falls under the second phase. Sheikh Mujib tried to develop bilateral relations of Bangladesh with India on the basis of sovereign equality. Mujib and Indira had common national ideology and world view. The bilateral relations during 1975-1996 i.e. during the era of the non- Awami League regimes, can be termed as third phase. The national ideology and the world view of Bangladesh were different from India during this period which influenced the nature of their bilateral relations. The installation of the Awami League regime in Bangladesh in March 1996 heralded the fourth phase of the bilateral relations. Trust, confidence and political understanding between the two countries returned. The fifth phase of Bangladesh- India relations is going on since October 2001 onwards, when BNP again came to power under Begum Khaleda Zia. During the present regime, Bangladesh-India relations are correct but not excellent because national ideology and world view of Bangladesh and India are different.

China is perceived in Dhaka as an important neighbour Sino- Bangla relations in different fields increased as a result of Zia's diplomatic initiatives. During Ershad's period the momentum of bilateral relations further increased. China is the single largest arms supplier to Bangladesh. The bilateral relations which began with negative commonality of perceptions towards India have slowly gained positive basis. The ongoing Sino-Indian detente has not affected the Sino-Bangla relations. As a result of the normalisation China has changed its policy of political support to the South Asian neighbours of India in their dispute with New Delhi. The BNP government did not change Bangladesh's policy of friendly cooperative relations towards China.

Pakistan recognised Bangladesh in February 1974 after which Prime Minister Bhutto visited Dhaka in June 1974. The visit failed to establish diplomatic relations because Sheikh Mujib wanted to settle the issues of the division of assets of the united Pakistan days and the repatriation of the Biharis from Bangladesh to Pakistan. The removal of the Mujib regime in a violent coup ended the hard approach towards Pakistan. All the non-Awami League post-Mujib regimes from Khondkar Mustaque Ahmad to Begum Khaleda Zia have positive perceptions about Pakistan and there have been similarities in their viewpoints with that of their

Pakistani counterparts on the issues related with South Asian security. Interaction in the field of defence through reciprocal visits by the defence personnel began during the regime of Ershad in the late 1980s. The coming to power of the Awami League brought a shift in Bangladeshi perception of Pakistan. The regime maintained its normal relations with Pakistan but the earlier warmth and confidence of the bilateral relations were missing. Begum Khaleda Zia once again came to power in October 2001 and again Bangladesh-Pakistan relations became good and positive. But, bilateral problems with Pakistan, a legacy of the secession are still unresolved and dormant.

Bangladesh has maintained excellent problem free relations based on common feelings and aspirations with Myanmar, Nepal, Bhutan and Sri Lanka, the other small South Asian states. Change of regime in Bangladesh has not affected its relations with these states.

In the broader context of Bangladesh's foreign policy, the launching of the South Asian Association for Regional Cooperation (SAARC) in Dhaka in 1985 comprising the seven countries of the region is an event of vital significance. It has been a major foreign policy initiative of Bangladesh which looks upon the organisation as an important instrument to promote individual and collective economic and social development and peace and mutual understanding in the region.

Bangladesh has supported the development of SAARC and has taken keen interest in it. Over the years SAARC has put in place an impressive number of agreements, institutions, programmes and activities towards the promotion of cooperation in South Asia. The subject committees called Technical Committees which currently total eleven in number are responsible for drawing up programmes and activities for cooperation and for overseeing their implementation. A number of socio-economic issues and matters of concern to South Asia, covering such diverse areas as education, health and population activities, tourism, agriculture, science and technology, are now on their agenda. SAARC agreements cover issues like terrorism, drugs and food security. A network of regional institutions and professional bodies (SAARC Agricultural Information Centre, SAARC Meteorological Centre, SAARC Chamber of Commerce and Industries, SAARC Law, and Association of SAARC Speakers and Parliamentarians, to name a few, have been usefully operating in their respective fields of competence for some time now.

One of the most important objectives of Bangladeshi foreign policy is to procure foreign aid. The aid diplomacy of Bangladesh has been routinised and formalised through experiences. The aid mobilising machinery-Economic Relations Division (ERD) has developed the process, technique and strategy for aid mobilization. Norms, rules and conventions for the donor- recipient relationship have been evolved. The formalisation and institutionalization of the internal work of the ERD and its outside interaction with the aid donors have made external resource mobilization easy.

The scope and influence of aid in the economy of Bangladesh has progressively increased with the passing of time. The ruling elite of Bangladesh have consensus on the role of aid in the economy. As an LDC, Bangladesh gets aid on very liberal terms and conditions from the developed countries who are regarded development partners of these states. The annual value of aid which Bangladesh receives is not a problem rather utilisation of the sanctioned aid is a problem.

The role of external trade in the economic development of a country has been recognised by the economists and proved by the development histories of different economies. Upto seventies the stress was on import substitution in trade policies of different developing states which has shifted to export promotion in the eighties after the success stories of the Asian Tigers. External trade is playing an important role in the development process of Bangladesh. Dhaka has progressively created different institutions and formulated policies for export promotion and export expansion to lower the balance of payment gap. There has been little change in its import structure since independence. Non-developmental i.e. consumer goods and raw materials for consumer goods account for almost 70 per cent of the import. This is a serious structural weakness in the foreign trade of Bangladesh. The share of jute and tea, the traditional export commodities of Bangladesh in the total value of export has declined and non-traditional items, like garments and frozen food have become main foreign exchange earning commodities. The share of garment export has shown a remarkable growth in Bangladesh. The weakness of this industry is the lower percentage of value addition in the country. In the late seventies the overseas remittances sent by the Bangladeshi migrant workers became the most important source of foreign exchange to the country. In 1989-90 the export earnings became 53 percent of the total foreign exchange which was higher than the remittances. It has maintained its position over remittances after that year.

The trade diplomacy of Bangladesh neither at bilateral level with the countries which imports its goods nor at multilateral level in the IMF to avail its different facilities for ameliorating balance of payment problems has been so effective. The onset of globalisation regime under WTO poses new challenges to Bangladeshi export. In the coming time all the privileges which is available to Bangladeshi export due to the LDC status of the country will be removed. The country has to prepare for a smooth transition from a positive discriminatory international trade regime to a non-discriminatory open international trade regime.

The third important economic task before Bangladesh foreign policy after aid procurement and trade promotion is the attraction of foreign private investment. All the developing countries are trying to attract more and more foreign investment in their economies. The need of foreign investment is higher in Bangladesh because the rate of domestic savings of the country is very poor. Mujib regime was very restrictive to any private investment so there was no foreign investment in that period. Zia started economic liberalisation which was further intensified by each successive regimes. As a result of liberalisation Bangladesh has gradually improved the terms given to the prospective foreign investors. Different institutions has been created to facilitate foreign investment. Some of the institutions are: the Foreign Investment Promotion and Protection Act 1980, Bangladesh Export Processing Zones Authority (BEPZA) established in 1983 and the Board of investment (1301) created in 1989. Inspite of all these Foreign Direct Investment (FDI) on an averages is about I per cent of the total foreign capital inflow, and about 0.8 per cent of total investment in Bangladesh. It is very small even in comparison to its South Asian neighbours. The reasons for the low FDI inflows are : the overall backwardness of the economy, political instability, administrative redtapism, official corruption, fear of labour unrest, small domestic market, very low credit rating and weak currency. The lower cost of labour is neaturalised by its low productivity.

External help in all desired forms has played very important role in the creation of the nation state of Bangladesh. The civil war or the Liberation War of Bangladesh is the first example of a successful liberation from a member state of the United Nations, which is responsible for the collective security of all its members. Leaders of the Liberation War solicited Indian help and New Delhi seized the opportunity, because creation of Bangladesh after dismembering Pakistan was considered vital for the security interest of India. The government of India and the Indian people provided all possible assistance to cause. The second important international event which proved crucial, for the success of the violent struggle was the signing of the Indo-Soviet treaty in response to Sino-American entente with the good offices of Pakistan during the Liberation War. Direct involvement of Moscow in support of New Delhi became decisive for the complete victory of India over East Pakistan and the emergence of Bangladesh.

Huge amount of Indian and international monetary and material assistance poured into the nascent state for the repatriation and rehabilitation of millions of refugees, restoration of law and order, organization of governance and administration and reorganization of the economy. The role of friendly states and institutions was not over for Bangladesh after its admission into the comity of nations and its recognition by all important nations. As a 'test case' of development Bangladesh has no option but to seek international help in different fields from friendly states and international institutions for its sustenance and development.

Foreign policy has been very important to the decision makers in Bangladesh at every stage of its national history. There has been continuity and changes in the foreign policy of the country from the days of the Liberation War to the present day. The changes have occurred in strategy, style, trends and direction of the foreign policy, some times in response to the changes in situations and some times as a result of the change in the nature of the regime.

VII

It can be said towards the end that the smaller countries of South Asia have often been faced with a crisis of identity.

This crisis has largely emerged due to the geo-politics in South Asia where India has a predominance. The smaller countries feel dwarfed against a big neighbour. These countries have multiple problems with India and they have a obsession that it is not possible for them to deal with India, that India has a hegemonistic attitude towards its neighbours and that their identity is submerged against a big neighbour. This crisis of identity has compelled these countries to use external factor as a tool against a possible regional hegemonism. But the crisis of identity has also been used by the smaller neighbours as an instrument to protect the interest of the ruling elite. Bangladesh has not been exception to this kind of situation. The outward looking approach of Bangladesh has also been largely shaped by its problems vis-a-vis India. It may also be noted here as pointed earlier, that India played a determining role in the emergence of Bangladesh. However, in the subsequent years this factor has both positive and negative connotations in the foreign policy of Bangladesh. One set of political elite has relied heavily on the positive connotations of India's role. Hence, it has a different kind of approach towards India. While the other set of political elite has relied on the negative connotations of India's role and followed a different kind of policy vis-a-vis India. Therefore, apart from other things the internal political development in Bangladesh also play an important role in shaping its foreign policy. The overall goal of Bangladeshi foreign policy has always been the same i.e., security and development along with sustenance. The foreign policy account of Bangladesh over all these years is a mixed bag of successes and failures in achieving the targeted objectives. There is scope for improvement both in foreign policy decision- making and its implementation to make it more effective.

Appendices

APPENDIX-1

TREATY BETWEEN THE GOVERNMENT OF THE PEOPLE'S REPUBLIC OF BANGLADESH AND THE GOVERNMENT OF THE REPUBLIC OF INDIA ON SHARING OF THE GANGA/GANGES WATERS AT FARAKKA

The Government of the People's Republic of Bangladesh and the Government of the Republic of India

DETERMINED to promote and strengthen their relations of friendship and good neighbourliness.

INSPIRED by the common desire of promoting the well-boing of thcir peoples. BEING desirous of sharing by mutual agreement the waters of the international rivers flowing through the territories of the two countries and of making the optimum utilisation of the water resources of their region in the fields of flood management, irrigation, river basin development and generation of hydropower for the mutual benefit of the peoples of the two countries,

RECOGNISING that the need for making an arrangement for sharing of the Ganga/Ganges waters at Farakka in a spirit of mutual accommodation and the need for a solution to the long-term problem of augmenting the flows of the Ganga/Ganges are in the mutual interests of the peoples of the two countries.

BEING desirous of finding a fair and just solution without affecting the rights and entitlements of either country other than those covered by this Treaty, or establishing any general principles of law or precedent,

HAVE AGREED AS FOLLOWS:

ARTICLE-I

The quantum of waters agreed to be released by India to Bangladesh will be at Farakka.

ARTICLE-II

(i) The sharing between India and Bangladesh of the Ganga/Ganges waters at Farakka by ten-day periods from the 1 st January to the 31 st May, every year will be with reference to the formula at Annexure I and an indicative schedule giving the implications of the sharing arrangement under Annexure I is at Annexure II.

(ii) The indicative schedule at Annexure II as referred to in subpara (i) above, is based on 40 years (1949-1988) 10-day period of average availability of water at Farakka. Every effort would be made by the upper riparian to protect flows of water at Farakka as in the 40-years' average availability as mentioned above.

(iii) In the event flow at Farakka falls below 50,000 cusecs in any 10-day period, the two Governments will enter into immediate consultations to make adjustments on an emergency basis, in accordance with the principles of equity, fair play and no harm to either party.

ARTICLE-III

The waters released to Bangladesh at Farakka under Article I shall not be reduced below Farakka except for reasonable uses of waters, not exceeding 200 cusecs, by India between Farakka and the point on the Ganga/Ganges where both its banks are in Bangladesh.

ARTICLE-IV

A Committee consisting of representatives nominated by the two Governments in equal numbers (hereinafter called the Joint Committee) shall be constituted following the signing of this Treaty. The Joint Committee shall set up suitable teams at Farakka and Hardinge Bridge to observe and record at Farakka the daily flows below Farakka Barrage, in the Feeder Canal, and at the Navigation Lock, as well as at the Hardinge Bridge.

ARTICLE-V

The Joint Committee shall decide its own procedure and method of functioning.

ARTICLE-VI

The Joint Committee shall submit to the two Governments all data collected by it and shall also submit a yearly report to both the Governments. Following submission of the reports the two Governments will meet at appropriate levels to decide upon such further actions as may be needed.

ARTICLE-VII

The Joint Committee shall be responsible for implementing the arrangements contained in this Treaty and examining any difficulty arising out of the implementation of the above arrangements and of the operation of Farakka Barrage. Any difference or dispute arising in this regard, if not resolved by the Joint Committee, shall be referred to the Indo-Bangladesh Joint Rivers Commission. If the difference or dispute still remains unresolved, it shall be referred to the two Governments which shall meet urgently at the appropriate level to resolve it by mutual discussion.

ARTICLE-VIII

The two Governments recognise the need to cooperate with each other in finding a solution to the long-term problem of augmenting the flows of the Ganga/Ganges during the dry season.

ARTICLE-IX

Guided by the principles of equity, fairness and no harm to either party, both the Governments agree to conclude water-sharing Treaties/ Agreements with regard to other common rivers.

ARTICLE-X

The sharing arrangement under this Treaty shall be reviewed by the two Governments at five years' interval or earlier, as required by either party and needed adjustments, based on principles of equity, fairness, and no harm to either party made thereto, if necessary. It would be open to either party to seek the first review after two years to assess the impact and working of the sharing arrangement as contained in this Treaty.

ARTICLE-XI

For the period of this Treaty, in the absence of mutual agreement on adjustments following reviews as mentioned in Article X, India shall release downstream of Farakka Barrage, water at a rate not less than 90% (ninety per cent) of Bangladesh's share according to the formula referred to in Article II, until such time as mutually agreed flows are decided upon.

ARTICLE-XII

This Treaty shall enter into force upon signature and shall remain in force for a period of thirty years and it shall be renewable on the basis of mutual consent.

IN WITNESS WHEREOF the undersigned, being duly authorised thereto by the respective Governments, have signed this Treaty.

Done at New Delhi 12 December 1996, in Hindi, Bangla and English languages. In tie event of any conflict between the texts, the English text shall prevail.

SHEIKH HASINA
12 December 1996
PRIME MINISTER,
PEOPLE'S REPUBLIC OF
BANGLADESH

H.D. DEVE GOWDA
12 December 1996
PRIME MINISTER,
REPUBLIC OF INDIA

ANNEXURE-I

Availability at Farakka	*Share of India*	*Share of Bangladesh*
70,000 cusecs or less	50%	50%
70,000-75,000 cusecs	Balance of flow	35,000 cusecs
75,000 cusecs or more	40,000 cusecs	Balance of flow

Subject to thc condition that India and Bangladesh each shall receive guaranteed 35,000 cusecs of water in alternate three 10-days periods during the period 1 March to 10 May.

ANNEXURE-II (Schedule)

(Sharing of waters at Farakka between 1 January and 31 May every year).

If actual availability corresponds to average flows of the period 1949 to 1988, the implication of the formula in Annexure I for the share of each side is:

Period	*Average of total flow 1949-88 (Cusecs)*	*India's share (Cusecs)*	*Bangladesh's share (Cusecs)*
January			
1-10	107,516	40,000	67,516
11-20	97,673	40,000	57,673
21-31	90,154	4000	50,154
February			
1-10	86,323	40,000	46,323
11-20	82,859	40,000	42,859
21-28	79,106	40,000	39,106
March			
1-10	74,419	39,419	35,000*
11-20	68,931	33,931	35,000
21-31	64,688	35,000*	29,688
April			
1-10	63,180	28,180	35,000*
11-20	62,633	35,000	27,000
21-30	60,992	25,992	35,000*
May			
1-10	67,351	35,000*	32,351
11-20	73,590	38,590	35,000*
21-31	81,854	40,000	41,854 *

Three ten-day periods during which 35,000 cusecs shall be provided.

APPENDIX-2

AGREEMENT BETWEEN THE GOVERNMENT OF THE UNION OF MYANMAR AND THE GOVERNMENT OF THE PEOPLE'S REPUBLIC OF BANGLADESH ON BORDER TRADE BETWEEN THE TWO COUNTRIES

In order to further strengthen the trade relations between the Government of the Union of Myanmar and the Government of the People's Republic of Bangladesh, the two government's have agreed to develop trade in border areas on the basis of equality and mutual benefit.

ARTICLE-I

The sale and purchase of goods under this agreement shall be carried out between the border areas of Myanmar, on the one part, and the border areas of Bangladesh, on the other part, Maungdow, on the one part, and Teknaf, on the other part, being the reserve points of delivery.

The buyers shall inspect and take delivery of goods at the seller's point of delivery.

ARTICLE-II

The goods to be traded on the border under this agreement shall be as permitted by both governments.

ARTICLE-III

The trade between the two governments shall be conducted in accordance with the export and import laws, rules and procedures and the foreign exchange regulations in force from time to time in their respective countries.

ARTICLE-IV

All contracts, invoices and other documents relating to the transactions to be effected under this agreement shall be expressed in US dollar or in currencies mutually agreed upon by the two governments.

ARTICLE-V

For the purpose of effecting payments arising from transactions under this agreement, the Myanmar Foreign Trade Bank, Yangon, and, the Sonali Bank of Bangladesh shall enter into separate banking arrangements.

ARTICLE-VI

The names, specifications and quantity of the commodities and the price, time of delivery, packing, inspection etc. of the commodities shall be in accordance with terms and conditions stipulated in the individual contract(s) or any other document(s).

ARTICLE-VII

This agreement shall be reviewed periodically by both sides to ensure successful implementation of its objectives. In case of differences relating to or arising out of this agreement, the same shall be amicably settled in the spirit of mutual cooperation and friendship.

ARTICLE-VIII

Amendment(s) or supplement(s) (if any) to this agreement shall be made by exchange of letters between the two government.

ARTICLE-IX

This agreement shall come into force with effect from the date on which it is signed and shall remain in force for one year from the date. It shall be automatically extended for a period of one year at a time unless one of the parties hereto gives notice in writing, three months in advance, of its intention to terminate this agreement.

This agreement is signed in Dhaka on the eighteenth day of May, nineteen hundred ninety four in two original texts in the English language, both texts being equally authentic.

(M. SHAMSUL ISLAM)
MINISTER FOR COMMERCE
GOVERNMENT OF THE PEOPLE'S
REPUBLIC OF BANGLADESH
FOR AND ON BEHALF OF THE
GOVERNMENT OF THE PEOPLE'S
REPUBLIC OF BANGLADESH

(LT. GEN. TUN KYI)
MINISTER FOR TRADE
GOVERNMENT OF THE
UNION OF MYANMAR
FOR AND ON BEHALF OF THE
GOVERNMENT OF THE
UNION OF MYANMAR

Bibliography

(A) BOOKS

A.T. Abbas, B.M., *The Ganges Water Dispute* (New Delhi: Vikas, 1982). Agwani, M.S. (ed.), *South Asia, Stability and Regional Cooperation* (Chandigarh : Centre for Research in Development, 1983).

Ahmed, Emajuddin, *Foreign Policy of Bangladesh: A Small State's Imperative* (Dhaka: University Press, 1984).

Ahmed, Emajuddin, *Military Rule and Myth of Democracy* (Dhaka: University Press, 1988).

Ahmad, Muzaffar and Kalam, Abul (eds.), *Bangladesh Foreign Relations: Changes and Direction* (Dhaka: University Press, 1989).

Ahmad, Salahuddin, *Bangladesh : Tradition and Transformation* (Dhaka University Press, 1987)

Ahmed, E. and K. Abul (eds.), *Bangladesh, South Asia and the World* (Dhaka: Academic Pub., 1992).

Ahmad, Moudud, *Bangladesh: Era of Sheikh Mujibur Rahman* (Dhaka University Press, 1983)

Ahmad, Moudud, *Democracy and the Challenge of Development : A Study of Politics and Military Interventions in Bangladesh* (Dhaka: University Press, 1995).

Ahmed, Nafis, *A New Economic Geography of Bangladesh* (Dhaka: University Press, 1976).

Ali, Ashraf, Islam, M. Faizul and Kuddus, Ruhul (eds.), *Development Ivsues of Bangladesh* (Dhaka: University Press, 1996)

AIi, S.M., *The Fearful State . Power, People and Internal War in South Asia,* (London : Zed Books, 1993)

Ali, S.M., *After the Dark Nights: Problems of Sheikh Mujibur Rahman* (Delhi: Thompson Press, 1973).

Al-Mashat, Abdul Monem M., *National Security in the Third World* (Boulder Westvies, 1985).

Anisuzzaman, *Identity, Religion and Recent History* (Calcutta: Naya Udyog, 1995).

Appadorai, A. and Rajan, M.S., *Foreign Policy and Religion,* (New Delhi: South Asian Publishers, 1985).

Arun Kumar Banerji (ed.), *Security Issues in South Asia . Domestic and External Sources of Threats to Security* (Calcutta : Minerva Associates, 1998) Ayoob, Mohammad, *India, Pakistan and Bangladesh* (New Delhi : ICWA, 1975)

Bajpai, U.S. (ed.), *India and Its Neighbourhood* (New Delhi : Lancer International, 1986).

Banerjee, Dipankar, *Security in South Asia. Comprehensive and Cooperative* (New Delhi: Manas Publications, 1999).

Bayes, Abdul and Mohammad, A., *Bangladesh at 25: An Analytical Discourse on Development* (Dhaka: University Press, 1988).

Begum, Khurshida, *Tension Over the Farakka Barrage : A Techno-Political Tangle in South Asia* (Dhaka: University Press, 1987)

Bindra, S.S., *Indo-Bangladesh Relations* (New Delhi : Deep and Deep Publications, 1982)

Biswas, Jayashree, *US-Bangladesh Relations: A Study of the Political and Economic Development during 1971-81* (Calcutta: Minerva Pub., 1984).

Block, J.F. and Thompson, K.W. (eds.), *Foreign Policies in a World of Change* (New York: Harper & Row, 1963).

Brands, William, *India, Pakistan and Great Powers* (New York: Praeger, 1972).

Brecher, Michael, *The Foreign Policy Systems of Israel : Setting, Images Process* (London : Oxford, 1972)

Calvert, Peter, *The Foreign Policy of New States* (Sussex: Wheatsheaf Pub., 1986).

Camilleri, J., *Chinese Foreign Policy: The Maoist Era and its Aftermath,* (Oxford: Martin Robertson, 1980).

Cassen, R. (ed.), *Soviet Interests in the Third World* (London : Sage, 1985). Chakravarti, Raghubir, *International Relations* (Calcutta: The World Press, 1970)

Chakravarti, S.K., *The Evolution of Politics in Bangladesh, 1947-78* (New Delhi: Associates Publishing House, 1978).

Chakravarty, S.R. (ed.), *Foreign Policy of Bangladesh* (New Delhi : Har Anand Publishers, 1994).

Chakravarty, S.R. and Narain, V. (eds.), *Bangladesh, Global Politics, Vol. III* (New Delhi: South Asian Pub., 1988).

Chaudhury, G.W., *The Last Days of United Pakistan* (London: C. Hurst, 1974). Chitty, N., *Framing South Asian Transformation: An Examination of Regional Views on South Asian Cooperation* (New Delhi : South Asian Publishers, 1994).

Chopra, P. (ed.), *Challenges of Bangladesh. A Special Debate* (Bombay: Popular Prakashan, 1971).

Chowdhury, Dilara, *Bangladesh and South Asian International System* (Dhaka: Academic Publishers, 1992).

Chowdhury, G.W., *India, Pakistan, Bangladesh and the Major Powers* (New York: Free Press, 1975).

Cohen, Stephen Philip, *The Security of South Asia: American and Asian Perspective* (New Delhi : Vistaar Publications, 1987).

Crow, Ben, Lindquist, Alan and Wilson, David (eds.), *Sharing the Ganges: The Politics and Technology of River Development* (New Delhi : Sage, 1995)

Dan, Haendel, *The Process of Priority Formation. U.S. Foreign Policy in the Indo-Pakistan War of 1971* (Colorado: Westview Press, 1977).

Deora, M.S. (ed.), *India's Role of Afro-Asian Movement and the Freedom Struggle of Bangladesh* (New Delhi : Discovery Publishing House, 1995). Dixit, J.N., *Indian Foreign Policy and its Neighbours* (New Delhi: Gyan Publishing House, 2001).

Dubey, Muchkund, *An Unequal Treaty: World Trading Order After GATT* (New Delhi: New Age International, 1996)

Dubey, Muchkund, *Indo-Bangladesh Economic Relations* (New Delhi: CPR, 1996).

Faaland, J., *Aid and Influence. The Case of Bangladesh* (London: Macmillan Press, 1981).

Franda, Marcus, *Bangladesh: The First Decade* (New Delhi: South Asian Pub., 1982).

Frankel, J., *International Politics: Conflict and Harmony* (London: Allen Lane, 1969).

Ghosh, S., *China-Bangladesh-India Triangle Today: Towards a* Solution?(New Delhi: Sterling Pub., 1995).

Ghosh, Pradip K., (ed.), *Developing* South *Asia: A Modernisation Perspective* (London: Greenwood Press, 1984).

Ghosh, S., *The Role of India in the Emergence of Bangladesh* (Calcutta Minerva Associates, 1983).

Ghosh, Sankar and Mukherjee, Somen (eds.), *Emerging South Asian Order: Hopes and Concerns* (Calcutta: Media South Asia, 1995).

Grover, Virender (ed.), *Encyclopedia of SAARC Nations, Vol.* 7 (New Delhi: Deep and Deep Pub., 1997).

Gupta, Sisir, *India and Regional Integration in Asia* (Bombay, 1964).

Hakim, Abdul S., *Begum Khaleda Zia of Bangladesh: A Political Bibliography* (New Delhi: Vikas Publishing House, 1992).

Harris, L., Craig and Wroden, Robert L, *China and the Third World: Champion or Challenger* (London: Croom Helm, 1986).

Hasanuzzaman, A.M. (ed.), *Bangladesh Crisis of Political Development,* (Dhaka : Jahangirnagar University, 1988).

Hossain, Akhtar, *Macroeconomic Issues and Politics: The Case of Bangladesh* (New Delhi : Sage, 1996).

Hossain, Golam, *Civil-Military Relations in Bangladesh: A Comparative Study* (Dhaka: University Press, 1991).

Hossain, Golam, *General Ziaur Rahman and the BNP: Political Transformation of a Military Regime* (Dhaka: University Press, 1988). Iftekharuzzaman and Ahmed, I., (eds.), *Bangladesh and SAARC: Issues, Perspectives and Outlook* (Dhaka: Academic Pub., 1992).

Iftekharuzzaman, and Sabur Abdus A.K.M. (eds.), *Bangladesh: Society, Polity, Economy* (Dhaka: Pragati Prakashan, 1993).

Islam, Nurul, *Development Strategy of Bangladesh* (Oxford: Pergaman, 1978). Islam, Sirajul (ed.), *History of Bangladesh, Vol. II* (Dhaka: Asiatic Society of Bangladesh, 1992).

Jackson, Robert, *South Asian Crisis: India-Pakistan-Bangladesh* (London: The International Institute for Strategic Studies, 1975).

Jacob, Lt. Gen. J.F.R., *Surrender at Dacca: Birth of a Nation* (New Delhi: Manohar, 1997)

Jahan, R., *Bangladesh Politics: Problems and Issues,* (Dhaka: University Press, 1980).

Jahan, Rounaq, *Bangladesh Politics: Problems and Issues* (Dhaka: University Press, 1980)

Jahan, Rounaq, *Pakistan: Failure in National Integration* (New York: Columbia University Press, 1972).

Jain, B.M., *South-Asian Security Problems and Prospects* (New Delhi: Radiant Publishers, 1985)

Jain, R.K. (ed.), *China, Pakistan and Bangladesh: Basic Documents, 1950□1976,* Vol. II (New Delhi: Radiant Publishers, 1977).

Jain, R.K. (ed.), *US-South Asian Relations, 1947-1982,* Vol. III (New Delhi: Radiant Publications, 1983).

Jayramu, P.S., *India's National Security and Foreign Policy* (New Delhi: ABC Publications, 1987)

Jeyaratham, Wilson A. and Dennis, Dalton (eds.), *The States of South Asia: Problems ofNation Integration* (New Delhi: Vikas Pub., 1982).

Johnson, B.L.C., *Bangladesh* (New York: Barnes & Noble, 1975).

Jolsti, K.T., *International Politics: A Fremework for Analysis* (New Jersey: Prentice-Hall, 1967)

Jones, Rodney W., *Emerging Powers-Defence and Security in the Third World* (New York: Praeger, 1986).

Joseph, Frankel, *International Politics: Conflict and Harmony* (London: Allen Lane the Penguine Press, 1969)

Kabir, M.G. and H. Shaukat (eds.), *Issue and Challenges Facing Bangladesh Foreign Policy* (Dhaka: Bangladesh Society of International Studies Pub., *1989).*

Kalam, Abul (ed.), *Bangladesh: Internal Dynamics and External Linkages* (Dhaka: University Press, *1996).*

Khan, Ataur R., *India, Pakistan & Bangladesh : Conflict or Cooperation* (Dhaka: Amader Bangla Press, *1976).*

Khan, Azizur Rahman and Hossian Mahabub, *The Strategy of Development in Bangladesh* (London: Macmillan Pub., *1989).*

Khan, Azizur Rahman, *The Economy of Bangladesh* (London: Macmillan, *1972).*

Khan, M.M. and Husain, S.A. (eds.), *Bangladesh Studies. Politics, Administration, Rural Development and Foreign Policy* (Dhaka, Centre for Administration Studies : Dhaka University, *1986)*

Khan, Muhiuddin Alamgir, *Development Strategy of Bangladesh* (Dhaka Centre for Social Studies, *1980).*

Khanna, D.D., *Strategic Environment in South Asia During the 1980s* (Allahbad: Department of Defence Studies, *1979).*

Khatri, Sridhar K., *Regional Security in South Asia* (Kathmandu: Centre for Nepal and Asian Studies, *1987).*

Kochenek, Stanley A., *Patron-Client Relations and Business in Bangladesh* (New Delhi : Sage Publications, *1993).*

Kukreja, V., *Civil-Military Relations in South Asia. Pakistan, Bangladesh and India* (New Delhi: Sage, 1991).

Kumar, Mahendra, *Theoretical Aspects of International Politics* (Delhi: Shiva Lal Agrawal and Company, 1978).

Lai, S., *Bangla-Pak Polities* (New Delhi : Election Archives, 1985).

Legg, Keith R. and Morrison, James, *Politics and the International System . An Introduction* (New York: Harper and Row Publications, 1971).

Lifschultz, Lawrence, *Bangladesh: The Unfinished Revolution* (London: Zed Press, 1979).

Macridis, Roy C. (ed.), *Foreign Policy in World Politics* (New Delhi: Prentice Hall of India, 1979).

Maniruzzaman, Talukder, *The Bangladesh Revolution and Its Aftermath* (Dhaka: Bangladesh Books International, 1980).

Mascarenhas, Anthony, *Bangladesh: Legacy of Blood* (London: Hodder and Stoughton, 1986).

Mathisen, Trygoe, *The Function of Small States in the Strategies of the Great Powers (Oslo:* Universitetsforlageet, 1971).

Matin, K.M., (ed.), *Bangladesh and UNCTAD V* (Dhaka: Bangladesh Institute of Development Studies, 1982).

Matin, Abdul (ed.), *Tribute to Sheikh Mujib. Fifth Death Anniversary* (London: Bangabandhu Society, 1980).

Mishra, P. K., *India, Pakistan, Nepal and Bangladesh: Media as a Factor in the Intra-Regional Interaction in South Asia* (Delhi: Sundeep Prakashan, 1979).

Mishra, P.K., *South Asian in International Politics* (Delhi : UDH Publishers 1984).

Modelski, G.A., *Theory of Foreign Policy* (London: Pall Hall, 1962). Morgenthau, Hans J., *Politics Among Nations. The Struggle for Power and Peace* (Calcutta: Scientific Book Agency, 1966).

Mostafa, Golam, *National Interest and Foreign Policy. Bangladesh's Relations with the Soviet Union and its Successor States* (New Delhi: South Asian Publishers, 1995).

Muhith, A.M.A., *American Response to Bangladesh Liberation War* (Dhaka: University Press, 1996).

Muhith, A.M.A., *Bangladesh. Emergence of A Nation* (Dhaka : Bangladesh Book International Ltd., 1978).

Muni, S.D. and Baral, Lok Raj (eds.), *Refugees and Regional Security in South Asia* (New Delhi: Konark Pub., 1999).

Muni, S.D. and Muni Anuradha, *Regional Cooperation in South Asia* (New Delhi: National Publishing House, 1984).

Myres, Ramon H.U.S., *Foreign Policy for Asia the 1980s and Beyond* (Stanford: Hoover Press, 1982).

Naik, J.K., *India, Rassia, China and Bangladesh* (New Delhi: S. Chand and Co., 1972).

Narain, Virendra, *Foreign Policy of Bangladesh* (Jaipur: Aalekh Publishers, 1987).

Nelson, J.M., *Aid, Influence and Foreign Policy* (New York: Macmillan, 1968).

Nixon, Richard, *The Memories of Richard Nixon* (New York: Grosset and Dunlop, 1978).

Novak, James J., *Bangladesh: Refection on the Water* (Dhaka: University Press, 1994).

Palmer, Norman D. and Perkins, Howard C., *The World Community in Transition: International Relations* (Calcutta; Scientific Book Agency, 1965). Palmer, Norman D., *South Asia and United States Policy* (Boston: Houghton Miffin, 1966).

Prasad, Bimal (ed.), *India's Foreign Policy: Studies in Continuity and Change* (New Delhi: Vikas Pub., 1979).

Puchkov, V.P., *Political Development of Bangladesh 1975-1985* (New Delhi: Patriot Publishers, 1988).

Rahman, A., *Foreign Aid and Self-Reliant Growth: The Case of Bangladesh* (Dhaka: Centre for Social Studies, 1984).

Raiz, Ali, *State, Class & Military Rule: Political Economy of Martial Law in Bangladesh* (Dhaka: Nadi New Press, 1994).

Ramakant (ed.), *China and South Asia: South Asia Studies Series 13* (New Delhi, 1988).

Rapur, H., *India's Foreign Policy, 1947-92: Shadows and Substance* (New Delhi : Sage Publications, 1994).

Rashid, H. Ur., *Geography of Bangladesh* (London: Westview Press, 1977).

Rizvi, Gowhar, *South Asia in a Changing International Order* (New Delhi: Sage Publications, 1993).

Roy, C. Mascridice (ed.), *Foreign Policy in World Politics* (New Delhi, 1979). Ruthnaswamy, M., *Principles and Practice of Foreign Policy* (Bombay: Popular Book Depot, 1961).

Sen Gupta, B. (ed.), *Regional Cooperation and Development in South Asia, 2* Vols. (New Delhi : South Asian Publishers, 1986).

Sen Gupta, J., *History of Freedom Movement in Bangladesh, 1943-1973: Some Involvement* (Calcutta : Naya Prakash, 1974).

Sharma, S.R., *Bangladesh Crisis and Indian Foreign Policy* (New Delhi Young Asia, 1978).

Shelley, M. Rahman, (ed.), *The Chittagong Hill Tracts of Bangladesh : The Untold Story* (Dhaka : Centre for Development Research, 1992).

Shelley, M. Rahman, *Emergence of a New Nation in a Multi-Polar World. Bangladesh* (Washington DC : University Press of America, 1978).

Singh, K., *India and Bangladesh* (Delhi: Anmol Publications, 1987).

Sisson, R. and Rose, L.E., *War and Secession . Pakistan, India and the Creation of Bangladesh* (New Delhi : Vistaar Publications, 1990).

Sobhan, Rehman (ed.), *From Aid Dependence to Self-Reliance: Development Options for Bangladesh* (Dhaka: University Press, 1990).

Sobhan, Rehman (ed.), *The Decade of Stagnation : The State of Bangladesh Economy in the 1980s* (Dhaka: University Press, 1991).

Sobhan, Rehman and Ahmad, Muzaffar, *Public Enterprise in an Intermediate Regime: A Study in the Political Economy of Bangladesh* (Dhaka : BIDS, 1980).

Sobhan, Rehman, *Bangladesh: Problems of Governance* (New Delhi: Konark Publishers, 1993).

Sobhan, Rehman, *The Crisis of External Dependence: The Political Economy of Foreign Aid to Bangladesh* (Dhaka: University Press, 1993).

Stremalic, John, H. (ed.), *Foreign Policy Priorities of Third World States* (Colorado: Westview Press, 1982).

Tajuddin, Muhammad, *Bangladesh and the Islamic World,* Azad Institute Paper-9 (Calcutta: Maulana Abul Kalam Azad Institute of Asian Studies, 1998).

Tajuddin, Muhammad, *China and South Asia: A Perspective for the Study of Bangla-China Relations,* Azad Institute Paper-5 (Calcutta: Maulana Abul Kalam Azad Institute of Asian Studies, 1996).

Tajuddin, Muhammad, *Foreign Policy of Bangladesh* (New Delhi: National Book Organisation, 2001).

Talukdar, Maniruzzaman, *Politics and Security of Bangladesh* (Dhaka: University Press, 1994).

Thomas, Raju G.C. (ed.), *Great Power Triangle and Asian Security* (Lexington Lexington Books, 1983).

Vajpayee, A.B., *Continuity and Change in India's Foreign Policy,* (New Delhi Ministry of External Affairs, 1978).

Vali, F.A., *Politics of the Indian Ocean Region . The Balances of Power* (New York : Free Press, 1976).

Venkatramani, M.S., *Undercurrents in American Foreign Relations* (London: Asia Publishing House, 1965).

Verghese, B.G., *Waters of Hope: Integrated Water Resource Development and Regional Cooperation within the Himalayan-Ganga-Brahmaputra-Barak Basin* (New Delhi : Oxford and IBH Publishing 1990).

Vernon, Hewitt, *The New International Politics of South Asia* (Manchester: Manchester University Press, 1997).

Wadhva, Charan, D., *Regional Economic Cooperation in Asia: Bangladesh, India, Pakistan and Sri Lanka* (New Delhi: Allied Publishers, 1987).

Watson, Adam, *Diplomacy: The Dialogue Between States* (Philadelphia: Ishi Publications, 1983).

Westergaard, K., *State and Rural Society in Bangladesh . A Study in Relationship* (London : Curzon, 1985).

Wright, D.A., *Bangladesh: Origins and Indian Ocean Relations (1971-1975)* (New Delhi : Sterling Publishers, 1988).

Zafarullah, H. (ed.), Policy *Issues in Bangladesh* (New Delhi : South Asian Publishers, 1994).

Zafarullah, H. (ed.), *The Zia Episode in Bangladesh Politics* (New Delhi South Asian Publishers 1996).

Ziring, I., *Bangladesh :Form Mujib to Ershad, An Interpretive Study* (Oxford Oxford University Press, 1992).

(B) ARTICLES

Abdul Hafiz, Md., "South Asia's Security: Extra-Regional Inputs", *BIISS Journal, Vol.* 10, No. 2, 1989.

Abdul, Sabur S.K.M., "Foreign Policy of Bangladesh: Challenges in the 1990s", *BIISS Journal, Vol.* 12, No.4, 1991.

Ahmad, Fakruddin, "Foreign Policy of Bangladesh: A Review of Past two Decades", *BIISS Journal, Vol.* 14, No.2, April 1993.

Ahmad, Imtiaz, "State and Foreign Policy: A Theoretical Abstraction", *BIISS Journal,* Vol.] 3, No.3, July 1992.

Ahmad, S., "Foreign Capital Inflow and Economic Growth in Bangladesh: A Two Gap Model for the Bangladesh Economy", *BDS, Vol.XVIII,* No. l, March 1990.

Ahmed, A.T. Salahuddin, "Bangladesh-China Relations: An Assessment", *BIISS Journal, Vol.* 13, No.2, 1992.

Ahmed, Kamal Uddin, "Aid Administration in Bangladesh", *Regional Studies* (Islamabad), Vol.X, No.3, 1992.

Ahmed, Kamal Uddin, "US Food Aid and Public Policy in Bangladesh", *Economic and Political Weekly, Vol.* 27, 27 March 1992.

Amin, Muhammad Ruhal, "Economic Diplomacy of Bangladesh: A Post-Cold War Perspective", *Journal of International Relations,* Vol.3, NO.1, July□December 1995.

Arora, V.K., "SAARC: Prospects of Cooperation", *India Quarterly* (New Delhi), Vol. 42, No. 1, January-March 1986.

Bhaskar, V. and M. Khan, "Privatisation and Employment: A Study of the Jute Industry in Bangladesh", *American Economic Review,* Vol.85, No.1, March 1995.

Bhattacharaya, Vivek, "India and Bangladesh", *India Quarterly, Vol. 41,* No. 1, January-March 1985.

Chaudhary, Ishfaq Ilahi, "Civilian Control of the Military in Bangladesh: Moving towards a Democratic Tradition", *BIISS Journal,* Vol.20, No.], 1999. Chaudhury, Nilufar, "The Indian Ocean: A Zone of Peace or a Zone of Conflict", *BIISSJournal,* Vol.6, No.2, 1985.

Chopra, P., "Foreign Policy in Changing World", *Economic and Political Weekly,* Vol.26, No. *14,* 6 April 1991.

Choudhary, Dilara, "Major Power Involvement in South Asia", *BIISS Journal, Vol. 7,* No. 3, July 1986.

Fowler, Peter, "The Bangladesh Economy : A Regional Perspective", *Asian Affair* (London), Vol.29, Part 1, February 1998.

Hafiz, M. Abdul, "Bangladesh-Pakistan Relations: Still Developing?", BIISS *Journal,* Vol.6, No.3, 1985.

Hakim, Muhammad A., "Fall of Ershad Regime and Its Aftermath", *Regional Studies, Vol.* 10, No. 1, Winter 1991-92.

Hossain, Golam, "Bangladesh in 1995: Politics of Intransigence", *Asian Survey,* Vol. 36, No. 2, February 1996.

Hossain, Kamal, "Bangladesh and South Asia, Priorities for the Nineties", *Man and Development, Vol. 14,* No.5, September 1992.

Hossain, Kamal, "Bangladesh's Sovereignty and an Independent Non-Aligned Foreign Policy", *Man and Development,* Vol. 7, No. 4, December 1985.

Huq, M. Shamsul, "South Asian Association for Regional Cooperation: Past, Present and Future", *BIISS Journal, Vol.* 7, No. 3, July 1986.

Husain, Syed Anwar, "Bangladesh's Contribution to Normalizing Relations with Muslim Countries", *Bangladesh Quarterly* (Dhaka), Vol. 18, No.3, March 1998.

Hussain, Akmal, "Geo-politics and Bangladesh Foreign Policy", CLIO, Vol. VII, June 1989.

Iftekharuzzaman, "Bangladesh in the Post-Cold War Era: Relevances of Experience of East Asian NIES", *BIISS Journal,* Vol.4, No.2, 1993. Iftekharuzzaman, "International Security in the Post-Cold War Era: Challenges Facing the UN", *BIISS Journal,* Vol.] 4, No.3, July 1993.

Iftekharuzzaman, "The Ganges Water Sharing Issue: Diplomacy and Domestic Polities in Bangladesh", *BIISS Journal, Vol.* 15, No.3, July 1994.

Irshad, Ashequa, "American's Changing Strategic Interests", *BIISS Journal, Vol.* 18, No. l, 1997.

Islam, M. Rafiqul, "The Effects of the Farakka Barrage on Bangladesh and International Law", *BIISS Journal,* Vol. 5, No. 3, July 1984.

Kabir, M.H., "Bangladesh's Participation in U.N. Peacekeeping Missions", *BFPS Quarterly,* Vol.2, No.3 (Dhaka: BIISS Publication), July-September 1996.

Khan, Abdul Rob, "Bangladesh in the Security Council: Opportunities & Challenges", *BFPS, MISS* Publication", Vol.6, No.2, April-June 2000. Khanduri, C.B., "Brief on Bangladesh", *Indian Defence Review,* April 1995. Kumar, Ravinder, "India Pakistan and Bangladesh: An Overview 1947-1990", *Mainstream,* Vol.29, No. 14, January 1991.

Lyon, Peter, "Bangladesh: Fashioning a Foreign Policy", *South Asian Review,* Vol. 5, No. 3, April 1972.

Mahanty, J.N., "China and the Emergence of Bangladesh : Role of Great Power Global Perceptions", *India Quarterly,* Vol. 39, No. 2, April-June 1983. Mahapatra, Chitamani, "Major Post-Cold War Trends in India's Neighbourhood", *Strategic Analysis,* June 1999.

Mahmood, Raisul Awal, "Bangladesh's External Economics Relation", *BIISS Journal, Vol.* 13, No.4, 1990.

Mostafa, Md. Golam, "Bangladesh Foreign Policy: The Middle East Factor", *BIISS Journal,* Vol.7, No. 1, 1986.

Murshed, Mansoob, "Aspects of Commercial and External Policies in Bangladesh", *Asian Affairs, Vol. 1,* No. 4, October-December 1989.

Rahman, S.M. Mahfuzul, "Economic Co-Operation Among the Developing Countries (1960-1985)", *Asian Affairs, Vol.* 9, No.

2, April-June 1987, Rahman, Ataur, "Foreign Policy Making in Bangladesh: Institutions and Processes", *BIISS Journal,* Vol.6, No.2, 1983.

Rahman, M. Samshur, "Role of Foreign Aid in the Economy of Bangladesh: A Bureaucratic Perception", *South* Asian *Studies* (London), Vol. 4, No. 2, July 1987.

Rahman, Samshur, "Foreign Direct Investment Prerequisites for a Healthy Fow", *BFPS* Quarterly(Dhaka:BIISS Publications), Vol.3, No.2, April-June 1997.

Rahman, Syed, "Issues and Agenda for South Asia Regional Cooperation: A Bangladeshi Perspective", Asian Survey, Vol. 17, No. 9, September 1977. Shaheen, Akhtera, "Determinants of Foreign Policy Behaviour of Small States in South Asia", *Regional Studies,* VoI.XIII, No.2, Spring 1995.

Shelley, Mizanur Rahman, "Bangladesh : The Quest for International Recognition", Asian Affairs, Vol. 5, No. 4, October-December 1983.

Silwal, Y.K., "SAARC: The First Decade" *South* Asian Survey (New Delhi), Vol. 3, No. 172 January-December 1996.

Sobhan, Rehman, "Foreign Aid and Domestic Resources Mobilisation in Banglaesh", The *Bangladesh Development Studies* (Dhaka), Vol. 16, No. 2, June 1986.

"South-South Cooperation", *World Focus,* Special Issue, Vol. 11, No. l, January 1990.

Tajuddin, Muhammad, "India-Bangladesh: A New Era", *Newsletter,* Maulana Abul Kalam Azad Institute of Asian Studies, Vol. 3, No. 2-3.

"United State-Bangladesh Relations", Asian Affairs (Dhaka), Vol.5, No. 111, July-September 1983.

Ved, M., "Bangladesh: 20 Years after Mujib", *Strategic Analysis, Vol. XVlI1,* No.5, August 1995.

Zafar, S.A., "Indo-Bangladesh Relations: Problems and Prospects", *Pakistan Horizon* (Karachi), Vol.46, Nos. 3&4, July-October 1993.

(C) NEWSPAPERS, MAGAZINES AND YEARBOOKS

Asia Year Book (Bangladesh)

Asian Recorder (New Delhi)

Asian Strategic Review (New Delhi) *Bangladesh Foreign Policy Survey* (Dhaka) *Bangladesh Observer* (Dhaka) *Bangladesh Quarterly* (Dhaka)

Beijing Review (Beijing) *BASS Journal* (Dhaka) *Dhaka Courier* (Dhaka) *Frontline* (Chennai)

IDSA News Review on South Asia/Indian Ocean (New Delhi) *India Today* (New Delhi)

Indian Express (New Delhi) *Ittefaq* (Dhaka)

Keesing's Record of World Events (New Delhi) *Mainstream* (New Delhi)

Morning Post (Dhaka) *Patriot* (New Delhi)

Public Opinion Trends Analysis and News Service (Bangladesh Series), New Delhi.

Telegraph (Calcutta)

The Bangladesh Times (Dhaka).

The Daily Star (Dhaka).

The Financial Express (New Delhi).

The Hindu (Madras)

The Hindustan Times (New Delhi)

The Morning Sun (Dhaka)

The New Nation (Dhaka)

The Pioneer (New Delhi)

The Statesman (New Delhi).

The Times of India (New Delhi)

The Year Book of World Affairs (New York)

Tribune (Chandigarh)

Index

❑❑❑